Puppetry: A Reader in Theatre Practice

Readers in Theatre Practices

Series editor: Simon Shepherd

Published:

Ross Brown: Sound: A Reader in Theatre Practice
Penny Francis: Puppetry: A Reader in Theatre Practice

Forthcoming:

Scott Palmer: Lighting: A Reader in Theatre Practice

Readers in Theatre Practices
Series standing order
ISBN 978–0–230–53717–0 hardcover
ISBN 978–0–230–53718–7 paperback
(outside North America only)

You can receive future titles in this series as they are published. To place a standing order please contact your bookseller or, in the case of difficulty, write to us at the address below with your name and address, the title of the series and the ISBN quoted above.

Customer Services Department, Macmillan Distribution Ltd
Houndmills, Basingstoke, Hampshire RG21 6XS, England

Puppetry:
A Reader in
Theatre Practice

Penny Francis

palgrave
macmillan

First published 2012 by
PALGRAVE MACMILLAN

Palgrave Macmillan in the UK is an imprint of Macmillan Publishers Limited,
registered in England, company number 785998, of Houndmills, Basingstoke,
Hampshire RG21 6XS.

Palgrave Macmillan in the US is a division of St Martin's Press LLC,
175 Fifth Avenue, New York, NY 10010.

Palgrave Macmillan is the global academic imprint of the above companies
and has companies and representatives throughout the world.

Palgrave® and Macmillan® are registered trademarks in the United States,
the United Kingdom, Europe and other countries

ISBN 978–0–230–23272–3 hardback
ISBN 978–0–230–23273–0 paperback

This book is printed on paper suitable for recycling and made from fully
managed and sustained forest sources. Logging, pulping and manufacturing
processes are expected to conform to the environmental regulations of the
country of origin.

A catalogue record for this book is available from the British Library.

A catalog record for this book is available from the Library of Congress.

10   9   8   7   6   5   4   3   2   1
21 20 19 18 17 16 15 14 13 12

Printed and bound in Great Britain by
CPI Antony Rowe, Chippenham and Eastbourne

For Henryk Jurkowski
My mentor and friend

Contents

Acknowledgements

The author, editor and publishers wish to thank the following for permission to reproduce copyright material:

Christopher Leith and Philip Sayer for the photo from *Scholastica* by Philip Sayer (1989)

Peter O'Rourke for his photo of *Giraffe* from The Little Angel Production of Roald Dahl's *The Giraffe, The Pelly and Me* (2008)

Patrick Baldwin for his photo from *Rubbished* produced by students of the MA in Advanced Theatre Practice at the Central School of Speech and Drama, London (2004)

Jack Sumberg and the Bread and Puppet Theatre for the photo of two masks by Peter Schumann: *Archbishop Romero* (1985) and *Blue General* (1977)

Maureen Kinnear and Sharmanka Kinetic Theatre for the photo from *Time of Rats* performed by Eduard Bersudsky's Sharmanka Kinetic Theatre, Glasgow (1991)

Josef Ptáček and DRAK Theatre Company for the photo of rod marionettes from a production of *The Three Golden Hairs* by the DRAK Theatre Company of Hradec Králové, Czech Republic (1998). Puppets by Marek Zákostelecky

Lyndie Wright for the diagram of a string marionette from John Wright's *Your Puppetry* (1951)

John Roberts for his photo of a large nether-rod puppet, designed and made by John and Lyndie Wright. Puppeteer: Christopher Leith

Holly Griffin for her photo of *Deirdre*, operated by Jacqueline Ilett of the Jacolly Puppet Company

Korinna Roeding and Mandy Travis for the photo from *The Lost Moon* by Mandy Travis (2008)

Mark Mander and Christophe Cohen for the photo of a humanette puppet, *Clementine*, made and performed by Mark Mander

Barry Smith and the Puppet Centre Trust for the sketch of a Barry Smith puppet in the technique of Bunraku-za from *Pierrot in Five Masks* (1980)

Stefan Fichert of the Puppet Players, Gauting, for the pastel sketch of a rear-rod puppet for a production of *Faust* (2008)

Simon Annand for his photo from Michael Morpurgo's *War Horse*, premiered in 2007. Puppets designed and crafted by Adrian Kohler of the Handspring Puppet Company, Cape Town

Central School of Speech and Drama for the photo from *Picnic Man*, a Central School Postgraduate Diploma project by students (1993)

John Franzen and In the Heart of the Beast theatre company for the photo of *Johnny Appleseed* from the book *Theatre of Wonder*. Puppet designed and built by Greg Leierwood (1989)

Trudie Lee and Ronnie Burkett for the photo of Billy and Sid from *Billy Twinkle* (2009)

Andy Rumball for his photo from *The Lost and Moated Land*, directed by Penny Bernand and Sue Buckmaster with scenography by Sophia Clist (1999)

Peter O'Rourke for his photo from *The Giraffe, the Pelly and Me* (2008) designed and directed by Peter O'Rourke

Liz Walker, co-founder of Faulty Optic, for her photo of 'Blue Face' from *Tunnelvision* (1998)

Damiet van Dalsum and Poppentheater Damiet for 'Silver Bird', a marionette from *Mijn Kleine Prins (My Little Prince)* (1998). Also reproduced on the front cover of this book

Penny Francis for her photo of a traditional Vertep cabinet theatre from the Ukraine

Mary Edwards for her photo of Punch drawing crowds to Brighton Pier (2008)

Alex Scherpf for the photo of a scene from Green Ginger's *Rust*. Netherrod, dual-operator puppet designed by Marc Parrett and Chris Pirie (2005)

The Edwin Mellen Press for pp. 20–21, 27, 31, 66–67, 104–105 and 118 from Henryk Jurkowski, *History of European Puppetry*, volume 1 (1996) and for pp. 320, 330 and 453 from Henryk Jurkowski, *History of European Puppetry*, volume 2 (1998) and 'Specificity in a New Guise' in an edited version from *Puppetry Yearbook*, Volume 5, pp. 79–96 (2002)

Johns Hopkins University Press for pp. 66, 252–253 from Harold B. Segel, *Pinocchio's Progeny: Puppets, Marionettes, Automatons, and Robots in Modernist and Avant-Garde Drama* © The Johns Hopkins University Press (1995)

The Oxford University Press for pp. 249, 336–337 from Steven Connor, *Dumbstruck: A Cultural History of Ventriloquism* (2000)

Crowood Press for pp.110–111, 41, 91–92, 42 and 45 from Tina Bicât, *Puppets and Performing Objects* (2007)

Jean-Louis Heckel for *Towards a Ludic Dialectic* (1993)

Kirsty Boyle for '*Karakuri Info*' © www.karakuri.info/history (2008)

Taylor and Francis Group for Penny Francis 'Interview with Howard Barker' in *Contemporary Theatre Review* (1999)

David Krut Publishing and Handspring Puppet Company for Basil Jones 'Puppetry and Authorship' in Jane Taylor (ed.), *Handspring Puppet Company* (2009)

Central School of Speech and Drama Publications and Simon Shepherd for Sue Buckmaster 'Object Relations' (2000); and J. Crouch and P. McDermott for 'The Pleasure Principle' in A. Dean (ed.) *Puppetry into Performance*, Issue 13 (2000)

Guardian News & Media Ltd for Tim Carroll 'Puppet Love: Why the Best Actors are Wooden' in www.guardian.co.uk (11 October 2007) © 2007

Taylor and Francis Group for essays by Joanna Enckell, Howard Barker, William Kentridge, Dennis Silk in Marion Baraitser (ed.), 'Theatre of Animation: Contemporary Adult Puppet Plays in Context', *Contemporary Theatre Review*, Volume 10, Issues 1 and 2 (1999), Harwood Academic Publishers

Playwrights Canada Press for excerpt from Ronnie Burkett's *Billy Twinkle: Requiem for a Golden Boy* (2009)

Henryk Jurkowski for 'Specificity in a New Guise: The Aesthetics of Puppetry at the Beginning of the 21st Century' (2002)

Brunella Eruli for 'The Use of Puppetry and the Theatre of Objects in the Performing Arts of Today' in Marek Waszkiel et al (eds) (2000) *L'art mondial de la marionnette/The Worldwide Art of Puppetry*, UNIMA 2000. France: I.I.M. and UNIMA

Hetty Paerl for 'Acerra and Pulcinella' (2007). Edited translation by Penny Francis www.pulcinellamuseo.it

Roman Paska (1990) for 'Notes on Puppet Primitives' in L. Kominz and M. Levenson (eds), *The Language of the Puppet*

Christopher Halsall for translation of the Heinrich von Kleist essay 'On the Marionette Theatre' (1810) in P. Francis (ed.), *Animations* Vol.6, No.6 1983 p. 3

Institut International de la Marionnette for Henryk Jurkowski, *Ecrivains et Marionnettes* (1991) pp. 3–4

Every effort has been made to trace rights holders, but if any have been inadvertently overlooked the publishers would be pleased to make the necessary arrangements at the first opportunity.

MY SPECIAL THANKS go to Eleanor Margolies, Simon Shepherd and Petra Jones whose editorial expertise was invaluable.

Also to Professor Henryk Jurkowski, John Bell, Brian Hibbitt and Ray DaSilva whose knowledge, time and practical assistance were generously given whenever they were needed.

Many other colleagues and friends have freely given their help and advice so that it is impossible to list them all here. All are active in puppetry in some manner and it is to them I owe most of what I have learned about their art. They include, in the Americas, Ronnie Burkett; Nancy Staub; the Center for Puppetry Arts, Atlanta; Eric Bass and Ines Zeller; Roman Paska; Eileen Blumenthal; Steve Tillis and Sandy Spieler.

In France: the Institut International de la Marionnette, Charleville-Mézières.

In Australia, Peter J. Wilson; Margaret Williams; Geoffrey Milne.

In Ireland, John McCormick; in the Netherlands, Hetty Paerl and Damiet van Dalsum; in the Czech Republic, Josef Krofta; in Sri Lanka, Jayadeva Tilakasiri; in South Africa, Basil Jones and Adrian Kohler.

In Britain, Steven Connor; Dorothy Max Prior; Mark Pitman; Lyndie Wright; Michael Dixon; Ronnie LeDrew; David Currell; Geoff Felix; Matthew Isaac Cohen; Gillie and Michel Robic; Mandy Travis; Nenagh Watson; Richard Medrington; Peter O'Rourke; Susan Tobin.

My warmest thanks to them all.

Penny Francis

Series Editor's Preface

This series aims to gather together both key historical texts and contemporary ways of thinking about the material crafts and practices of theatre.

These crafts work with the physical materials of theatre – sound, objects, light, paint, fabric, and – yes – physical bodies. Out of these materials the theatre event is created.

In gathering the key texts of a craft it becomes very obvious that the craft is not simply a handling of materials, however skilful. It is also a way of thinking about both the materials and their processes of handling. Work with sound and objects, for example, involves – always, at some level – concepts of what sound is and does, what an object is and does … what a body is.

For many areas of theatre practice there are the sorts of 'how to do it'-books that have been published for at least a century. These range widely in quality and interest but next to none of them is able to, or wants to, position the *doing* in relation to the *thinking about doing* or the thinking about the material being used.

This series of books aims to promote both thinking about doing and thinking about materials. Its authors are much more than mere editors, however. All are specialists in their field of practice and they are charged to reflect on their specialism and its history in order, often for the first time, to model concepts and provide the tools not just for doing but for thinking about theatre practice.

At the heart of each craft is a tense relationship. On the one hand there is the basic raw material that is worked – the wood, the light, the paint, the musculature. These have their own given identity – their weight, mechanical logics, smell, particle formation, feel. In short, the texture of the stuff. And on the other hand there is theatre, wanting its effects and illusions, its distortions and impossibilities. The raw material resists the theatre as much as yields to it, the theatre both develops the material and learns from it. The stuff and the magic. This relationship is perhaps what defines the very activity of theatre itself.

It is this relationship, the thing which defines the practice of theatre, which lies at the heart of each book in this series.

Simon Shepherd

List of Illustrations

Introduction

The theatrical potential of a puppet, an animated figure or object, was until the 1990s 'the best-kept secret of theatre' (Allen and Shaw, 1992), but the secret is out. Puppetry, a medium that consists of an amalgam of theatre and the fine arts and crafts, has been widely absorbed into contemporary performance, in adult work as in children's. The use (and abuse) of animated figures and objects may be observed in mainstream as well as in fringe productions, in opera and dance and, inevitably but proudly, in most productions for children. While the cinema has been pushing the frontiers of animation in one form or another for over a century, theatre animation only found its own language and thereby recognition towards the end of the 1900s. This is no longer a performing art 'on the brink of belonging', but a regular ingredient – worldwide – of the diet of twenty-first century theatregoers.

A survey undertaken now would find innumerable examples of productions which include puppetry (as a greater or lesser ingredient) playing in the grandest mainstream theatres and in small studios and arts centres, and rather less often in the traditional venues: school halls, squares, streets and fairgrounds.[1] As well as its own myriad dedicated events, puppetry also finds a presence in prestigious music and multimedia festivals (e.g. Avignon, Edinburgh) in most countries. Innovative work for adults and children can be seen everywhere: in Europe, the Americas, Australasia and throughout Asia where puppets are more reluctant to abandon their traditional spiritual and religious significance. The dynamism of the art form is incontrovertible, evidenced as much in Japan and South Korea as in Scotland and Brazil.

The book's focus is on puppetry's evolution from the 1990s to the present. The accent is on developments observed from a modern west European perspective, but with references to those ancient traditions from both west and east which have exerted the strongest influence on most of today's performance modes. These include the *Bunraku-za* of Japan, and the *wayang* of Indonesia, and the indispensable and universal comic anti-heroes descended from the *commedia dell'arte*, for example Pulcinella and Punch.

The spiritual and ritualistic aspects of puppetry will be only briefly addressed, although they are by no means extinct, and are essential to an understanding of an ancient performing art that has at its source human

---

[1] At the time of writing puppets are taking or have very recently taken leading roles in productions staged, for example, in London, England: at the Royal National Theatre, the Royal Shakespeare Company, the English National Opera, the Royal Opera House, the Lyceum, the Gielgud, the New London, the Lyric Theatre Hammersmith, and the Barbican Arts Centre. In New York there is a similar rich mix on and off-Broadway.

Venus and Adonis based on the Shakespeare Masque staged by the Royal
Shakespeare company with the Little Angel Theatre in 2004 and 2007. Design,
Lyndie Wright. Director, Greg Doran.
Reproduced by permission of the Royal Shakespeare Company.

belief in a spirit world (Nelson, 2001). Here lie the origins of the performing
puppet, attendant on the emergence of every indigenous society, preceding
theatre, preceding any organized religion.

Like acting, puppetry has a long and often disreputable history, and has
only recently attracted the attention of non-specialist theatre-makers.
Although it inspired the artists of the Modernist movement, the professional
puppeteers were slow to catch up with their ideas and until well into the
second half of the last century few in the west, with the notable exception of
the French (who have been setting the pace for innovation for at least a
century), applied puppetry to adult experimental theatre. If the reader is interested in a brief overview of puppetry's history in western cultures, it may be
found in the seventh chapter, where I briefly trace the steady upward trajec-
tory, in terms of quality and quantity, which object and figure animation in
theatre, television and film has followed, particularly since the 1980s. I believe
that a sampling of current productions with puppets on offer, taken with a
light study of our subject, will reveal to the reader an independent and fascinating art form, a complement to the other more familiar theatre disciplines.

Written material in English underpinning puppet theatre is still compara-
tively sparse, difficult to locate and largely directed at the specialist practitioners, although the situation is changing. If you have ever expressed a need

to be better informed, so as to enjoy, produce, practice, evaluate and 'read' puppetry with a degree of understanding and knowledge, I hope to go some way towards answering that need in these pages where much other reading is signalled. The explorer will find few books about modern puppetry in libraries or bookshops, and those few are often limited to its history, or to puppet-making and performance for beginners. The histories are usually excellent, and there are some colourful and informative picture books for adults.[2] Most of the more thoughtful writing (in English) on the genre resides in essays scattered in anthologies, journals and other publications of limited circulation, poorly publicized outside the enclosures of the specialists. To bring them to the notice of a wider readership many extracts are here included, with a short list of relevant reading appended to each chapter and a more general bibliography at the end. Too many of the works cited are out of print, and many important ones are excluded because they await an English translation. I have therefore taken the painful decision to include mainly writings available in English, with a few indispensable exceptions.[3]

My own exploration of puppetry in performance has taken me around the world, observing, discussing, editing, reviewing, commentating and finally teaching in the prestigious Central School of Speech and Drama, London. (A growing number of theatre schools all over the world now include what is, after all, an essential component of the performing arts).

This book brings together the lessons I have learned during the most fertile period, to date, in the evolution of puppetry. My mission is to attract the widest possible public to its surprises and pleasures, and to promote understanding of a unique medium of expression. I came to puppetry from a position of scepticism as to its value in a modern adult theatre context, but on closer acquaintance I became excited by its inventiveness and possibilities, its unusual admixture of the visual, dramatic and auditory which together contribute to the best of contemporary theatre.

For the reader unfamiliar with the art form's potential and its achievements I aim to add to their knowledge of its techniques, language, dramaturgy and aesthetics. For all theatre practitioners, critics, tutors, students and the enquiring theatregoer, I hope the information and ideas will be stimulating and useful.

---

[2] Two of the more recent are: Blumenthal, Eileen (2005), *Puppetry and Puppets*, London: Thames and Hudson. Also published in the US as *Puppetry: a World History*, New York: Harry N. Abrams. Jurkowski, Henryk, *Metamorphoses* (2009), France: IIM and Editions L'Entretemps.

[3] The following journals and book series are invaluable as resources for research and information: *Animations Online*, www.puppetcentre.org.uk/animationsonline; *Total Theatre Magazine*, www.totaltheatre.org.uk; *Puppet Notebook*, www.unima.org.uk; *Puppetry International*, www.unima-usa.org/publications; *PUCK: La marionnette et les autres arts*, France: Editions Institut International de la Marionnette (IIM), and Fisher, J. (ed.) (1995–1997; 2000–2005) *The Puppetry Yearbook Vols. 1–6*, Lewiston, NY: Edwin Mellen Press.

Chapter

1 *Approach*

This book is intended for every category of theatrophile, all of them surely remarking on the growing presence of puppetry in mainstream and fringe productions. At the same time many are realizing that their experience, training or education in theatre has included little or nothing of puppetry. Some will want to know where it has come from and how it began; some will question its *raison d'être* in a modern theatre. Writers and critics will want to evaluate what they see, others will want to discover how it works. All these questions are, to some extent at least, addressed, with indications of where to discover more.

The three subjects of this chapter are first, puppetry itself; second, the puppet, including a distinction between the animated/manipulated 'figure' and the animated/manipulated 'object'; third, the puppeteer, whether actor-manipulator, designer-craftsperson or all of these. I offer an approach in the context of modern theatre practice, focusing on the period between 1990 and the present, with interventions and insights by many other writers.

It will become clear that we are dealing with a genre of the performing arts – intriguing and shape-shifting – for which there are few rules. Definitions and instructions are usually debatable, and any edicts and precepts given here and indeed in most other books on puppetry may be regarded only as points of departure for discussion and experiment.

In the context of today's 'western' theatre practices, any producer and practitioner of non-literary and non-naturalist theatre, including the genres inexactly labelled 'visual' and 'physical', 'music-', 'dance-', 'circus-', or 'object-theatre', will find themselves considering puppetry as a medium of expression to include in their productions.

All the most significant developments in theatre of the last hundred and twenty years have seen set, light and sound design gain in importance and critical attention; opera and ballet have renewed themselves in contemporary dance and music theatre; *commedia dell'arte* is revived in improvised, masked and circus-based shows often called 'physical theatre' which are some distance from classical mime; children's productions have revolutionized their dramaturgy and their standards of performance, attracting innovative artists and in many cases statutory funding. Puppetry, now allied and aligned with the other performing arts, has similarly evolved, broadening its brief to include endless forms of creative experiment, often unrecognizable as puppetry, often produced by artists trained in other disciplines. It has grown into a dynamic performing art, taking its position alongside all the others. The renewal is, crucially, engaging the attention of a youthful adult public.

Most theatre people, including its audiences, have come to the dramatic theatre through its literature, the printed plays. The teaching of 'drama' is usually located in school and university departments of English and a verbal text is still widely considered the central pillar of a production. However the growth of a paying public for another kind of theatre is an undeniable fact – it is a theatre whose performance text is concerned as much with scenography, sound design, music and other new visual media as with words. Among its resources puppetry sits naturally, concerned as it is with design and sculpture, with action, movement and music, usually more than with dialogue.

PUPPETRY, THE ART AND THE ACT

The term 'puppetry' denotes the act of bringing to imagined life inert figures and forms (representational or abstract) for a ritual or theatrical purpose – for a *performance*. The perceived investment of the inanimate with *anima* or spirit is effected through the convincing transference of a performer's energy to one or more of these figures and forms, endowing them with motion (normally), voice (if necessary) and presence (always). The transference is effected through the natural or manufactured 'controls' of the puppet, combined with specific performing skills, innate or acquired, directly and immediately applied (in 'real-time') to the thing animated. The execution of the performance may be live, recorded, and in a growing number of cases actioned by technological as opposed to handmade or hands-on control, but the hands or the body of the puppet operator are always in attendance, to effect and affect the performance of the figure or object.

The animation of objects, i.e. puppetry, can be directly traced to the atavistic, universal belief in the spirit life hidden within and embodied by natural phenomena, things and materials. This belief forms the core of the animist religion and is intrinsic to the understanding of the puppet's origins. Animism was humankind's first belief system and informed the early stages of awakening to its small world, its place in that world and its first questions as to the reason for its existence. Uncertain of their own power, unconscious of their mental capacities, but certain of their dependence on nature, humans deified everything that they feared or that brought them comfort and sustenance, investing any *thing* which represented the forces around them with *anima*.

In a paper presented at a 1992 conference in Poland on the trends in world puppetry research, the Catalan academic and writer, Maryse Badiou, charts the intermediaries by which humans connect to the sacred. In descending order they are: venerated natural objects, the image, sculpture (volume) and the cinema (motion), the puppet and the shadow, the dancer, the actor and finally the human. She confirmed first, the widely held belief that puppets and shadow theatre have been present since the first manifestations of humanity, in every culture of the world, and second, the human's 'insatiable thirst' to capture the volume and the movement of beings and things:

> [They play] their part in the community's most important occasions – birth, death, marriage and so on – through rituals, religious ceremonies and traditional celebrations; they are, without any doubt, the memory of the human condition in all its expressions. (Badiou, 1992: 61, trans. PF)

American academic Frank Proschan, a professor of anthropology, introduces an essay to be found in an edition of the periodical *Semiotica* devoted to the semiotic study of puppets and performing objects thus:

> Among the most ancient and widespread of cultural traditions is the use of material objects in narrative or dramatic performance [...] Dancers who wear masks, bards who use scroll-paintings [...] to illustrate their narrations, children who create dramatic scenes in dollplay, worshippers who bear icons in a religious procession, [...] all manifest the urge to give life to non-living things, as they animate objects in dramatic performances and use material images as surrogates for human actors. Whether the dramatic actor is a miniaturized wood-and-cloth puppet or a gigantic, extra-human phantasm, and whether the performance context is one of secular entertainment or sacred ritual, the creative energy that animates the images is the same – the impulse to create objects to act in our stead. Objects through which we can project intensified, artistic and often holy speech and action. (Proschan, 1983: 3)

In modern times, when many but by no means all societies have 'freed' themselves from animistic beliefs, the freedom can seem superficial when confronted with the animation, the apparent stirring of life, in a 'dead' object. It is my claim that at the very least a residue of animism, the belief in the spirit residing within everything that is apparently inert, is universally present in twenty-first century humans; that this explains the power of the staged puppet.

You may identify two kinds of performance: one in which the puppetry is the principal medium of expression, which is referred to as a *'puppet show'* or *'puppet theatre'*. The other is a production in which the puppetry is only a greater or lesser component, and thus can be referred to as a *'theatre with puppets'* (it seems necessary to note the difference, albeit obvious).

Puppetry springs from two taproots: one nourishes its magic and illusion, its dramaturgy of ritual and religion, fairy tale, legend and folk memory, and the other nourishes the broad branches of its comedy, parody and satire. As a performance medium ritual and religion have been employed for thousands of years to produce sacred representations of gods and spirits, to evoke fear and awe, and to conjure demons, revelations of the divine and reminders of death.

In a 2000 interview the French director Grégoire Callies, after directi[ng] Büchner's *Leonce and Lena* with puppets, expressed the opinion that [the] theatre of object and puppet was more relevant than it was 40 or 50 years ag[o]

> I get the impression that I could link this change to the emergence of new concepts, new thoughts, like those of Deleuze and Foucault, even to the evolution of modern philosophy. Is it not simply linked to the return of the barbaric, to the end of a certain humanism, to another way of thinking about the burden of life and the role of death?
>
> The puppet, after all, speaks only of that, of the relationship between life and death. Doesn't it also correspond to our need to interrogate our power; literally to create life, to play the demiurge? (see Paska, 2000: 86–88, trans. PF)

Ritual and religion are dominant in most African and much of Asian practice, and both can be found in western puppet theatre too, for example in performances for children, such as Jesus' nativity at Christmas and some Jewish festivals, and also in the adult work of a few artists such as Christopher Leith, an English wood sculptor whose hieratic figures illustrate solemn tales of the saints. Divinities appear in myriad worldwide puppet-performed versions of myths and legends: a recent Royal Shakespeare Company production of the Shakespeare poem *Venus and Adonis* drew full houses, while devils and demons inevitably appear in the perennial puppet versions of *Faust* and *Don Juan*, and in episodes from the *Mahabharata* and the *Ramayana* epics. Every country has its ancient tales of mythical creatures and heroic adventures.

The repertoire for school-age children has broken the restraints of anodyne fairy and folk tales, and productions may now include unsanitized versions of the Grimm folk tales, Angela Carter's bloody fairy stories and other strong meat.

Figure 1.1   Christopher Leith's *Scholastica* (1989, but often revived since). 36 inch (1 metre) marionettes with heads and hands carved in limewood. The touching story of St Benedict and St Scholastica.

© Philip Sayer. Reproduced by permission of Christopher Leith.

Puppetry's close affinity to things fantastic effectively reflects children's darker fantasies.

Puppetry's other root gives rise to the knockabout, vulgar comedy of shows featuring Punch, the stereotypical anti-hero born of *commedia dell'arte*'s Pulcinella (and probably of ancestors reaching far further back into pre-Christian times). He is the embodiment of the man-in-the-street protesting against all forms of authority. Profanity, trickery, slapstick and even lewdness are joyfully expressed in his shows and those of his worldwide cousins (Petrouchka, Polichinelle, Kasper, Vitéz László, Vassilache, the Mamulengo, Karagöz, Karaghiosis, Mubarak, Gerolamo, the much later advent of Guignol and Tchantchès, and many others of the type). Since the nineteenth century, in Britain the antics of Punch are commonly thought of as suitable entertainment for children, a curious subversion of the original Punch and Judy street show in which the comedy depends on anarchy, violence, misogyny and social satire! Today Punch and Judy may be a bowdlerized version of the original,[1] yet even now, in the twenty-first century, after several hundred years of life, the highly schematic antics of Punch and his international brotherhood are a staple of puppetry and continue to draw crowds.

Parody, for which the miniature, manipulated characters imitate and mock their human counterparts and their activities, has been a constant in the puppet theatre probably since antiquity. It is not as often found as it once was, although in the Brussels bar-theatre called 'Toone' parodies of operas, melodramas and political shenanigans are still enjoyed, even after many years of the company's existence. The Sicilian *'pupi'* also perform what have evolved into amusing parodies of the conflicts of the Saracens and Christians in Crusader times. The Sicilian companies with their magnificently armoured figures could be seen all over the island even as late as the 1980s, but their numbers are now much reduced. In Britain the excellent Mark Mander parodies celebrities, using figures which are part human, part rear-rod puppet (a form known as 'humanettes', described in the next chapter), miming to songs and speech with uncanny accuracy.

With his satirical teeth drawn Punch is widely tolerated, in spite of the pressures of political correctness which confine any strong satire and lewdness to political and social cabaret in pubs and clubs. A puppet is a natural transgressor, entering where no human dares. Pornography is an underground offshoot, where puppets lend themselves more acceptably than humans to representations of acts of sex and violence, and this arena is growing. Where the puppets in action often produce an effect more comic than titillating (Jurkowski, 1988: 97–112) there are now more serious seams of cruelty that some puppeteers are mining.

Good professional live puppetry, solemn or comic, is predicated first on

---

[1] In 2005 the great Ken Campbell originated *Attack of the Clowns* which more accurately restored the show to its original crudity but with twenty-first century comic relevance.

the spectator's complicity and engagement with the animated characters, so that acceptance and credulity overcome scepticism; and second, on the skills of the puppet-maker and above all the puppet operator who must be capable of sustaining the spectator's attention. Having witnessed on many occasions (nowadays mercifully rare) puppet shows incompetently conceived, crafted and animated, I have been surprised by the intense engagement of the average spectator with the weakest of them. The magnetism of the moving figure, even poorly made and animated, goes some way to explaining its survival throughout the centuries, against all the odds. High levels of manipulation skills seem not to have been required of western puppet operators until the late eighteenth century, when the popularity of the *fantoccini*, the trick marionettes on strings, demanded a good measure of dexterity and preparation. I do not of course speak of the age-old skills of the trained professionals of Asia, the marionettists and shadow artists of China, the *ningyo joruri* players of Japan, the dalangs of Indonesia and other master puppeteers performing a traditional, popular puppet repertory that is in many of these regions still closely associated with ritual and ceremony. Today's puppetry exacts more and more from every manipulator of puppets and objects; audiences are becoming educated to recognize skill in both the performers and their instruments, as the former become more numerous, trained and increasingly aspirational.

The criteria to apply to the evaluation of contemporary performances start, however, not with the crafting skills but with an estimation of the content of the production – the dramaturgy – and its suitability, its *validity* for puppet play, of which more in Chapter 5. The best performance text is usually expressed in a dynamic series of staged pictures, while other measures of the show's quality are the unity of aesthetic which comprises the materiality of the puppets, the sensitivity of the soundscape, the level of skill in the manipulation of the figures, and the appropriate stylistic of the acting, all to be enlarged on in the third chapter on performance practicalities.

A leaflet advertising a recent (2007) exhibition of puppets in the United States bears witness to the change in the modern perception and appreciation of puppet play:

> As a form of popular theater, invested with high artistic values and ambition, puppetry continues to thrive, especially in parts of Eastern Europe, Asia, and Africa. In contemporary Western culture, where animation is increasingly prevalent in art and entertainment, the puppet renews its capacity as a psychological abstraction, social commentator and playful entertainer.[2]

The sentence could hardly have been written before this present century. It indicates that observers are able to recognize expertise in puppetry as they

---

[2] From the publicity leaflet for *The Puppet Show*, a touring exhibition produced by the Institute of Contemporary Art in Philadelphia, United States, 2007.

have long recognized it in, for instance, dance, where for years it has been impossible to present a professional company whose members were not highly trained.

'PUPPET THEATRE' AND A 'THEATRE WITH PUPPETS'

If puppetry is the art and the act, *'puppet theatre'* or *'the puppet show'* is the staged production.

Professor Henryk Jurkowski, a Polish teacher and writer, will be widely quoted in this book since he is the most prolific writer to date on the history and theories of puppetry. In 1988 his first book in English was published: *Aspects of Puppet Theatre* is a collection of essays which quickly became required reading for every student of the art form. The first essay was titled *Literary Views on Puppet Theatre* in which he traced references to the puppet in the works of various prominent authors from classical times to the present. In it Jurkowski proposes a definition of puppet theatre, having established that *its characteristic features are the changing relationships between its iconic signs of character, its driving power and the source of its vocal expression*:

> The puppet theatre is a theatre art: the main and basic features that differentiate it from the live theatre is that the speaking and performing object makes temporal use of the physical sources of its vocal and driving powers, which are present beyond the object. The relationship between the object (the puppet) and its power sources changes all the time, and these variations are of great semiological and aesthetic significance. (Jurkowski, 1988: 31)

The common name given to puppetry in live performance is 'puppet show'. Once, the expectation was that puppets would be operated by the hands of hidden operators working from below within a booth or behind a screen or from above on a bridge. The troupes were constantly on the move, travellers with a great deal of baggage, literal and metaphorical. The social status of all performing with the puppet show was lowly. Another term given to the puppet show in England in the sixteenth and seventeenth centuries was 'motion'. Edward Gordon Craig revived it for his series of witty playlets which he called *The Drama for Fools, Five Motions for Marionettes*.[3]

Since those early times the puppet theatre's status and that of the puppeteer have made a long journey into respectable society. The puppet show, even when its popularity faded in the early twentieth century, maintained upward mobility with the attention of the high-art Modernists, in revolt against naturalism and in search of art's spiritual values. Their

---

[3] See Craig, E. Gordon, *The Drama for Fools by Tom Fool: Five Motions for Marionettes*, Florence 1918, supplemented by a further collection hitherto unpublished and acquired in 2004 by the Institut International de la Marionnette, Charleville-Mézières, France.

embrace awarded puppetry the status of an art form, and they left a legacy which has contributed to its present-day prominence – and the search for another description.

By the second half of the twentieth century *'puppet theatre'* had become the smart title[4] in English when the term 'puppet show' was thought to sound unbecoming to the latest productions with their higher aspirations. The new title became currency, especially when the Communist-dominated countries poured subsidies into what Moscow considered an ideal educational medium. Because of generous funding, enabling the engagement of well-known artists from the human theatre and the schooling of new talent, the Soviet productions often had great merit. In response, from the 1960s, a handful of western production companies, such as the Caricature Theatre of Wales and the Cannon Hill Puppet Theatre of Birmingham, modelled themselves on the eastern European state companies, setting themselves ambitious goals which attracted new respect and finance, though the subsidies were minuscule compared with the Soviet largesse. However 'puppet show' has stubbornly remained the common English label.

Peter Schumann was a catalyst of the twentieth century's puppet theatre revival. Still active, he will live in the history of theatre and puppet theatre for his courage, breadth of mind, his genius as a sculptor and the application of his talents to a company – the Bread and Puppet Theatre – that made an immeasurable contribution to the respect now afforded to puppetry. The work of the Bread and Puppet theatre has drawn attention to injustice and tyranny in many parts of the world, including those of Schumann's adopted homeland, the United States. His productions are of giant scale, performed usually in the open air by effigies with metre-high heads and vast hands. They are held aloft by a small army of puppeteers and locally recruited, voluntary assistants accompanied by musicians and banners. The shows, not only because of their scale, are impossible to overlook, as a force for protest, freedom and hope. The company has travelled to various troubled parts of the world where injustice is rife. Much has been written of the company's activities and he himself has written many pungent essays.[5] This is an extract from one, *The Radicality of Puppet Theatre*:

> Puppet theatre, the employment and dance of dolls, effigies, and puppets, is not only historically obscure and unable to shake off its ties to shamanistic healing and other inherently strange and hard-to-prove social services. It is also, by definition of its most persuasive characteristics, an anarchic art, subversive and untameable by nature, an art which is easier researched in police records than in

---

[4] In Germany many adopted the term 'Figurentheater' and in English there were other substitutes intended to avoid the humble 'puppet' word. 'Theatre of Animation' was one, 'theatre of animated forms' another.

[5] See the two volumes of *Peter Schumann's Bread and Puppet Theatre* (1988) by Stefan Brecht for the most comprehensive account.

theatre chronicles, an art which by fate and spirit does not aspire to represent governments or civilizations, but prefers its own secret and demeaning stature in society, representing, more or less, the demons of that society and definitely not its institutions. [...]

And yet, despite the general tendency of our cultural effects to be subservient to the power of the market, to money-making and to the associated steeping of our souls in as much nonsense as possible, despite the fact that puppet theatre exists mostly in the feeble manner of an art obedient to the demands of the entertainment business, puppet theatre also exists as a radically new and daring art form: new, not in the sense of unheard-of newness, but in the sense of an uncovered truth that was there all along but was so common it couldn't be seen for what it was. Radical in the sense of not only turning away from established concepts, it also succeeded in a widening of the heart that allowed for greater inclusion of more modern art into the ancient art of puppetry. (see Schechner, 1991, 75–83)

In the late 1980s and still growing like a triffid, the phenomenon of a '*theatre with puppets*' arrived to take over a large proportion of puppetry practice. To illustrate the difference between a *puppet theatre* and a *theatre with puppets*: the company Tartana of Madrid produced a version of *King Lear* in 1987 in which human-sized, animated figures were the principal medium, playing all the characters, thus clearly 'puppet theatre'. Complicite, a company based in England, frequently employs animated objects in its productions, a theatre with puppets, for example *Mnemonic* (1999), *Light* (2000), and *Shun-kin* (2009).

The current western mainstream and fringe repertory holds many examples of theatre with puppets. It refers of course to a production of mixed means of expression and while hardly an accepted label or category, it serves as a useful description of the last development in the evolution of staged puppetry; certainly it has proved successful in attracting for the first time a large number of artists, producers, directors and designers from mainstream theatre, including opera and dance. Since the 1980s these theatre-makers have come to regard the art form as accessible and attractive, where before most puppetry had allowed itself to degenerate into a ghettoized entertainment suitable only for the very undemanding. Children were thought to be the ideal public for a puppet show, but were frequently offered poorly conceived and executed productions as unsuited to them as to the adults accompanying them. It is true that children still constitute the greater proportion of audiences for puppetry, but today they are more likely to witness productions that pre-suppose their intelligence and sound judgement, developed at an early age through contact with the high production values of television and the cinema. Adults too are increasingly beguiled by the art form and are now catered for by the puppeteers regularly. Adult productions are growing exponentially: an international puppet festival may programme more shows for adults than for kids. Puppets are winning back some of their old ground.

All the twenty-first century productions have been heavily influenced by the latest available technological resources, and, crucially, more generous subsidy. The shows play in arts centres and prestigious theatre spaces rather than in school or parish halls, and there is a proliferation of national and international festivals where the puppeteers absorb new ideas and new contacts.

Whether as a 'puppet show', 'puppet theatre' or a 'theatre with puppets' the genre has become an accustomed addition to the spectrum of the performing arts.

Having located puppetry in an innovative contemporary theatre context, is it possible to define the puppet itself?

THE PUPPET: ANIMATED FIGURE AND OBJECT

You will find a variety of definitions of a puppet, a different one in almost every book on the subject. For me, the puppet is a representation and distillation of a character, the repository of a persona perceived by both creator and spectator within its outward form. It can be any thing, any object, if brought to imagined life through the agency of a human player who inspires it and controls it directly. The control may be through corporeal contact (hands-on, hands-in), or via strings, wires, wooden or metal rods. The figure animated electronically or even remotely is still a puppet if the performer is present at the other end of the cable or the machinery, controlling the movements, just as at the end of a simple string or rod.

The writer and educator A.R. (Panto) Philpott (1919–1991) in his *Dictionary of Puppetry* (long out of print but little out of date) wisely observes:

Perfect definition eludes theorists, historians, puppeteers, dictionary-makers. It is easier to state what a puppet is NOT: it is not a 'doll' … Dolls are for personal play: puppets are essentially theatrical in function. (Philpott, 1969: 209)

It is not an automaton either, although there is no doubt that automata are cousins and even assistants to the puppet, so that the dividing line is sometimes blurred (as further explained in the next chapter). The automaton, when set in motion by clockwork or some other mechanism and not directly operated by human hands, is pre-programmed, repetitive in its action and therefore not, in my view, a puppet.

In pursuit of other perceptions of the puppet I quote Eric Bass, a prodigiously talented American auteur-puppeteer, who sees the puppet through the eyes of a Jewish poet and comedian. He claims that 'puppets are poetic' and goes on:

They are, because they are not human, immediately metaphors. Their world is a poem, not a short story. They are by their very nature images come to life. When the puppet bridges the gap between his seeming limitations and his coming to life, he has made a moving comment on the human condition. And even the puppet's death can be moving as, having given us the gift of his breath, he then takes it back. And yet, in the next moment, he lives again, immortal, a dream or memory in the actor's hands. The actor can play this role, too, but the puppet *is* the role. He is naturally tragicomic, naturally abstract, a detail. In the human world, he is a visitor and we must see ourselves through his eyes. (see Staub, 1992: 10)

Miles Lee, a writer and puppeteer, and pioneer of the art form in Scotland, wrote a book in 1958 entitled *Puppet Theatre Production and Manipulation,* about many aspects of puppet-specific production which remains a good resource and is full of sensible guidance:

> The main life and purpose of the puppet is its movement and what it does in an actual performance. Action and movement are the prime life factors of the puppet, voice and speech being secondary components. (Lee, 1958: 51)

Lee's statement should be qualified, however. Stillness can be as effective in the life of a puppet character as motion. Belief in the thing's life can be projected onto a motionless object, through the focus and conviction of the other characters on the stage conveyed to the spectator who in turn becomes convinced of its *anima.*

Peter Brook's production of *Le Costume* provides a good example of the life perceived in an immobile object. The play told of a vengeful husband who, having caught his wife at home *in flagrante delicto,* places the abandoned suit of his wife's lover, who has fled, over a chair at the end of the marital bed as a permanent reminder of her guilt. For spectator and actors, the suit was invested with a powerful presence – a torturous reminder of her adultery.[6]

Was it then a puppet? Or is the thing never a puppet when it is inert? It must remain a question of individual perception.[7] The figurative puppet at rest will yet be perceived as puppet, given its distinctive manufacture. Specially designed, shaped or modified to be a stage or screen character, attached to some sort of control mechanism, even if it is onstage but unmoving, then it will be seen as a puppet, since the intention of its maker and its theatrical employment are obvious: it is a potential performer, whether ritualistic or dramatic. The object-puppet, unmodified and unmoving, is simply

---

[6] *Le Costume,* directed by Peter Brook, was produced in London in 2001 and 2003. The play is an adaptation by Mothobi Mutloatse and Barney Simon of the short story, *The Suit,* by South African writer Can Themba.

[7] Compare the occasion when shortly after the death of Kantor in 1990, in the Centre Pompidou in Paris, the company placed the same chair onstage as the director had occupied during rehearsals of *Today is my Birthday.* The company announced that it would stay unoccupied during the performance. 'The stage ... was filled with objects and people from Kantor's "Room and Inn of Imagination/Memory" [...] a big picture frame [...] stage right was occupied by Kantor's double, the Self-portrait, a man in a black suit and a long black scarf, who sat on a chair with his back to the audience' (Kantor, 1993: 366).

a useful or useless artefact. A polythene bag performs only when given life and breath in a performance by a puppeteer, when the spectator may perceive its life as a symbol or a ghost, even a human character. The same polythene bag, put aside by the puppeteer, is, in the perception of the average spectator, an object again.

The form of a figurative puppet can be realistic or abstract, exquisitely sculpted or roughly made. It can represent a human or animal or the concrete expression of an emotion, the symbol of an idea. Fantastic characters – many of them creatures from the outer limits of man's imagination – appear as variations on the theme: monsters, extra-terrestrials, robots. I have seen animated numbers and letters of the alphabet, mathematical shapes, personified images of the seasons, of spirits, archetypal depictions of destitution or grandeur.

Sometimes a puppet is hardly crafted at all: its appearance must depend on the dramaturgy and the aesthetic of the production in preparation. All will be manipulated as depictions of characters in dramatic or comic performance not performable by the human actor, in what has been called a 'theatre of the impossible' (Vella and Rickards, 1989) – impossible, that is, for the flesh and blood performers, constrained by the weight and frailty of their physicality and by gravity.

The question of the definition of a puppet has been complicated by producers exploring the potential of the latest technologies in relation to

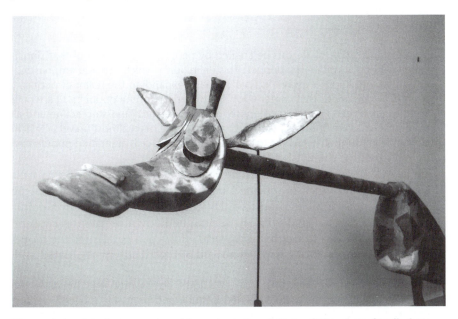

Figure 1.2   Art, design and craft in a single head. Peter O'Rourke's Giraffe from the Little Angel production of Roald Dahl's *The Giraffe, the Pelly and Me* (2008).
© Peter O'Rourke, who also designed and directed the production.

their puppetry. Hardly a performance is given without some inclusion of projection, video or filmed animation in the constant stream of experiment. It remains an academic question whether the mediated, screened image can ever be termed a valid puppet to accord with my definition above, although a plausible contribution in favour of its entitlement is given in an essay by the American academic and writer Steve Tillis, 'The Art of Puppetry in the Age of Media Production' (Tillis, 2001). It is a long essay, cleverly argued, and worth seeking out to read in full.

Tillis lists three types of 'media figure': those generated by computer graphics, those 'moved' by stop-action photography and those activated by electronic ('animatronic') controls. He discusses the widely insisted-on criterion of the puppet performing in 'real-time', and argues that media figures – most obviously those created through computer graphics – cannot generally be said to lose their presence in time and space when presented by their particular medium, for their presence is actually created by the medium. That is to say that they are not media reproductions but original productions made possible through media (Tillis, 2001: 173). He notes that the 'real-time' criterion refers to 'a synchronicity between the puppeteer's control and the puppet's resultant movement' and suggests that an 'alternate meaning of real-time would refer to a synchronicity not only of control and movement, but of audience reception as well'. Going on to discuss a 1994 essay by Stephen Kaplin (Tillis, 2001: 18–25), to be found in the same volume, *Puppets, Masks and Performing Objects*, Tillis draws out Kaplin's implied definition of puppetry.

> [If] the signification of life can be created by people, then the site of that signification is to be considered a puppet. This definition – which I should emphasize, I have read into Kaplin's essay – is revolutionary, expanding the realm of puppetry beyond all definitions that center upon the materiality of the puppet [...] It would seem to encompass not only computer graphics images (and stop-action and all animatronics as well), but also forms of art that have been almost universally held distinct from puppetry, such as the cel (also known as cell) animation popularized by Walt Disney. (Tillis, 2001: 175)

Tillis then explains the complicated but interesting means by which the computer graphic figure is produced, Having joints and articulation points like those of a puppet, and with the technique known as 'motion capture' generated in real-time through the physical efforts of a performer, the movement of the figure on the screen can be said to be directly manipulated:

> To create from the keyboard the walk of a figure across a room [...] involves the bringing together of separately defined gestural and proxemic movements: first one uses handles to define the gestures that constitute walking, and then one defines the animation path and speed of the walk. This bringing together of movements is analogous to the way that puppets are moved. A marionette, for example, also has specific gestures of walking, created primarily with its leg strings; these

walking gestures are brought together with a proxemic path along which the marionette is transported by its main support strings. [...] The main difference between
the keyboard-created walking of a computer graphics figure and a puppet is that
the walk of the former is painstakingly composed over an extended period of time,
while the walk of the latter is created all at once, in real-time. (Tillis, 2001: 177)

Tillis approaches the question of whether the figure's intangibility should be
taken into account if it is to earn its place under the heading of 'puppet'.

Computer graphics figures are not tangible [...] As we have seen, there are striking similarities in the creation of computer graphics figures and puppets: the
creation of both involves the construction of a figure imbued with articulation
points that is then given surface design features. Both, in short, are artificial
human constructs designed for manipulation (of one sort or another) by people.
And, as I suggested earlier, both share the crucial trait of being sites of signification other than 'real' living beings. (Tillis, 2001: 178–79)

Noting that puppets made of wood or cloth are tangible objects, while
computer graphics figures are not, Tillis proposes that traditional puppets
should be thought of as 'tangible' puppets, while computer graphics figures
are thought of as 'virtual' puppets. Another point in favour of the argument
concerns the manipulator of this kind of figure: can a person working at a
keyboard be called a puppeteer? Certainly the virtual puppet still depends
on human control 'of one sort or another'.

There follows an explication of the stop-action puppet, which can never
perform on a stage as its action depends on the movement from one attitude
and gesture to another by a photographer and a trained manipulator. Each
movement is shot so that, strung together, the finished film is indistinguishable by an average viewer from the cell animation of, say, a Disney cartoon.
Tillis describes stop-action figures as closely related to puppets 'as we have
known them' except in one crucial respect: 'the absence of even the possibility of real-time control is the defining characteristic of these figures' (Tillis,
2001: 182).

According to Tillis, these three types of animated forms – tangible, virtual
and stop-motion – should all take their rightful place under the rubric of
'puppet', but only, he says, if the criteria of 'real-time' action and 'tangibility'
are discounted. I have not used either of these in my definition above; I'm
therefore ready to be convinced that the stop-action, the animatronic and the
keyboard-operated computer figures are screen puppets: the first two, after
all, have a trained performer controlling the movements. Of the third I am
less convinced: here the keyboard is the control, moving the character. Can
this be said to be a means of manipulation, even if 'operated' by the hands
of a puppeteer? I leave it to the reader.

While technology is discovering new techniques for animating the puppet,
new materials for its construction are invented. There are no longer any rules
here, unless the figure is intended for a strictly traditional performance when

there will indeed be strict rules, as in the making of a figure for the Bunraku theatre, which takes years of intensive practice.

The answer to the question 'what is a puppet?' depends, as Margaret Williams explains, on just 'how the question is posed'. Like Vella and Rickards Williams is Australian, an academic who taught theatre, including puppet theatre theory and practice, in the University of New South Wales and whose first-hand experience is incalculable, having also married a puppeteer, Richard Bradshaw, and toured the world with him and his shadow show. In her essay, *Including the Audience: The Idea of 'the Puppet' and the Real Spectator*, she writes

> Any definition necessarily reflects the writer's pre-existing conceptual framework and excludes what does not confirm it. Yet there seems a persistent need for individual perspectives on puppetry, even personal preferences, to be framed in terms of a universal definition.
>
> Roger-Daniel Bensky notes that a puppet is not only a medium of artistic expression but an object of reflection – aesthetic, psychological and metaphysical. There are many valuable semiotic and aesthetic analyses of puppetry and its relation to the theatre of human drama, and of specific puppet forms. But it is the *idea* of 'the puppet' that is the subject of much theoretical debate, an idea which Jurkowski says would persist even if all puppets cease to exist. [...] The most common definition of a puppet is the oxymoron of a 'living object', what Jurkowski calls the 'magic' puppet. But 'magic' implies something more than just the apparent miracle of life in the inanimate: the puppet is seen as the bearer of an archetypal or collective memory, the heir to a long tradition of belief that inanimate matter moulded into human form has magical power. (Williams, 2007: 119–20)

THE ANIMATED OBJECT

Be that as it may, the puppet can appear as a realistic or abstract figure, a piece of unformed material or a non-performative object. At this stage it is important to explain the distinction between the animated *figure* and the animated *object*. The first is manufactured to depict a stage character, the second is a thing in its natural state or manufactured with no thought of any future as a stage player. In performance, animated and manipulated, *both* are puppets.

The '*object-puppet*' may be almost any thing not intended for performance, made or in its natural state: a garden tool, an item of clothing, a flexible table lamp, newspaper, a stick or a plant. To convince the spectator of an object's breathing presence, to imbue it with character, that is to make it become a puppet, is, by the way, more difficult for most puppeteers than the animation of a recognizably human or animal figure. The energy needed to 'enliven' the object has to be powerful enough to carry to the audience who, if complicit, conveys their conviction (of the object's liveness) back to the puppeteer. A delicate triangle of projected energy and response from the puppeteer through the object to the audience has to be formed, but is rarely sustainable for long.

The Human Among Objects was the title of a lecture given at a meeting of the members of the British Centre of UNIMA, the international association for puppetry, in Brighton in 1994. Jurkowski as the invited speaker traced the rise of interest in the object as an animated character as opposed to the portrait or caricatured figure, in this 'new age of artistic expression'. He said:

> Distinct from puppets, common objects are manufactured for some practical use. Naturally each has its own iconicity which allows people to recognise it. If a performer produces an object in order to turn it into a stage character, his task is more complex than the task of presenting a puppet character. By means of his acting and manipulation he has to transform the object (for example, an umbrella) into a character (for example, a woman). First he has to contradict the iconic and practical value of the object and next he has to endow it with new functions and new appearance to make it recognisable as the intended character. (Jurkowski, 1994: 9)

Successful object animation in theatre comes in short episodes or vignettes which are comic or tragic. A few longer pieces have been successful: there was for instance a forty-minute show by Peter Ketturkat with a strong storyline, *Keine Angst vor Grossen Tieren!* (*Don't be Afraid of the Big Animals!*), a classic success of the puppet theatre, created in the 1970s and produced again in 2006. The characters were all kitchen or garden implements, most modified in some way (attached eyes or hair for example), but some as unadorned as their manu-facturer intended them. The 2005 touring version of this show was reviewed by Beccy Smith, dramaturg and director, in the periodical *Animations Online*:

> Ketturkat's work is renowned for its playful reinvention of object theatre. The long narrow playboard provides a simple wide-screen framing, the lighting state is fixed and the bizarrely varied sound effects voiced by the strange objects of his world are created one-man-band style by the two performers hidden within. Yet the precision and aptitude with which Ketturkat characterises his objects, testing every physical property of each item, matching movement to shape, rhythm to mechanisms and deftly mixing human qualities with the surreal, give a sense that we're witnessing a liberation of the essence within each form. There's no over-arching structure to the piece, instead spoons, corkscrews, garlic crusher and tubing ... seemed to live out their inner life before us, before vanishing back to obscurity and, presumably, the kitchen drawer or garden shed – but remaining forever transfigured in our imagination.[8]

---

[8] I have quoted the 'statements' of several artists from a booklet produced in 1992 (see http://www.puppetcentre.org.uk/animationsonline/aofifteen/reviews.html) to accompany an exhibition of the work of the United States' greatest puppeteers. As this claims to be a serious work, I have not included in the main text the statement by the peerless performer-comedian Paul Zaloom, but I cannot resist reproducing it here:

> 'I am interested in puppetry because puppets show up to rehearsals on time. I like puppets because you can hurt them and throw them out the window and not get into

'Object animation' is more than 'object manipulation' – the former means the projection of life into the object; the latter only demands dexterity in its 'handling'. Both will affirm the object's characteristics and materiality, showing its dramaturgical significance, but only the first will imbue it with breath.

Tadeusz Kantor (1915–1990), visionary Polish theatre-maker, designer, and, in his early years, puppeteer, was perennially interested in the employment of 'low status objects' which he dedicated to the creation of 'a "different" reality'. In one of his lessons, the *Insegnamento*s, he agreed that

> There must be a very close, almost biological symbiosis between an actor and an object.
> They cannot be separated.
> In the simplest case, the actor must attempt to do everything for the OBJECT to stay visible; in the most radical case the actor and the object must become one. I call this state a BIO-OBJECT. (Kantor, 1993: 240)

In the course of the production of *La Ballade de Mister Punch* by Alain Recoing's Théâtre des Mains Nues in Paris in 1976 Antoine Vitez, the respected French director, commented on the pleasurable interrelationships to be discovered between a human actor and a scenic environment consisting mainly of objects in transformation:

> Now I would like to say something perverse: the transformation of the object is the concern of contemporary theatre, leading us to the wellsprings of performance. In my work I have often used transformation. In the show *Friday or the Natural Life* from the novel of Michel Tournier which I produced in Chaillot, an umbrella became a magic arrow, then a flute, a parachute, a parasol, a scarecrow, and a stage character. Each object gradually changed its function during the course of the play. (Vitez, 1976: 19)

Encapsulating the neo-modernist passion for the impersonal theatre at its most extreme, an English-Israeli writer, poet, actor and puppeteer Dennis Silk (1928–1998) saw life in every kind of object, even a knife and fork on a table. Silk was a surrealist with a unique vision who formed a company he called 'Thing Theatre':

---

trouble. Another significant advantage of puppets is that I can play many different characters without changing my pants ["trousers" to the British]. The reason I've dedicated my life to puppetry is that I love schlepping around a thousand pounds of stuff wherever I go.

I work with found objects because they are cheap. "Found object" is a pretentious word for "thing". My shows are too weird for T.V. and not weird enough for the avant-garde. The only people who cannot understand my work are non-English speakers and television executives. Avant-gardists understand my work and thus don't like it'.

Thing Theatre? What does that mean? It means a theatre where things are granted a higher dramatic status than in the theatre of the personal actor. A playgoer may ask: Isn't it a little frivolous, a little whimsical, to deprive the personal actor of part of his function, and to search out instead the dramatic life in a shoelace, a bicycle-pump, a hair-dryer? The *thing* novelty will wear off soon enough, a playgoer will say. Can a packet of sewing needles outtalk Chekhov?

That playgoer is wrong. It's because the personal actor has lost the thing in himself, the strong concentrated thing, that we turn to a theatre of the thing. He's squandered his strength in a hundred personal emotions which he then inflicts on his role. But the thing-actor has guarded its strength, it's a form of locked-up energy waiting for the right outlet. The personal actor should be locked up in a furniture warehouse for an entire week, and study the concentrated life in a chair, a table, a commode ... the unhurried life. The warehouse should be his school. (Silk, 1996: 228)

Silk's long essay on *The Marionette Theatre* goes to the mystery at the heart of puppetry, but will seem eccentric to anyone who is not a poet or a puppeteer or an animist, preferably all three. Here is a taster:

The umbrella teases. It opens. Then folds back on itself. Really it's two umbrellas. Yet it's one. A villager would have to have two minds to grasp it. Moreover its mode of arrival draws attention to itself. So they build a shrine to it. Best to abandon it to mystery ... In the street outside the small red spinning top has been hoarding its conversation for a long time ... Speech after long silence. And its cousin, the yo-yo, opens and shuts shop. The balloon declared itself at half-past nine this morning ... Then went back into tininess ... The umbrella should make a place for them in the shrine. It should hold a nest of gods. Umbrella, yo-yo, spinning-top, balloon. A cotton-reel. ... The flag over the shrine waits. Waits for a lucky wind to give it life. Unfolds and flaps in the wind. (Silk, 1996: 238)

If a Theatre of Objects is concerned with the presence of things or raw materials rather than crafted, mimetic figures, it is nevertheless notable that in the playing, almost every manipulated object recalls a human or animal character, with, for example, a location (if only hinted) for its head and eyes. Perhaps there is a case to be made for a theatrical exploration of the pure thing-ness of an object in its essential, non-humanoid form. Enno Podehl, German academic, performer and director cites a production of a company who tried to do exactly that. In an essay from the journal *Das Andere Theater* (The Other Theatre) written in 2002 and titled 'Parlament den Dingen' (Parliament of Things) this was the final paragraph:

In the piece 'Mousson' (Monsoon) by the 'Au Cul de Loup' company from Paris, objects perform without any assigned roles. They are just themselves, unwieldy or soft, transparent or expansive, and most of all filled with sound. At first sight they don't tell you much. It is only in movement that they develop their specific world of sound and space – the world of the monsoon. Through their weight, their form and their musical qualities the objects themselves pass on movement impulses to the performers who allow them to resonate within themselves and then return them, intensified, to the objects to allow every possibility contained in them their full expression. The players are not only performers but discoverers. They no longer direct the flow but respond to the impulses coming from the objects. We experience how objects handled by sensitive people become personal musical instruments, and how people can be transformed into dancers by objects. We become witness to the visualisation of music.

This form of object theatre rehabilitates the independence of objects. The rules and gestures of the game find themselves in a mutually respectful exchange, like a spirited dialogue between player/performer and object. The performing objects – at first sight quite peculiar – have been chosen specifically for this performance. They are the subjects of this play. The dramatic structure grows from the impulses they pass on to the performers. (in Podehl, 2002: 3–44)

For both figure-puppet and object-puppet the intention is to convince those watching that the thing contains breath, that it is inspired, that it is alive. In the course of a performance more often than not the conviction depends on many variables, including the age and experience of the spectators, their technical knowledge of the art form, and the skill of the puppet operators. All but the most naïve spectators will find themselves now convinced, now unconvinced that the creature before them has life; they will focus on the puppet, then the manipulator and the method of control (when the manipulator is visible), and back again to the puppet. If the puppeteer is hidden they will shift focus between the puppet and, say, the setting. The changing focus is evidence of an alternating belief and unbelief in the puppet's autonomous existence. The condition has no scientific label that I can find, but has been described (poetically) as the 'opalization effect' (Jurkowski, 1988: 41–42) and (confusingly) as 'double vision' (Tillis, 1992: 59). Probably the most accurate word, 'oscillation', is used by T.A. Green and W.J. Pepicello (Green, 1983: 157).

The more child-like an audience member – of any age – the more engaged by the puppet he or she will be and the oscillation effect will be less; and vice versa, the more sophisticated the viewer, the more difficult it is to enter and remain in the illusion, so oscillation between belief and unbelief is more frequent. It is, however, worth reporting the true anecdote of a worldly man of the theatre, not a Christian, who found himself reaching for his handkerchief during an amateur 'nativity' play depicting the sentimental legend of the Christmas rose. He believed in what he was seeing for the duration of the story. Similarly one was conscious at every performance of the hundreds of spectators visibly moved by the plight of the injured puppet animals in the current adaptation of Michael Morpurgo's story *War Horse*. Puppets can evoke profound emotion.

Few members of an adult public would describe themselves as 'child-like', I suspect; nonetheless the animated figure touches our collective memory of innocence, the simple acceptance of a fiction, such as normal children enjoy. We imbue the puppets with our imagination and experience a

Figure 1.3 *Rubbished*, a devised production by students of the MA in Advanced Theatre Practice at the Central School of Speech and Drama, London (2004). The central character is Pinky, a toddler with attitude.
© Patrick Baldwin.

deceptive empathy, deceptive because empathy assumes feeling in the recipient. The puppet only mimics feeling through attitude and movement.

The Spanish modernist playwright Jacinto Benavente (1866–1954) described his 1908 play *Los Intereses Creados (The Bonds of Interest)*, as a 'puppetesque farce in the style of the commedia dell'arte'. In it the central character Crispin says:

> The author is well aware that so primitive a spectacle is not the most appropriate for the sophisticated audience of the present time. Therefore he begs the protection of your refinement and good will. He asks only that you become as young as possible in spirit. The world is already old and in its dotage. But Art is not resigned to growing old, and in order to seem a child plays at nonsense ... And that is why these old puppets presume to amuse you today with their trifles. (Benavente, [1908] 2004: Prologue)

Simultaneous actions – inspirational, manual, vocal, mechanical – via one or more human operators, visible or screened, are what give the puppet its physical life. It acts as an outline, so to speak, for the eye to fill with character and colour, from the projection of the spectator's fantasy, born in the silence of the head, arising from memories, ideals, concerns, dreams. In successful puppet play the audience cooperates actively, and will afterwards swear that this or that figure changed expression; that it grew taller during the action, or that it effected a range of movement, all impossible.

THE PUPPETEER

The primary characteristic of puppeteers is a belief in the hidden life of *things*. A crushed piece of paper, a kitchen chair, a box or a book can appear to breathe in their hands. Another hallmark, especially of the designer-maker, is a visual creativity that they wish to express in scenic terms. They see a performance text through a prism of moving pictures; they see camels in clouds, dancers in daffodils, an old man in a black bin liner, wolves in walls.

Peter Schumann, world famous founder of the Bread and Puppet Theatre, wrote:

> The considerable talents for the puppeteer's bag-of-tricks showmanship all originate in their preoccupation with things. The puppeteers harvest piles of human-like and yet other worldly qualities from their observation of objects, especially from their practice of moving these objects [...] The manipulation of puppets is over and above the wilful targeting which aims for certain results from an audience. The puppeteers' only hope of mastering their puppets is to enter their puppets' delicate and seemingly inexhaustible lives. (see Staub, 1992: 22)

Puppeteering as a profession and even the word puppeteer are as yet an immature presence in theatre histories. After the 1930s, the formally trained professional arose only through the establishment of the first higher education specialist schools throughout the Soviet Union and its satellites as in Bialystok (Poland), Jaroslavl (Russia), Prague, Budapest and East Berlin. They were provided by the authorities in order to mobilize and prepare the human resources needed for the scores of state puppet theatres established throughout eastern Europe.

The puppeteer, trained or not, can be showman or shaman, exhibitionist or poet. Practitioners in western countries with no specialist formation will usually have a qualification in sculpture, painting and/or scenic design, even architecture – rarely in acting. Many play musical instruments, and you will be hard put to it to find one who is not musical. Most vocational puppeteers were in the past male and many I have met identified their vocation at a pre-pubescent age, a fact that may well be of interest to anthropologists. In northern Europe since the 1980s the profession has by contrast attracted many women and at least half the younger puppeteers are now, I estimate, female.

Their ranks may be divided into three: the builder of puppets and sets who may also be the overall designer of a show, the performer-operator, and those adept at both construction and performance. At the time of writing the majority belong to the third group, but scenography for puppetry is being slowly recognized as a specialist discipline.

The first group, the designers and/or makers, often prefer to remain in the workshop, with little desire to confront an audience. In this category you see the Pygmalion, the sculptor or painter wishing his or her creations to be endowed with breath and motion. Although the best puppet-makers are fine artists their figures and settings are rarely seen in art galleries however high their plastic value. They are primarily making theatre, a theatre of movement and transformation difficult to reconcile with still-life exhibits.

The second group, the freelance performers, is the smallest, but it is growing rapidly. Puppeteer-performers are rarely actors, although they understand many of the techniques of acting. They are a different breed. They do not create their puppets, only animate them, manipulating and often speaking for one or more of the characters. Sometimes they themselves act in a human role alongside their puppet(s), and this duality of performance demands great skill. If they can act, dance or sing they have a better chance of employment in today's multi-disciplined performing companies. Although they are the animators, not the makers, any of them will tell you that it is difficult to work comfortably with a figure not custom-fitted to suit the manipulator's physique. As with all performing objects the puppet should handle and be handled as if it were an extension of its operator.

In the third group are the all-rounders, the puppeteers as capable of designing and crafting as performing. Amongst professionals of the western tradition this group has been until now the most commonly found, but their numbers as a proportion of the whole are diminishing. Reasons for this lie in the structuring of the formal training now available in schools and courses all over the world. In the pioneering Soviet establishments, many of which continue their activity, the actor-puppeteers and the designer-puppeteers have found themselves in separate schools. In most western training grounds the separation of performance from design and construction is not an appealing policy, as most would-be puppet practitioners wish for at least some knowledge of both, for reasons practical, artistic and economic. A few schools offer all-round training, as for example the prestigious Institute in Charleville-Mézières, France, which gives the students theories and practicalities of theatre, construction and manipulation, and in addition encourages creative theatre-making in a three-year course.

The training of puppeteers gives rise to much debate and examination of alternative methods. While formal provision is everywhere growing most would-be professionals still serve an apprenticeship with existing companies, learning on the job. The prospect facing most of them, although their horizons are expanding, is in some respects unchanged from the end of the twentieth century. Those who are producers, builders and performers will be likely to earn their bread within an independently formed small-scale touring company of two to six people, answering the demand for imaginative and educational entertainment for children and families. They play at weekends and through school holidays, in puppetry festivals, arts festivals and folk festivals. Many tour abroad. Their life is a hardworking round of preparing shows, fundraising for the periods of preparation (when performance income can normally not be earned), booking venues and tours, and finally performing a new or revived show for the public. They frequently act as their own production, stage and accounting managers, driving a van all over the country and humping sets and puppets into and out of the playing space. The most active accept as many bookings as they can fit into the schedule, sometimes playing four shows in a weekend in four different venues, sometimes luxuriating in a week when a show has been booked into a single venue. The temptation to experiment with a production based on an unknown story is small: the safe repertoire is the fairy and folk tale or (as at present) an adaptation of a popular children's book or television favourite. However the statutory funding bodies (at least in Europe) encourage adventurous work that explores new dramaturgies and modes of expression, and it is hoped that the circuits will gradually present more and more of it.

Freelance performer-puppeteers with no company of their own have a precarious existence, like any actor. They wait to be engaged, perhaps by a puppet group, or a theatre company needing specialist input, or most lucrative of all, a television or a film company making a commercial (of which a surprisingly large number feature animated figures and objects). Certainly the freelance category of puppeteer has swollen to a surprising extent since the 1990s.

The designer-maker puppeteers have also increased their market share. More productions mean more work, and the best have plenty of work. Theatre prop-makers are of course asked to make puppet figures, but the experience of the specialist puppeteer is irreplaceable, involving as it does knowledge of the arcane arts of jointing and weighting, of the materials suitable for the production's aesthetic and so on.

As much as the puppeteers of all these three types have found their world growing and their chances of employment increasing, it is rare to find a puppeteer, however regularly employed, who does not struggle to earn a decent living. As with actors, they must break into television or lead a company whose standards of excellence will be smiled on by sponsors and awarded generous and regular subsidy if they are to pay the mortgage.

A singular example, working from New York but frequently invited to direct abroad, is Roman Paska, a puppeteer-poet and film director whose productions are of some intellectual stature and whose one-person stage company was Theatre for The Birds, now the Dead Puppet company. In 1992 he wrote:

> It's one thing to work with puppets, it's something Other to be a puppeteer ... I can think of many good aesthetic and poetic reasons why I work with puppets, but they can't explain what really moved me to become a puppeteer. Or what behoves me to be one. Apparently that choice was made before the age of Reason, with the kind of unreasoning instinct that comes from below. And while I still can't make up my mind, demon instinct tells me things my mind can never

fathom; that, for instance, the puppet is more intent on being real than being symbolic; that therefore puppet theatre is a 'theatre of possession' and that the only fully realized puppeteers are shamans or madmen, holy or insane ... I try to believe that there is still some rational justification for what I do, some conventional use or necessity. But deep inside I know that puppet theatre is as irrational and unnecessary as nature. Like a bird, a planet or a disease. And despite all efforts to feather a nest for puppet theatre in contemporary society, it remains a fundamentally deviant, subversive, marginal art form. That may be the most strange and marvellous thing about it. Anyway, it's one good reason why I call it theatre for the birds ... In an iron age of reason, someone has to carry the golden torch of Folly. (see Staub, 1992: 20)

Hundreds of puppet artists, few of them publicly recognized by name or appearance unless they have a television or film profile, are working all over Europe, and thousands if you include other parts of the world. After centuries of separation and concealment they and their art have 'come out' of their self-made closet, both in a physical and metaphorical sense. Even for the curtain calls of a major production instead of hiding behind their puppet character, they now by right bow on their own behalf.

It is evident that in most performances the unconcealed puppeteers have become the accepted convention, except for an uninitiated public which may still demonstrate surprise and even indignation at seeing the puppeteer at work on his puppet, as if robbed of a treasured illusion. But illusion is no longer the *sine qua non* of puppetry, as it is no longer the stuff of theatre, for the truly modern theatre-maker. The rows of bulky spotlights are unmasked, like the marionettes' wooden controls. The playwright and theatre-maker Anna Furse writes:

Illusion and disbelief are often opposed to materiality and flatness on the live art aesthetic, while the politics of this debate remain caught up in principles of fair play. There is an idea that if you beguile the spectator, or mystify them with charisma, you are somehow cheating them, assuming authority over their freedom to interpret. But I would argue that visible puppetry offers precisely an opportunity for illusion to be stripped bare. What makes any suspension of belief exciting and fair is that it is, as we say, 'willing'. Even a five-year-old knows that a monkey puppet is a puppet when they see the puppeteer leap around the stage with it. But it is their choice to play the game – the *jeu*.

It seems to me that actor-puppeteers open up all kinds of questions about collaboration, hierarchy, liveness, presence, persona, performer, actor, and most importantly what spectators are actually looking at when they sit and watch. Puppeteers are unlike any other actors because they are entirely committed to the Other [...] what puppeteers contribute to the art of the performer is an almost ethical question. It is a question of attention and the places that the performer draws attention to and from. Rather than draw attention to themselves, actor-puppeteers devote their attention to guiding ours outside, leading our attention away from their own bodies via the body itself. This lack of ego, or 'indicative attention-seeking' that tells the audience 'I'm here but look at this or that now' produces an extraordinary concentration, and a particular kind of focus [...] You're not thinking about your own body except in how to adapt it to the need of the puppeteering activity, moment by moment. (see Margolies, 2009: 20–21)

Furse was asked to adapt the traditional Japanese story of 'The Peach Child' for the Little Angel Theatre in London. She was invited to 'extend the language of the puppet show' and bring her particular way of working with the body and visual narrative to the project, through a prolonged rehearsal period during which she worked the puppeteers hard, employing physical exercises including Tai Chi to improve co-ordination and concentration.

Some of the most effective manipulation – from the spectator's point of view – results from the puppeteer's unconscious ability to project visual and spiritual imagination into the figure being operated. The puppeteer is projecting the complete conception of a role, from above, behind or below, its character expressed in gait, clothes, gesture – as if into a reversed reflection in a mirror. The puppet is an entity which absorbs its operator's energy and is thereby able to convince the spectator of its vitality. It is a matter of transferred, not duplicated, kinesthetics. If the puppeteer is projected 'into' the puppet character, it cannot but be the cynosure, it cannot make a wrong gesture; it cannot produce the wrong voice. A distinguished Polish designer, Jadwiga Mydlarska-Kowal (1943–2001) put it in a nutshell:

> The actor in the dramatic theatre is himself the plastic material. In the puppet theatre, by contrast, the actor puts the space and the plastic forms that I have created, as the designer, to work. I think that the actor, in puppet theatre, has to have an enormously strong visual imagination. He has to make the form move, he must live the form, he must sense the form. His task is very important. And that is what distinguishes the actor in puppet theatre from the actor in the dramatic theatre. (see Jurkowski, 1998: 152)

It is to be noted that the illusion of the autonomous puppet has been ruptured and the puppeteer has emerged undisguised, in accordance with twentieth century tendencies in western modes of theatre. The influence of Brecht and various elements of post-modernist culture, when mystification and magic fell out of favour, were contributory factors: faith in the supernatural seems to many in the richer countries more and more suspect. But, as Victoria Nelson argues in her fascinating book *The Secret Life of Puppets*, on the 'displacement of the supernatural' into the realm of psychology, the 'repressed religious' is

> visible in representations of puppets, robots, cyborgs and other artificial humans in literature and film. It endures as a fascination with the spiritualizing of matter and the demiurgic infusion of soul into human simulacra – a fascination that manifested itself, in the twentieth century, both in avant-garde theatre and in popular entertainments. (Nelson, 2001: 20)

The puppeteer's presence alongside the figures and objects being animated is now taken for granted in the collage of staged media, and has given rise to a great number of deliberations on its meaning. In the chapter on aesthetics are two exemplary essays by Paska and by Roland Barthes on the subject.

Puppets are operated by many different categories of visible performer – dancer, singer, dramatic actor, comedian, musician, and the convention of the hidden puppeteer is usually reserved for shows following tradition. However, in spite of its ceremonial connotations, Asian puppetry, as seen in the technique of the Bunraku-za, the Indonesian wayang, the dance puppetry of Cambodia, for example, all display the puppeteer as an essential physical element of the spectacle. This must be accepted as a fact which has exerted another strong influence on western performance.

Writing as a puppeteer-designer-producer and film-maker, Julie Taymor, best known for her authorship of the staged production of *The Lion King*, enlarges on this:

> In my work in the theatre I often choose to juxtapose live actors with puppetry and masked dancers. This allows for the pinspotting of human elements of the live characters. In most naturalist theatre the human face along with the details of the body, its flesh and gestures, are taken for granted. But when you isolate the exact moment of exposing these human elements their presence is magnified and the humanity of the character is heightened. The scale and form (shadow, hand, rod, bunraku, etc) of the stylised figures in the production determine their importance and depth of meaning and emotion. In designing or choosing the style of puppet or mask an artist has complete control over the depth of meaning and range of expression of a given character or image. Through the juxtaposition of humans, puppets, and masks a work can have a multilayered texture operating on many levels of reality.[9] (see Staub, 1992: 26)

For some the presence of the puppet operator is 'not so much a disruption of illusion as the potential for a different kind of focus, with the imagination of the spectator now engaged as much with the visible craft of the puppeteer'[10] as with the otherness of the puppet. The exposure of the techniques, for example the source of the puppet's voice and the control of its movement, the absorption of the performers in their puppet, or their interaction when playing two separate characters, intensifies the interest for many of the spectators, rendering the 'oscillation' of their focus a deliberate, not an involuntary choice. Illogically the process rarely destroys the spectator's belief in the life of the character, if it is animated and not a simple prop. Halina Waszkiel, Polish critic and teacher, wrote that 'the essence of puppetry lies in the mysterious bond linking the puppet and its manipulator'. This was for her

[9] Simon Shepherd, editorial comment on a draft of the chapter.
[10] Ibid.

the crux of the matter – 'there can be no magic of the puppet theatre without masterly manipulation' (Waszkiel, 2008: 23).

Perhaps the revelation of the puppeteer is a fashion of the times and the pendulum may swing. We may witness a renewed pursuit of mysteries and magic, a return to the hidden manipulators wishing to give all the focus back to their puppets, or to restore a pre-secular repertoire. Even in the 1980s a stirring of dissent was detected in the words of a respected German producer and performer: Peter Waschinsky declared himself tired of revealing all the secrets of puppet theatre to the audience. Believing that this particular experimental process had been exhausted as a scenic genre, he decided 'to restore the puppet's right to its illusionist function':

> I do not say that this 'deconstructive' kind of theatre can never be interesting, but in most cases it is not: first of all the rather primitive 'alienation effect' within it is quickly exhausted. Brechtian actors, at least the best ones, knew perfectly well how to create illusion in their acting. They applied the distancing effect in order to emphasize certain moments so they would seem special to the audience, so that they really would be alienated. This means that in order to limit or to distort illusion it is necessary to create it first. The same applies to the puppet theatre. (see Jurkowski, 1998: 330)

Since Waschinsky's disquiet has not stemmed the tide of *distanciation* in puppet play, it will by now be clear that there must be a growing demand for the puppeteer with acting skill to complement that of manipulation. In parallel there is a growing demand for actors who can manipulate a puppet. In my experience few vocational puppeteers are natural actors, though they may well be able to dance, sing, speak lines intelligently, and so on. Historically, most have not entered the profession to be a performer on a stage, often preferring to remain actually or metaphorically hidden. It has already been pointed out that actors can be equally inadequate when asked to animate a puppet. There is a gap between the necessary talents of the traditionally trained actors, whose instrument is their own physique and personality, and the necessary talents of the traditional puppeteers, whose instrument is a figure, a character that is an extension of themselves, their hands and/or body, with a personality and appearance unlike him or herself. The actor must be able to interpret a verbal text, to represent the psychological makeup of a character via changes of facial expression (largely), whereas the facial expression of the puppet has been painted or sculpted so that its character is apprehended mainly through gait, clothing and gesture. Thus, if a producer demands actors who know how to operate a puppet, or puppeteers who can act, he or she has, up to the time of writing, been looking for a rarity.

Required to operate a puppet, actors, dancers or singers occasionally discover a hitherto unrealized skill, (this applies most often to dancers, used as they are to the strict control of physique and gesture). Latent talent reveals itself as soon as any performer handles a figure, in the instinctive neutralizing of their own 'presence' as their vitality is transferred to the puppet. Many performers are surprised to find how demanding puppet animation is, mentally and physically. The designer Tina Bicât, after close study undertaken for her excellent book *Puppets and Performing Objects* says:

> Actors present *themselves* onstage [my emphasis]. They may be disguised and adopting a character far from their own, but they are looking through their own eyes at the audience and hearing with their own ears. Actors must be self-conscious [in order] to perform. They have to be certain that all eyes are drawn to them [...]
>
> The puppet is selfless and breathes only with the help of its animator. The actor must discard the stability of his or her own body and learn to look through the puppet's eyes, hear through its ears and breathe for it. [...] The actor can believe in, and in many ways become, another person. It is one step further in the process to send this belief down your arm and into an inanimate object in order to make it, not yourself, the star of the show. It requires a rearrangement of many of your instincts as a performer. (Bicât, 2007: 110–11)

There is much that the actor can learn from acquaintance with puppet play. In 1921 Edward Gordon Craig, always devoted to the arts of puppetry, wrote an essay named 'Puppets and Poets' claiming the puppet was both 'the ABC of the actor' and 'the actor's primer'. He recommended the puppet as 'an example of the perfect distillation of human movement and form. Every actor should keep a puppet at hand in everyday life, so as to learn from it incessantly' (Craig, 1921: 18).

I contend – as did George Bernard Shaw – that as a theatre discipline, the animation and manipulation of a puppet should be a mandatory discipline taught in any modern programme of performer-training. Actors learn from the puppet's disassociation from any superfluous and intrusive emotion, in the constraints of its physicality and therefore in an economy of movement; they learn about the submission of their own personality to that of the character they are playing. The puppet has no ego to shed, no self-consciousness. The point is elegantly made in the 1810 essay *On The Marionette Theatre* by Heinrich von Kleist, included in almost every treatise on the art form, including this one, in the chapter on the aesthetics of puppetry.

In stylistic contrast to this approach and as further illumination for a theatre of animated objects, I have appended to this chapter a vivid account of a puppeteer-creator's pleasure and challenge in a solo performance with objects, by the French pedagogue, puppeteer and director Jean-Louis Heckel.

FURTHER READING

Batchelder, M. (1948) *The Puppet Theatre Handbook*, London: H. Jenkins.

Bensky, Roger-Daniel (1969) *Structures Textuelles de la Marionnette de Langue Française*, Paris: Editions A-G Nizet.

Craig, Edward Gordon (1921) *Puppets and Poets, The Chapbook – a monthly miscellany*, no.20, London: The Poetry Bookshop.
Curci, Rafael (2002) *De los objetos y otras manipulaciones titiriteras*, Buenos Aires: Instituto Nacional de Teatro and Universidad de Buenos Aires.
Knight, Malcolm (ed.) (1992) 'Proceedings of the Soviet/British Puppetry Conference, Glasgow, November 1989', *Contemporary Theatre Review*, 1, 1.
Margolies, Eleanor (ed.) (2009) *Theatre Materials*, London: Centre of Excellence in Training for Theatre, Central School of Speech and Drama.
Pasqualino, Antonio (1978) *L'Opera dei Pupi*, Palermo: Sellerio.
Plowright, Poh Sim (2002) *Mediums, Puppets and the Human Actor in the Theatres of the East*, Lewiston, NY: Edwin Mellen Press.
Schechner, Richard, (1991) 'The Canon', *TDR: The Drama Review* 35, 4.
Tillis, Steve (1996) 'The Actor Occluded: Puppet Theatre and Acting Theory' *Theatre Topics*, 6, 2, 109–119.

APPENDIX TO CHAPTER I

The following was written by Jean-Louis Heckel in 1993. Heckel founded a company called NADA which played a form of object theatre of original invention. He was appointed head of studies of the Ecole Supérieure Nationale des Arts de la Marionnette (ESNAM) at the Institut International de la Marionnette (I.I.M.) in Charleville-Mézières, and is also artistic head of La Nef, a training and producing centre in Paris. I have translated it from the French and have M. Heckel's permission to reproduce it, but neither of us remembers where or whether it has been published before.

TOWARDS A LUDIC DIALECTIC by Jean-Louis Heckel

Seated in the darkness, silent, attentive, impatient, they have come into this auditorium to be told a story. A new adventure, another fable, an old tale revisited, a poem, some silent moments, some images – but above all, a story.

So, I tell them a story. But I move into it with great speed: I rise up, my mouth makes the sound of wind, then a storm, then I take a twig and draw a map with it across the stage, I slide a cushion under my shirt to become fat, I borrow a scarf and become a magician. It's as simple as child's play. But the further you go into the action, the more the simplicity is perceived to be rich with digressions and transformations. My stick and my staff become a character, the cushion a mountain, my wind noises a dialogue … Little by little I am elaborating a world of objects that surround me, markers on the story of my journey. My imaginary characters become real before my eyes, and start to challenge me. With almost nothing I learn to use my body, my imagination, to express anything, to tell everything.

I renew my pleasure in play, I stop my cinema, my personal comedy, and start to make theatre. To bring the spectator into my world – sometimes even, when the show is success, into a whole new universe – I am working exclusively with two tools: the performer (body and voice) and the object (a thing manipulated on the stage, under the lights).

The author
It is impossible to play without the body. Thus the player starts by warming up his muscles, stretching his limbs; he practises control over the breath which will carry his voice, learns that certain gestures will provoke certain sensations, that each attitude he strikes will make resonances within a space, that each movement has a colour, a motivation and a purpose. We are talking about a gymnastic that is as much mental as physical. I articulate my body and my mind to reconstitute their unity. This is the first manipulation. If I do not master this prime tool, I cannot hope to aspire to my role as manipulator. That is why I cannot conceive of a puppeteer who would not be a performer, and even a distinct actor. At some stage he will make use of mask, mime, verse. He is the supreme performer, in that he should be capable not only of incarnating a character, but also of giving life to a piece of cloth or paper to make it into an animal, a person and so on.

The object
Once this first tool has been mastered (but it will always need work) it is necessary to make everything from nothing. Far from apologizing for a 'poor theatre' (a phrase now sadly pejorative) the 'nothing' is a question of choice and of artistic exactitude. To every text, every theme, there belongs a certain material. There is a strange alchemy between a story and its base matter. To the unity at the heart of a theatre text, be it libretto, drama or adaptation, there is a corresponding unity of form specific to each story. This might be stones and goatskins; vegetables (Ubu); an edible set (Hansel and Gretel). The object is more than a single element, it is one of a collection of materials that corresponds to an aesthetic statement, and also to the dramaturgy. It frames the improvisational work, an irreversible constraint. The constant resistance of the material forces the actor and the director into a constant look-out for the incongruous, the irresistible, the unconscious chance. In this risky world the decor, the costumes, lighting, sound – all should be onstage from the first day of rehearsals. The intellectual possibilities and the dramaturgical development cannot be effected without the concrete bases. One could compare this work to the starting point of a jazz musician who only discovers the joy of real freedom after absorbing and integrating a mountain of constraints.

The player manipulates the object, the object manipulates the player: it is a demanding dialectic, but a ludic one, a game of constant comings and goings in which the director plays the part of umpire, of leader of the game. Once it has 'taken' he has nothing more to do than to efface himself and leave things to the lonely performer-manipulators. At the point when he can no longer separate the actor from the manipulator, the gamble is won. Puppet production, theatre of figures, theatre of objects, spectacle: no more insistence on labels, categories. You learn to unlearn, to forget stereotypes, niceties of language; you whittle away and sandpaper down until you have found the mythologic figures which will, at last, lead us into the story.

So then, seated in the darkness ...

Chapter

2 *Related Arts*

Close cousins of the puppet theatre are the genres of ventriloquism, masks and automata when applied in performance. All are concerned with the animation of objects, all are embedded in theatre's most ancient history, in its origins of ritual and magic, all have functioned as universal, artificial aids for the evocation of awe and fear and the exercise of power. In contemporary theatre all have become a secular medium of entertainment, for western audiences at least, while retaining their more or less residual spiritual liaisons. Another common characteristic is their basis in the manual and corporeal crafts: as with puppetry, these three genres demand a high degree of acquired skill, needing long periods of study and unremitting practice.

MASKS

Like puppeteers, *masked players* lose their own personality to assume the physical attributes of the character of their mask, when they are not working with the 'neutral' mask, which holds no expression and when the players assume a character and a physical bearing as circumstance demands, often in the training process. Another stylistic is the 'character' mask which itself proposes a personality, as it has always for the comic characters, now known as the *zanni*, of the *commedia dell'arte*. A player in a commedia troupe was often known for his or her interpretation of a single mask, the word becoming a synonym for 'role', as in '[Colombina's] love affairs with Arlecchino, Pulcinella or some other mask brought about quarrels and peace-makings between her and Pasquella' (McKechnie, 1931: 66). Mask play is an effective route to puppet play: the masked performer acts as a self-manipulated figure, his or her normal bearing, voice and mannerisms subsumed in the dictates of the mask.

First encounters with a mask, as with a puppet, can be disorienting both for the performer and the spectator: some are designed to terrify and subdue, or, in contrast, to evoke hilarity in extremes of farcical action, usually in concert with a distorted and unrecognizable voice. The connection with both puppets and ventriloquism is evident: the alienation and otherness intrinsic to many kinds of masks, as it is to the ritual puppet and the conventional vent doll with its aggressive, perpetual grin, evoke fear or at least apprehension, even in the most experienced and blasé adult. It is not surprising: the disguise of the mask, the uncanniness of many puppets and the effect of the displaced voice on the baffled listener were essential ingredients of the mystifying rituals of earliest human societies. People believed that these instruments served to strengthen or defend man's power against alien spirits, especially the power of a masked priest or chieftain, whose proximal contact with the substitute image, (the mask or puppet figure), or the conjuring of a disembodied voice, seemed to prove intimate contact with gods, demons, and other spirits.

Ronald Duncan, poet and playwright, wrote prophetically in the 1961 reissue of Chambers' Encyclopaedia, when realism in European theatre prevailed:

> The early history of drama is essentially an account of the origin of the use of masks. They were an important element of the classical theatre. They helped [...] to increase the stature of the actor, and they represented the role, comic or tragic, that he was to perform. Early drama was wholly mimetic in character. The first plays were ritualistic and in these masks were worn by the deity, the devil or some religious or symbolic character. [...]. Indeed, demonology and drama had a common root, as is shown by the gargoyles on early church buildings, which are very similar to those portraying pagan spirits.
>
> Later, as [Christian] drama moved from inside the church to performance outside, it developed from its purely liturgical origins into the comedies and tragedies of the middle ages, carrying the mask with it as part of its convention [...] For similar purposes masks were used in a wholly symbolic way, as in the *Commedia dell'arte* they portray Harlequin, Columbine or Pantaloon.
>
> A mask did more than disguise an actor; it suppressed his personality and kept drama from the purely realistic representation into which it has fallen [...] Because drama is now realistic and makeup copies nature, masks are no longer used.
>
> But it would indeed be a mistake to assume that the mask has no place in the theatre of the future. For if drama returns to its own original conventions, which were essentially unrealistic, it will no doubt find a use for the mask. When it does so the drama as a whole will be changed: its character will be immediately lifted from purely realistic language into poetry, which is the natural vehicle of symbolism. (Duncan, 1961: 140)

It is also a natural vehicle for puppetry, as I have demonstrated. The heightened language of caricature, the broad character brushstrokes of musical theatre, the crafts of dance and song so strikingly shown in shows like *The Lion King* in which all the characters are masked by makeup and costume, would have amazed and I dare say delighted Ronald Duncan.

Thirty-seven years later, confirmation of Duncan's prophecy comes opportunely from the entry for Mask in Patrice Pavis' *Dictionary of the Theatre*:

Contemporary Western theatre has revived the use of the mask. This rediscovery (it had already been used in classical Greek theatre and *commedia dell'arte*) coincides with the *re-theatricalization* of theatre and the promotion of body expression.

[...] there are several indications for their use in theatre, particularly the ability to observe others while being protected from observation oneself.

[...] By hiding one's face one voluntarily renounces psychological expression, which generally provides the greatest amount of information, often very detailed, to the spectator. The actor is forced to make a considerable physical effort to compensate for this loss of meaning and identification. The body translates and amplifies the character's inner self by exaggerating each gesture. This reinforces the theatricality and makes the actor's use of space considerably more important. The opposition between a neutral face and a body in perpetual motion is one of the essential aesthetic consequences of wearing a mask. The mask does not have to represent a face; a neutral mask or a half-mask is enough to immobilize facial expression and concentrate attention on the actor's body.

The mask denaturalizes the character by introducing a foreign body into the relationship of identification between spectator and actor. It is therefore often used when the mise-en-scène seeks to avoid emotional transference and defamiliarizes the character.

[...] Masks are meaningful only within the mise-en-scène as a whole. They are no longer confined to the face [for example, 'body-mask'], but retain close links with facial expression, the actor's overall appearance and even the scenery. (Pavis, 1998: 202)

The rigorous teaching of Jacques Lecoq (1921–1999) in his Paris-based International School has much to do with the re-adoption of the mask, through his emphasis on corporeal expression in theatre-making and in the training of performers. Steven Whinnery, one-time student at the school confesses:

I was bamboozled, challenged, tearful, confused and a very bad student. But in the friction, burn and deep immersion something got right into my bones and the fundamental tenets of his teaching stayed with me and influenced all my subsequent work. (Whinnery, 2007: 14–15)

It is no exaggeration to say that Lecoq's influence led many of his students to subsequent professional success in the vanguard of theatre, having awoken in them a desire to re-evaluate and regenerate contemporary performance in general, in a reaction against the realistically presented literary play in particular.

In addition to the neutral mask and the character mask Lecoq's 'list' included the categories of 'Larval', and 'Clown' or 'Red Nose', to which Michael Chase, a British leader in the field of mask-making and mask training would add the 'Acoustic' mask, an 'open-mouthed helmet', the nearest

Figure 2.1   Masks by Peter Schumann of Bread and Puppet Theatre. Archbishop Romero, 1985, 12 ft. and Blue General, 1977, 14 ft.
© Jack Sumberg. Reproduced by permission of the Bread and Puppet Theatre.

to that of classical Greece. Chase has devoted his life to mask-work, and knows about the art of animating an object:

> For the mask to remain alive on the stage it cries out for three living relationships: the first is the performer in relationship to their creative impulse and inner spontaneous life, the playful essence; the second is the relationship with the other performers, the other masks on stage. And the third is the mask in relationship with the audience, the world. Whether this is in dance, mime or drama the same relationships need to be maintained [...] if the relationships are maintained, a new world begins to emerge on the stage, as if by magic ... (Whinnery, 2007: 13)

A pupil of Jacques Lecoq in the 1980s, puppeteer Mark Pitman (1959–), who also teaches mask-work, explained in an interview on 14 January 2010 that the first principle that students need to understand is how to 'keep the mask alive' even when the player is still, through the practice of 'small breath' – just as with the motionless puppet. The performer is trained to reach for a good understanding of his or her body and its movement through total control, concentration and precision – just as in puppetry. Pitman said:

> Neutral mask is used mainly for workshops and teaching or learning. Precisely because of its neutrality it is dramatically the strongest of all masks, magnetically drawing the attention of the spectators. It is the best teacher of stillness and the importance of breath, just as a puppet is. The students learn through watching each other in action, through simple exercises such as waking up, looking around, picking something up, throwing it. Motivation and mood are expressed through the body, sometimes aided by vocality.
>
> In the school of Lecoq we were taught with the neutral mask in the first year, commedia and character masks in the second. The difference lay in the increased energy and strength the latter needed from the performers to express their character, although control and stillness were still very necessary. (Pitman, 2010 in interview)

The making of masks demands flair as well as craftsmanship. Two examples of great makers are the Italians Amleto and Donato Sartori in whose honour the Museum of the Mask was created in 2004, near Padua. The best commedia masks were and are made of leather but character or 'expressive' masks may be made of papier mâché, neoprene, silicone, plaster bandage and other materials both traditional and modern. Pitman explains the importance of finding 'movement in the form': the mask can be 'sharp-edged, knife-like, or soft-featured and passive' to accord with the role of its wearer.

Before covering the face and starting to perform, masked performers take time to gaze at their mask, contemplating its character. Given enough time (for they may perform with more than one figure) the best puppeteers will do the same, absorbing the object's spirit and appearance and thence finding its voice and gait. Like the puppet, the mask will seem to some practitioners to exert an uncanny force over the performer, to be in control. Whinnery ends his article (quoted above) with the words 'Don't get involved with masks; they do strange things to you'.

AUTOMATA

Automata, mechanical contrivances engineered to be 'self-operational' when set in motion, are not in themselves uncanny, but can create mystery and incredulity if the mechanism is concealed beneath or within figures which then appear to be moving 'automatically', with no visible human control. The same is largely true of puppets invisibly manipulated.

The creation of automata has been known universally at least as far back as antiquity, attesting to a universal desire among (not always male) mechanicians, pseudo-magicians, mathematicians and physicians to create intricate models to be set in motion to the satisfaction of the maker and the amazement of the spectator. American marionettist Helen Joseph recounts how

Eminent mathematicians interested themselves in perfecting the mechanism of the dolls [...] In the writings of the celebrated Heron of Alexandria, living two centuries before Christ, one can find a very minute description of a puppet show for which he planned the ingenious mechanism. He explains that there are two kinds of automata, first those acting on a movable stage which itself advanced and retreated at the end of the acts, and, second, those performing on a stationary stage divided into acts by a change of scene. The *Apotheosis of Bacchus* was of the first type, the action presented within a miniature temple wherein stood the statue of the god with dancing bacchantes circling around, fountains jetting forth milk, garlands of flowers, sounding cymbals, all accomplished by a mechanism of weights and cords. It was an extremely elaborate affair. Of the second type of puppet show Heron cites as example *The Tragedy of Nauplius,* the mechanism for which was invented by a contemporary engineer, Philo of Byzantium. There were five scenes disclosed, one after the other, by doors which opened and closed: first, the seashore, with workmen constructing the ships, hammering, sawing, etc.; second, the coast with the Greeks dragging their ships to the water; third, sky and sea, with the ships sailing over the waters which begin to grow rough and stormy; fourth, the coast of Euboë, Nauplius brandishing a torch on the rocks and shoals whither the Greek vessels steer and are shattered (Athene stands behind Nauplius, who is the instrument of her vengeance); fifth, the wreck of the ships, Ajax struggling and drowning in the waves, Athene appearing in a thunderclap! This play was probably taken from episodes of the Homeric legend and, although Heron does not so state, the action of the puppets was most likely accompanied by a recital of the poem upon which the drama was founded. (Joseph, 1922: 18–20)

The automata entertainment described here seems to be a classical forerunner of the spectacular genre of theatre known as *theatrum mundi* or *teatrum mundi*:

Gottfried Hautsch, who died in 1703, [...] constructed in Nurnberg a mechanical automaton with many figures, which was nicknamed his 'little world'. This is a kind of automaton which, to distinguish it from others, is technically indicated by the term *theatrum mundi*. The *theatrum mundi* for centuries provided the traditional afterpiece of the wandering marionette theatres; by means of small movable figures running on rails it showed a diversity of scenes, such as the creation of the world and Noah and the Flood. Flockton's show, which was exhibited in England at the end of the eighteenth century, utilised five hundred figures, all employed in different ways and manners. Here there were movable figures of a peculiarly ingenious kind: swans, for example, which dipped their heads in the water, spread their wings and craned their long necks to clean their feathers [...] It was only with the success of the film that these mechanical shows declined, but not so long ago one could still see, as a lively and boisterous afterpiece to a popular puppet show, the battle of Sedan, the siege of the Taku forts, sledging, storms at sea, etc. (Boehn, 1972: 11)

The 'figures' were probably mechanically operated, moving on tracks in the stage floor in a detailed, pre-constructed series of spectacular scenes operated by various mechanisms backstage. Victoria Nelson returns us to the history:

Late Antiquity's high traditions of religious images and scientific innovation, meanwhile, [were] kept alive in the Arabic and Byzantine cultures after the collapse of the Roman empire. [...] Throughout the Middle Ages in Europe, a muted Neo-Platonic, theurgic element would survive in two areas outside the church: non-religious automata and folklore around constructed or resurrected human bodies. [...] the considerable medieval fashion for automata – both real contrivances and those imagined contrivances mentioned in romances such as the Arthurian cycle – involved the familiar but now forbidden fascination with the theurgist's imitation of God's powers as Creator. The phenomenon of oracular statues and busts, so prevalent in Late Antiquity, also survived as a folk tradition in the Middle Ages: Pope Sylvester II was rumored to consult such a 'talking head' on difficult matters of theology, as were the monk Roger Bacon and the Dominican friar and natural philosopher Albertus Magnus. References in medieval English miracle plays to 'gods on strings' – true marionettes now? – date from 1200, and the occasional contrived wonder is noted, such as a crucifix in Boxley, Kent whose eyes and head were made to move by the monks at significant moments and puppets used by the pre-Reformation English priests to enact the Passion. (Nelson, 2001: 49)

The story told by James Michener in his monumental study of Spain, *Iberia*, I find blackly amusing: in the middle of the fifteenth century Queen Isabella of Castile, decided that the Conde de Luna posed a threat and must be eliminated. In Toledo:

[s]he organised a cabal of nobles who ... gave him a drum-head court-martial and sped him to the execution block. He was buried in the Capilla de Santiago [where] his family erected over his grave a life-sized portrait statue so articulated that when Mass was being said at the main altar some twenty yards away, a servant who followed the motions of the priest could manipulate a series of underground chains which made the statue stand, sit or genuflect at the proper points of the service, creaking loudly as it did so. So far as we know this was the world's first mechanical man and it became so notorious that more people watched it than the priest. This continued for some thirty years until one day Queen Isabel said sternly 'Get that thing out of here!' What became of the praying statue no-one remembers. (Michener, 1968: 132)

Automata was never buried, but it was not until the eighteenth and the early nineteenth century that its popularity in Europe grew so great as to breed a desire among theatre producers to develop an attraction evidently capable of drawing crowds. Before they were harnessed to the theatre, the automata and their makers had to rely on demonstrations in exhibition halls, fairground tents or private homes. Sometimes they drew large numbers of spectators, but not for long. Any single machine, no matter how amazing, is a repetitive phenomenon, inescapably driven by its mechanism, of itself incapable of responses to an audience, so never a dramatic character, although mechanical aids to puppet animation and human aids to the automaton have been employed all through their long history.

Around the turn of the century (eighteenth to nineteenth) this attempt to 'theatricalize' the automata resulted briefly in the reappearance of the *theatrum mundi* already referred to, described as a series of small-scale spectacular mobile set-pieces strung together on a stage to tell a story using astonishing effects of light and sound in scenes of naval battles, thunderstorms, fireworks and erupting volcanoes. The show was made possible by miraculously delicate and intricate weights, levers and chains, revolving or unrolling panoramic backcloths, some set in motion by clockwork, the whole organized backstage by the energetic proprietor and his assistants. Jurkowski believes that

> The universal dream, the creation of an artificial moving human was followed by the dream of creating an artificial setting for him, also movable. In other words the craftsmen of the eighteenth century wanted to bring to life all the elements of a painted landscape or seascape [...] One which was greatly appreciated was a representation of *le chateau de Saint-Ouen*:
>
> 'We can imagine Madame de Pompadour – because it was her property – contemplating the moving scenery, accomplished by the mechanisms. You could see dogs appear, run one after the other and vanish behind the isolated building in the park. A little further on two marquises make multiple reverences before a lady of high quality who in her turn, touched by their gallantry, returns a graceful bow. A coachman, some sheep, and a brave peasant woman pulling the bridle of her cow parade along the road ... Workers on the river try to make their wood float, and in the boats cheerful gentlemen and ladies take refreshment, while the washer-woman beats their linen rhythmically and an angler, unconcerned, pokes playfully at a gudgeon'.
>
> It sufficed to make this kind of 'living picture' bigger and the subjects more variable to arrive at the mechanical theatre later known as *Theatrum Mundi*. (Jurkowski, 1996: 221)

In another work Jurkowski writes:

> All these engineers took their work seriously, trying to combine the beauty of sculpture with mechanical perfection. Especially in the century of the Enlightenment their belief in the unlimited possibility of human technical skill led them to surprising results in their works, enchanting both court and popular audiences [...] There is a strong analogy between automata and puppet shows if we consider them as market activities appealing to the same human instinct, that is the human fascination for the creation of artificial life [...]. Puppets did not lose in the competition with automata. After the first moments of surprise the automata with their repetitive mechanical movements, disappeared into oblivion. (Jurkowski, 1994: 6)

The rise of the variety show in the mid nineteenth century encouraged the production of short, highly diverting 'numbers' or 'turns' as Ian Steadman confirms in *the Cambridge Guide to Theatre*:

> [It was the] most widespread and widely attended form of urban entertainment in the 19th and early 20th century. The element of variety is common to popular

theatre, which seeks to engage limited attention spans with a diversity of skills. [...] A major contributory factor to its prominence was a new proletarian public, who had lost their village traditions and were receptive to less demanding, cheaper and more colourful amusement than the 'legitimate' theatre offered. Variety can be identified by its series of attractions, 'turns' or 'numbers', unconnected by any theme. (see Steadman, 1992: 1036–37)

The demand affected the shows of the mechanicians, the puppeteers, the ventriloquists and even the masked players. The first explored the possibilities of transformations; the second exploited the amusement value of the short sketch and the 'trick figure', given to eye-popping changes of appearance and character; the third, the ventriloquist, as we shall see, took to the compact format of the 'knee-figure', simple to stage with only one performer and one or two vent 'dummies' as they came to be called. The masked players continued to present their dances and comic and knockabout interludes of the *commedia* stock characters, often for the opening and closing of many music hall and variety programmes.

The metaphor of man reduced to the function of machine or robot under the various tyrants and wars of the early twentieth century appealed to the dramatic writing and imagery of the Modernists. After World War I the aesthetic of the Bauhaus was centred on geometric forms in space, mechanized figures, humans as marionettes in motion, as in Oskar Schlemmer's *Triadic Ballet* (1912 and 1922) and *The Mechanical Ballet* (1923). They illustrated the general fascination with the machine shown by the avant-garde theatre artists in the Modernist period, offering 'further testimony of the grasp on artistic consciousness of modern technology and the complex pattern of responses to the new age' (Jurkowski, 1998: 321). In a comprehensive work on the employment of puppetry in European Modernist theatre Professor Harold B. Segel, American historian, writes:

The experimental theatre of the renowned Bauhaus gradually began to take shape after Oskar Schlemmer joined its staff in 1921. Together with Laszlo Moholy-Nagy and Farkas Molnár, Schlemmer created an unusual laboratory essentially of the actor and devoted principally to the translation into spatial terms of the 'emblems' of contemporary society. These emblems he determined to be abstraction, mechanization – which Schlemmer describes as 'the inexorable process which now lays claim to every sphere of life and art' – and the new potentials of technology and invention [...]

The endeavor to free man from his physical bondage and to heighten his freedom of movement beyond his native potential resulted in substituting for the organism the mechanical human figure [Kunstfigur]: the *automaton and the marionette*. E.T.A. Hoffman extolled the first of these, Heinrich von Kleist the second.

The English stage reformer E.G. Craig demands: 'The actor must go and in his place comes the inanimate figure – the Übermarionette we may call him'. And the Russian [Valeri] Bryusov demands that we 'replace actors with mechanized dolls, into each of which a phonograph shall be built'. (Segel, 1995: 319–21)

If in this the twenty-first century automata rarely appear as stage entertainment, theatre and, especially, film artists are still magnetically attracted to the mechanized figure and the new technologies of animation: robots, cybermen and their ilk. The German Harry Kramer (1925–) with his *Mechanical Theatre* and the Russian Eduard Bersudsky (1939–) with his *Sharmanka Kinetic Theatre* are still to be seen: the latter's 'performance' is a series of intriguing, harmonious, linked 'scenes' programmed to 'come to life' (with no visible human presence) one after the other, enhanced by changing backgrounds of light and sound. *Sharmanka* has a home in Glasgow, and may sometimes be seen on tour and as permanent exhibits in Science and other museums. It has a rich pictorial presence on the internet. The show attracted thousands of spectators to London's Theatre Museum for a fourteen-month season in 2002–3.

An ancient Japanese theatre tradition, this one tying the animated figure to the arts of automata, is the *karakuri ningyo* which consists of large-scale

Figure 2.2 Automaton. *Time of Rats* (1991) by Eduard Bersudsky's Sharmanka Kinetic Theatre, Glasgow.

© Maureen Kinnear. Reproduced by permission of the Sharmanka Kinetic Theatre.

intricate mechanisms operated by six or more manipulators, carried on chariots through the streets for festivals and sometimes presented as a transformational form of storytelling; a performance in a theatre space. American professor Jane Marie Law, whose book *Puppets of Nostalgia* is 'the first major work in any Western language to examine the ritual origins and religious dimensions of puppetry in Japan' explains:

> The word 'Karakuri' means a mechanical device to tease, trick, or take a person by surprise. It implies hidden magic, or an element of mystery. In Japanese 'Ningyo' is written as two separate characters, meaning person and shape. It loosely translates as puppet, but can also be seen in the context of doll or even effigy. (Law, 1997: 18)

Kirsty Boyle has contributed a comprehensive, authorized internet site on the karakuri ningyo. There you may learn that

> The Japanese Karakuri puppets utilise subtle, abstract movements to invoke feeling and emotion. There are three main categories of Karakuri. 'Butai Karakuri' are puppets used in the theatre, 'Zashiki Karakuri' are small and can be played with in rooms and 'Dashi Karakuri' puppets perform on wooden floats used in religious festivals. Traditionally Karakuri appeared in religious festivals, performed re-enactments of traditional myths and legends and entertained the public with their sophisticated, symbolic and graceful gestures.
>
> The Karakuri tradition of invisibly concealing technology extends beyond puppetry and robotics, and continues to manifest itself in popular culture. Karakuri influenced the Noh, Kabuki and Bunraku theatre arts and directly contributed to the industrial modernisation of Japan. During the Edo period Japan was completely isolated from the rest of the world, during which time a unique cultural heritage developed away from outside influences. Despite isolation, Western technology was uniquely adapted to produce Karakuri Ningyo puppets (SUEMATSU 2001b). Essentially, Karakuri is the realisation of the symbiotic relationship between Eastern tradition and Western technology (KUROKAWA 2001). The history of the Karakuri Ningyo highlights anthropomorphic approaches to sociable robot development, and how they differ between the East and West. It is the starting point from which Japan's love of robots and technology has developed. (Boyle, 2008)

The genre has shed most of its connections with religious processional worship. When I have seen them, the mechanisms have been revealed, attracting interest from spectators curious to see the workings of the transformations. No mechanical show is more complicated; the machines are an engineering wonder.

Mechanical figures in motion are still a draw, indoors or out, although it may seem that marvels are nowadays commonplace for a public steeped in unceasing technological advances, but still fascinated by machinery seemingly invested with ghosts.

Meanwhile their great subjects the god-dolls live on in the popular entertainments of the present day so well known to us all – the mummy from ancient Egypt revived to wreak havoc; the doll or mannequin come to life through the efforts of a charismatic creator or soul-bestower; the puppet turned robot-android-clone-cyborg seeking humanity and immortality at the same time. (Nelson, 2001: 61)

VENTRILOQUISM

Ventriloquism has evolved into a branch of the puppetry arts, since it is now mainly manifested in the apparent endowment of speech by a performer to one or more human or animal dolls, for public entertainment. Its essence lies in the human voice and the projection of that voice, rather than in the animation of a thing. The briefest study of its history reveals that for many millennia the primary skill, illusion and purpose of ventriloquism lay in making the spectator believe that a medium or intermediary with the spirit world could cause a disembodied voice to speak from across a room, across a street, from within a suitcase or the depths of a cellar. It could also put words in another person's mouth, for mischievous or sinister purposes.

Steve Connor in his book on the history of the art form, *Dumbstruck,* tells us that the 'beginnings of ventriloquism, or at least of the documentation of its practices and effects, lie in classical Greece' (Connor, 2000: 49). Many believe that the miraculous Oracle at Delphi spoke her prophecies with a voice thrown by a ventriloquist. The word means a 'stomach-speaker' from a compression of the Latin *venter,* stomach or abdomen, and *loquor,* to speak. Ventriloquists are born with a talent as real as the native talent of a gifted gymnast: with practice they develop the ability to alter and 'throw' the voice greater or lesser distances without appearing to speak. There are two types of ventriloquial voice: one that originates in the entrails and creates the 'inner effect' (high-pitched, hollow or stifled sounds) and the second that produces the 'outer effect', the 'thrown' voice, seeming to come from a place distanced from the speaker, with a breathier, higher timbre, from the region of the diaphragm.

In a naïve and superstitious age the voice of prophecy, doom or command, apparently emanating from a spiritualist medium, a statue, a tree, an Oracle or an invisible Power was thought to be caused by the presence of spirit beings. Ventriloquists have been subject to every form of malevolence and suspicion both because and in spite of the unusual skill involved in their practice. Until the eighteenth century females were usually held responsible for the phenomenon, in the belief that the vaginal aperture was where the evil spirit resided, the source of the supernatural voice. Society as usual blamed solitary old crones or women of dubious reputation who were frequently executed as witches.

From the seventeenth century onwards, the spirit of the Enlightenment sought to demystify the hitherto unexplained, including all forms of the supernatural, and by the nineteenth century 'the practice had undergone radical change, beginning to find its place within what would become a culture of mass entertainment', becoming both 'more familiar and more trivial, [moving] from a condition of spiritual malady to a form of expertise'.

At the same time it became the province of the accomplished male rather than the 'mystic' or 'possessed' female, and little by little the ventriloquial demonstrations – which in the distant past would happen in the open air, or anyway in large enclosed spaces with scenery and staging – became from the end of the nineteenth century a music hall 'turn', as already mentioned above. The professional ventriloquist acquired the visual aid of the now familiar 'dummy'. What was primarily an auditory show of mystic power was balanced with optical illusion. Connor again:

> As the old joke has it, ventriloquism is for dummies. It no longer has associations with voices produced from the hidden interior of the body, or even with the so-called 'throwing' of the voice into the empty air. Ventriloquism has become for us the art of making certain kinds of visible anthropomorphic object appear to talk. So powerful is the fixative effect of the dummy that we find it hard to understand how ventriloquists could ever have functioned without dummies. And yet the dummy is a relatively recent addition to the repertoire of the ventriloquist. Of course it would not be quite true to say that ventriloquism has been practised entirely without dummies until the nineteenth century. As long as there have been dolls and puppets, busts and statues, fashioned to look like human beings, people have been tempted to imagine them talking, or to try to make them talk. Lucina tells the story of Alexander, who actually made a hybrid figure out of a living snake and a false head, built of canvas, representing the god Asclepius. (Connor, 2000: 249)

But Alexander cheated and hired some hidden person to speak into a tube attached to the puppet. Different forms of conjuring and sleight of hand and eye were more and more employed in this way – and mechanisms too. These have today matured into electronic devices and computer-generated energy, adding to the repertory and capabilities of the ventriloquist turned puppeteer-mechanician, allying the art to that of the automatist.

> From the middle years of the nineteenth century, automata were used to make visibly present on the stage the groups of interlocutors whom artists of the previous generation had summoned up invisibly or themselves embodied. [...] In the last three decades of the century Lieutenant Walter Cole had a very popular entertainment called 'Merry Folks' in which he was accompanied by a group of life-size automata, representing characters such as the solemn Quaker [...], the querulous old couple, a little girl and the toping Ally Sloper. [...] Cole's automata walked as well as talked [...] Multiple automata performances continued to appear until at least the turn of the century. [...] Subsequently the development of actual technologies for amplifying, recording and transmitting speech, technologies that tended towards ever greater disembodiment and abstraction, would leave the figures of the ventriloquist and his dummy stranded, as it were, at a more primitive technological stage of crude visibility. However, the history of technological forms is characterized by anachronistic loops and pleats, and the very arrestedness

of the ventriloquist's dummy allows it to enter into some interesting encounters with later technological forms. (Connor, 2000: 336–37)

Ventriloquism is not a past without a present, as Connor believed (Connor, 2000: 415). There are still voice-throwers and stomach-speakers plying their trade on the stage with and without mechanical or technological aids; there are still underground mediums and other 'engastrimyths' causing spirits to be 'summoned', creating fear and mayhem in different contexts. Rarely would they call themselves puppeteers or automatists, even fewer mask-workers, although there is an argument that the self-revelatory nature of the average ventriloquist's 'dialogue' turns the dummy into a form of masking.

The ubiquitous use of the synchronized moving mouth puppet, made popular by the Muppet figures of Jim Henson's television production company, can appear very close indeed to the art of the ventriloquist when seen live (or in 'real-time'), on television, even if in this case little attempt is made by the puppeteers to displace their voice into the head of the manipu-lated figure or to hide their moving lips. The late Wayland Flowers (1939–1988), an American famous for his television work but also well-known as a live performer of the cabaret stage, was able to synchronize his words to the mouth movement of the puppet held above him at the end of his arm so exactly and with such an evident fusion of spirit with the charac-ter he held, that his performance convinced many in the audience that it was the puppet who actually spoke. For me he was the ideal puppeteer, an exam-ple of the technically consummate with an ability to lose himself in a puppet character that verged on the uncanny.

Other theatre forms draw on the arts of object animation, but none I think are as closely linked as these three. I have sketched: the mask, the automa-ton and ventriloquism. Their relationship to puppetry and to each other is evident, at least in their contemporary practice.

FURTHER READING

Boyle, Kirsty (2008) www.karakuri.info/origins/index.html, accessed 19 Jan 2010.
Hutton, Darryl (1974) *Ventriloquism*, New York: Sterling Publishing.
Johnstone, Keith ([1981] 1989) *Impro*, London: Methuen Drama.
Lecoq, Jacques (2000) *The Moving Body*, trans. D. Bradby, London: Methuen.
Smith, Derek (2003) 'A Brief History of Automata', www.smithsrisca.co.uk/automata-history.html, accessed 30 September 2010.
Wilshire, Toby (2006) *The Mask Handbook, A Practical Guide*, London and New York: Routledge.
Vox, Valentine (1981) *I Can See Your Lips Moving*, Tadworth: Kaye and Ward.
Wood, G. (2002) *Living Dolls: A Magical History of the Quest for Mechanical Life*, London: Faber and Faber.

Chapter
3   *Techniques*

An acquaintance with the most widely employed types of puppet and the methods of their operation and construction will contribute to the appreciation of their performance. In that belief I will describe most of the classic techniques with something of their aesthetics and applications. If the reader does not aspire to building a puppet (as I never have) or staging a show, then even the best 'how to do it' books are more or less unnecessary, although a modicum of knowledge of the workings, labels and dramaturgical potential of the various types of figure and some indication of their staging and activities may be useful.

Given the good books available on 'making puppets' I will not dwell on construction methods, but will list some of the best of these at the end of the chapter. With their many illustrations the books provide sound guides for building several types of traditional puppet, remembering always that in modern productions there are as many methods of construction and operation as the puppeteer can invent – and puppeteers are infinitely inventive. Respected authors include H.W. Whanslaw, Günter Böhmer, Peter Fraser, John Wright, H-J Fettig and David Currell, their books serving as useful guides to the classic forms. New methods and materials are constantly used, so that no survey of present practices in puppet-making can be comprehensive. In a later chapter (Chapter 5 on Dramaturgy) I will recall some recent shows which included figures that seem not to belong to any of the categories that follow.

Puppets as scenic characters are, or should be, designed and made with materials to accord with the aesthetic of the production in preparation. From driftwood to the most refined wood carving, from a bathroom tap to a giant moving sculpture, from pierced animal hide to plastic sheeting, from aluminium foil to sticky tape, the scenery and/or the animated character itself – figure or object – can be made from any one substance or combination of stuff, as long as it is stylistically and dramaturgically valid. An example might be a pastoral tale with scenery and characters recalling a farm and the countryside, made of sacking, wheat sheaves and agricultural tools, all in a blend of earth colours. Similarly ideas for staging – the architecture and construction of the settings – will arise naturally from the theme, style and scale of the production and from a score of practical considerations such as what manipulation technique will be employed and where the puppet operators will be placed.

ROD AND STRING MARIONETTES

To a European public, the *marionette* and the *hand* or *glove* puppet are the most familiar.[1] 'Marionette' for the English speaker has come to mean a figure operated from above, either by a rigid rod to the middle of the head (and perhaps to one hand), and a small number of strings to the limbs – the *'rod marionette'*; or by an indeterminate number of cords of varying thickness attached to the head, shoulders, back, limbs, and so on, according to the actions the character is required to make – the *'string marionette'*.

The *rod marionette* was known and practised throughout Europe before the string marionette and even, from the evidence of many excavated arte-facts, since antiquity. The evidence includes the holes in the limbs for the attachment of strings or thongs, and perhaps a single larger hole in the top of the head for the rod. This head rod gives the figure its name and is usually of metal, attached by a hook and screw eye to (or through) the head, and held by the manipulator above by a large hook or alternative handle on the end of the rod. Strings or wires to at least one of the arms may supplement the head rod. The technique tends to give the rod marionette a less fluid, more definite movement than that of its string counterpart.

It is the only type used by the traditional players in Sicily, for the purposes of the monumental *'opera dei pupi'*. These tall (up to a metre and a half), heavy wooden characters move with a dynamic force that well suits their melodramatic vehemence, their battles and the macabre comedy tricks of decapitations and dissections that distinguish the genre, depicted with the liberal use of painted gore. The stories most often performed concern the enmity between the Saracens and the Crusaders of the Middle Ages. The puppeteers working the characters from above and from the side of the painted backcloths stamp their feet to emphasize the puppets' steps, declaim the speeches, shout exclamations, operate the fights with scimitars and swords, and generally call on good muscular and vocal powers. The thick head rods add to the puppets' weight and with these they tilt the figures forward from the hip and swing the legs (which have no controls attached), using theories of pendular motion and gravity to effect the warriors' strides. The hero common to most of the stories is Orlando (best known from the sixteenth century poem *Orlando Furioso* by Ariosto), always recognizable from a misalignment of one eye, a strabismus.[2] He always wins his battles, often fought to rescue his beloved Angelica from the dastardly Saracens.

In his *Dictionary of Puppetry* A.R. Philpott describes the *opera dei pupi* as 'one of the few surviving forms of folk puppetry, of tremendous vigour in itself, but only to be found in an ever-dwindling number of theatres' (Philpott, 1969: 236). While Philpott sees the puppets reflected in 'the little

---

[1] In French, the generic word for an animated figure is *marionnette*: in English it is *puppet*.
[2] Interestingly, the hero-prince of the Indonesian Ramayana is also painted with a gentle squint.

Figure 3.1 Rod marionettes from *The Three Golden Hairs* (1998) by the DRAK theatre of Hradec Králové, Czech Republic. Note the hands, part of the aesthetic of this kind of puppet theatre. Puppets by Marek Zákostelecky.

© Josef Ptacek. Reproduced by permission of the DRAK company.

articulated figurines found in ancient tombs and ruins', and the stories stemming from the *chansons de geste* of twelth century France, no documentation of the tradition has yet been found that dates it earlier than the nineteenth century. The stories once included the lives of the saints and bandit folk tales, with the puppeteers or a hidden performer speaking for the characters, improvising the lines around a familiar text in a show which could go on for hours. This was the first form of puppet theatre to be recognized in 2001 as an example of the world's cultural treasures, awarded the honorific of Intangible Cultural Heritage by UNESCO.

The rod marionette can be seen in other European countries, notably in Belgian folk puppetry where the average size of the figures is much smaller. Their unnatural gait predisposes them to comedy, and their popularity still fills a few cellar theatre bars in Belgium, most famously the Brussels bar-theatre of Toone, founded in 1840.[3] (The current leader of the theatre is Toone VIII, Nicolas Géal, the latest in line of the Toone dynasty).

The manipulation is similar to the big Sicilian figures, by the hook in the head, the handle at the end of the rod, and one or two other operating rods or strings. Here too the operator leans over a painted scenic backdrop, and part of the enjoyment is derived from the unapologetic appearances of the human hands invading the fiction of the play.

In the Czech Republic the rod marionette, also smaller and more delicate than the Sicilian version, is widely used. A traditional type it may be, but the most avant-garde director will creatively make use of its simplicity of movement and manipulation. The DRAK company of Eastern Bohemia, for example, has used them since the 1970s in adaptations of comic opera and more

---

[3] See 'Royal Theatre of Toone', www.ilotsacre.be/site/en/curiosities/toone_theater.htm, accessed Jan. 2009.

serious works by Shakespeare, Schwartz and Schultz, alongside human actors and musicians.

From the hitherto sparse documentary and archaeological evidence, most if not all European marionettes from the ancient world up to the end of the eighteenth century had – at an educated guess – a rod rather than a string to the head. A revived performance said to date from the early sixteenth century, can be seen in Evora, Portugal, now the home of the *Bonecos de Santo Aleixo*. The old puppets and sets have been restored and revived to tell naïve stories full of ironic humour about, for example, the Creation of the World and Jesus' nativity, with songs and texts handed down via folk memory.[4]

It is probable that Punch, first recorded by Pepys in 1662, appeared in England from Italy as a glove puppet, but it is certain that he later appeared as a rod marionette, becoming something of a national hero of the stage, a trouble-making character in a host of parodies and plays that drew the gentry as well as the ordinary folk.

In the surviving pictures and figures of the fashionable operas of that period the rod marionette also prevails. The operas spread Europe-wide and were sought after as fashionable entertainment by the Court and the nobility, the puppets acting as mobile actors enlivening the arias sung by the human singers. Composers for the puppet opera were of the quality of Accaioli, Haydn and Mozart.

The technique and the repertoire of the *string marionette* are widely documented in Germany, Italy and Britain where the puppeteers of the nineteenth century took to them readily and even profitably (see McCormick, 2004 and Jurkowski, 1996). String marionettes can be found worldwide and were, along with shadow puppets, the technique most often seen in eastern practice. They were, and are, manipulated with a variety of controls ranging from the Rajasthan method of using only one or two strong cords looped over the fingers with which they manage a surprising range of movements to the Japanese multi-stringed wooden control. The Burmese marionette is instantly recognizable by its thick, numerous cords attached to a relatively simple wooden control; and by its feet, turned outwards in the manner of Burmese dancers. (There are many who maintain that the puppets taught the dancers, not the other way round). The puppets, both figures and animals, are pleasingly crafted and richly costumed, as befitted their once elevated social role, as the Burmese artist and writer Ma Thanegi explains:

> In the past Burmese marionettes enjoyed a rare and powerful privilege as speakers for both King and subjects. Never merely for entertainment, puppetry was a high art held in much esteem by all classes. Marionettes were a means of making people aware of current events; a medium for educating the masses in literature, history and religion; a display of lifestyles and customs. At the same time they

---

[4] http://www.cm-evora.pt/pt/conteudos/eventos/Bonecos%20de%20Santo%20Aleixo.htm accessed Feb. 2009.

functioned as mouthpiece for the people in the days of royalty, tiny hands in state and social affairs. These 'Small Dolls', *yoke thei* as they are termed in Burmese, enjoyed greater freedom of speech, dress and movement than live performers. (Thanegi, 1995)

At the beginning of this century performances of Asian marionettes still consist almost entirely of the string version (as opposed to the rod). A Chinese figure, like the English, will have thin strings, perhaps thirty or more, controlled either by a simple aeroplane (crossbar) mechanism, or, depending on the range of movement the character has to perform, by the most wondrously complicated set of wooden or metal controls, needing the dexterity of a harpist.

All over Europe the string marionette continues to be widely and proudly employed in numerous dramatic contexts, small-scale or life-size, often in contemporary re-workings of fairy tales and legends. The marionette can be a moving sculpture of beauty and grace, able to fly and hover pleasingly, suited to 'underwater' ballets, a mid twentieth century tradition that survives in shows such as Basil Twist's *Symphonie Fantastique* (1998–2003 – this one literally under water, the marionettes being forms made of cloth); or musical illustration, cabaret acts or spiritual encounters. The string puppet may be part of an ancient tradition, but shows little sign of dying out.

Through management of the control and the strings, with which they need complete familiarity, the puppeteers have to be capable of sensing and judging the placing, tension and weight of the marionette. Long rehearsal is needed until all of this becomes second nature. It is easy for the figure to flop, to buckle at the knees, to lose focus and thus credibility.

Although Miles Lee, in *Puppet Theatre Production and Manipulation*, opined that marionettes 'possess a remote and super-human quality [which] makes it difficult for them to portray humour' (Lee, 1958: 46–47), remoteness and super-humanity are by no means their only characteristic. String marionettes can be fast and funny too – examples are the brilliantly executed, action-packed stories of some productions by the Chinese marionette troupes, the world-travelled 'Clown Gustaf' of the German master Albrecht Roser, the comic characters of the prodigious Canadian Ronnie Burkett, together with the variety 'artistes', the circus clowns and animals that survive from the nineteenth and twentieth centuries.

The length of the strings that reach from the character to the operator's hands will be as the movement and the production aesthetic demand. Control of the figure is more or less positive according to the length – the longer the weaker the impetus and therefore the softer the movement. There are productions with strings three metres long; on the other hand the company Puppet House from St. Petersburg played a version of *Sleeping Beauty* featuring puppets with strings less than a metre long, operated in a booth stage that framed the head and hands of the puppeteer, providing contrast in scale and distancing the spectator from the cuteness of the little characters. Otherwise manipulation of the string figure is commonly either at ground level, with the manipulator standing alongside the puppet character, holding the control chest-high, or leaning over the rail of a bridge out of sight above the playing area.

All puppets are difficult to operate well but (arguably) the string puppet is the most difficult. To operate one convincingly needs rigorous practice, although few attempt to equal the level of skill of the traditional Chinese marionettist, severely trained from youth, who develops manual dexterity born of many hours of painful exercises. No equivalent of their methods of training exists in the west, there are some fine western solo marionettists too, as noted above, albeit self-taught and self-motivated.

NETHER-RODS

In the east, in Japan, China and Indonesia for example, the *rod puppet* as a figure operated from below has been in use for centuries. The best known came to Europe from the Indonesian islands where they are called *wayang golek*, or *wayang klitik*. We will come later to the two-dimensional shadows known as *wayang kulit*. *Wayang*, roughly speaking, is the generic word for puppet, as *ningyo* is the Japanese equivalent. The colonizing of the East Indies by the Dutch ensured that these stylized figures were brought to the Netherlands, usually as ornaments for the home.

The rod puppet operated from below (I call it the nether-rod technique) was not practised in Europe until the delicacy and artistry of the wayang figures found favour with Modernist currents of art in the early twentieth century and captured the attention of certain puppeteers. The most notable of these was the Austrian Richard Teschner (1879–1948) whose taste was for the fantastic and the exquisite and who famously displayed his uniquely spectacular productions (more a succession of carefully composed *tableaux vivants* than action stories) behind a very large round lens which was carefully lit. The puppets were typically operated from below on a wooden rod attached to the body and fixed in the head, with long slender rods, often metal, visibly attached to the hands, with one end of the arm rods in the puppeteer's hands. Extra string controls – e.g. for the head – might be threaded into the rods.

> [Teschner] achieved an incomparable mastery in the construction and operation of figures of this kind. He was an exponent of the late Jugendstil (or 'art nouveau') with a versatility amounting to genius, and in him were combined technical ingenuity and a pronounced sense of the purely artistic. To his first encounter with the Wayang Golek puppets Teschner owed the decisive stimulus for the mechanical and aesthetic conception of his figures. (Böhmer, 1971)

One of the first Europeans to use the nether-rod, Teschner had discovered some *wayang golek* figures while on honeymoon in Holland, where many

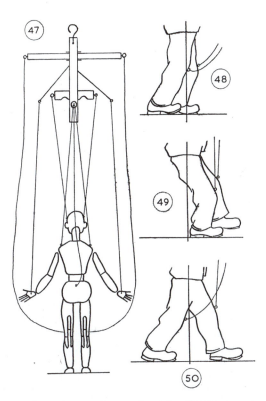

Figure 3.2 Diagram of a string marionette by John Wright, founder of the Little Angel Theatre, London. From *Your Puppetry* by Wright (1951).

Reproduced by permission of Lyndie Wright.

Indonesian rod (and shadow) puppets had been imported by the Dutch colonists.

He would have been surprised to know that the technique – though adapted – was about to become the most widely-used of all until the 1990s, thanks to its ubiquitous and almost mandatory application in the scores of puppet theatres established throughout the Soviet bloc and other Communist-ruled states. Here, during most of the second half of the twentieth century, puppet performances took place in large theatres with audiences numbering in the hundreds and even thousands, using a large and heavy version of the nether-rod puppet, developed as the dominant technique. These figures may still be seen in the countries of residual Soviet influence such as Cuba, India (Bengal) and even China, though hardly at all in Russia itself. The nether-rod can have one to three operators, normally hidden behind a high screen stretched across the width of the stage, though I can report a production seen in Shanghai on an open stage: the skills of the puppeteers were on show and their acrobatic action and that of the puppets they manipulated were breathtaking. The control mechanisms were often so well-engineered as to make the characters' movements uncannily lifelike. Some of these rod puppets, in particular those of the Chinese and the model company, the Central State Puppet Theatre of Moscow, achieved a precision of movement superior to anything seen in the west. A few of the characters were strung internally with twine or wire threaded through the rods up to the head and along the limbs, thus operated with no visible controls. The technique seems to have been sometimes employed in the *neurospasta* of ancient Greece and was developed, secretively (as I found out when we went backstage), by the Moscow theatre under its powerful and talented leader, Sergei Obraztsov. In the twentieth century puppeteers could still be secretive about their specialist techniques.

Normally the Soviet model has a jointed head and neck, little corporal flexibility but a range of expressive head and arm gestures effected either by long thin rods to the hands or by triggers which the puppeteers operated at the lower end of the rod. Although the general brief was to produce work for children, the Moscow-approved repertoire became wide, and included

Figure 3.3   A large nether-rod puppet designed and made by John and Lyndie Wright. From a production of *Noah* (1985) by the Little Angel Theatre, London. Puppeteer: Christopher Leith.

© John Roberts.

Figure 3.4   A variation on the rod puppet technique. Jacqueline Ilett of the Jacolly Puppet company operating 'Deirdre'. Puppet by Holly Griffin.
© Holly Griffin.

productions of adult texts which the authorities accepted as suitable for young people in their teens. Socialist Realism featured for a while, but was hardly suited to puppets, and was soon followed by a return to folk and fairy tales, classic dramas with plenty of action (the nether-rod puppet can move swiftly), lavish musicals, parody and propagandist satire often targeting the countries on the other side of the 'Iron Curtain', particularly the USA.

The period of most use of the nether-rod figures was prolonged and elaborated with various moving parts and a number of good texts, comic or tragic, by well-known authors such as Kafka and Pushkin. The unseen puppeteer(s) held the character above the screen as high as the arm would allow, the supporting rod often in a pouch on the stomach or slotted onto the back of the playboard,[5] one hand on the thumb trigger to move the head and the other hand holding one or two of the slender rods controlling the hands and arms. The action mimed the speaking or singing of the story, sometimes live but usually recorded; the manipulation of one figure often took two operators possessing strong arm and shoulder muscles. In fact a strong physique and voice are assets for any puppeteer.

Throughout all of this epoch, roughly 1950–1990, the nether-rod puppet,

[5] The playboard is the puppets' narrow stage fixed at the front of the booth or screen.

large and small, operated by generally invisible operators was ubiquitous. Now, in the early twenty-first century, for reasons artistic and economic, the tall heavy figure is rarely to be seen, although its ancestor, the refined wayang golek still plays in its homelands of the east and wherever else it has put down its delicate roots, planted by expatriate devotees.

GLOVE OR HAND PUPPETS

If your puppet character wants to express itself in wordy improvisation then the *glove* or *hand puppet* is your instrument. Folk puppetry all over the world uses it more than any other. One would not imagine that an apparently simple figure worn on the hand (or on both hand and forearm or even on two hands) could possibly have many differing methods of construction, nevertheless it is so. It can be made to accommodate one, two or even three fingers in the head, preferably so that an asymmetric shoulder height – the Quasimodo look – is avoided. It may have a mouth that opens and shuts in which the puppeteer's fingers mime the speech: this type can be called a 'clap-mouth' puppet, reflected in the German title of the Klappmaul theatre group of Frankfurt who perfected their use.

As a direct contact and interlocutor with the audience, quick in repartee, able to grasp and handle props, the lively and usually comic glove figure has been in use since at least the middle ages. Its expert manipulation is far more difficult than most people imagine, as an expert performance is hard to come by, at least in most of Britain and Europe, and is something of a revelation when it is observed. The German expert Gunter Böhmer writes:

> The hand puppet is the simplest form of puppet ... although it demands aptitude, effort and capacity for psychological understanding to transform a figure consisting merely of a head, the shell of a costume, and short little arms into a living, vehemently mobile being, and at the same time to give it a precise, typical and unmistakable character. (Böhmer, 1971: 15)

Glove or hand puppets usually perform in a classic booth, with the operator hidden below the playboard, but able to spy on the audience through a camouflaged 'window' in the booth's covering. With arms upstretched, he or she moves the figure with one, two or even three fingers in its head, the remaining fingers in the arms. Although the figure is likely not to be seen below the torso, a character, Punch for example, may have a pair of legs which, as Böhmer puts it, 'are swung high-spiritedly over the front of the stage to dangle indolently when the figure sits down on the playboard'. He goes on:

> Participation by the spectators, who are encouraged to interject comments to which the puppet instantly reacts, makes possible a contact with the public which no other form of puppetry can attain [...]

> The simple and popular appeal of hand puppetry has not prevented the modern artistic puppet theatre from making use of this vital and lively medium, which allows the puppeteer to exploit every incident and inspiration of the moment. (Böhmer, 1971: 15)

In my experience the highest manipulation skills in glove puppetry have been attained by the Germans and – as one would expect – the Chinese. The latter are able to accomplish astonishing feats with their tiny figures, such as removing an overcoat and throwing it to the puppet at the other side of the booth which deftly catches it and puts it on. The Chinese shows consist usually of stories framing a series of short variety turns that can include balancing and twirling a pile of plates on the end of a stick held in the puppet's mouth, or whirling like a dervish before flying to the other side of the booth, to be caught in the other hand of the puppeteer, and other such tricks which must take countless hours of practice. In Germany glove puppetry is widely employed in contemporary pieces; I remember for example a production of the Dadaist writer Kurt Schwitter's *Tod mit Happyend (Death with Happy end)* by the Theater Handgemenge company, wherein the operation of the small birdlike glove characters by a trio of puppeteers hidden in a booth was exceptionally accomplished, the aesthetic of the show mirroring the darkly comic text. Glove puppets play humour naturally, in part because they can make quick movements, instantly reacting to jokes, executing comic business and handling props, able to race across the stage or dip and surface on the playboard. When offstage the puppet is usually hung upside down on its own hook inside the booth so that the player's hand can easily be lowered to remove itself from one character and slip inside another while the other hand continues performing on the playboard. The newly unhooked character can then be held up to face the spectators, ready to play.

For the shows given by the Punch family the booth was and usually still is the normal play space, fronted by a presenter, often the showman, whose job is to engage Punch in banter. He or she has frequently to moderate and even translate the outrageous and sometimes indistinguishable words of the puppet protagonist, especially when the puppeteer is speaking with a swazzle or *pivetta* pressed against the upper palate (its manufacture is a trade secret, but basically it consists of a flattish sandwich of fine metal wrapped around with cord). This essential adjunct to the Punchman's skill renders the voice harsh and squawking. Punch's Neapolitan name, Pulcinella, may be derived from 'little chicken', and there are old masks and sketches which suggest that his paunch, his hump and his hooked nose might well come from the outline of a cock or chicken. However Allardyce Nicoll, the great historian of theatre, does not believe the etymology to be entirely proven, even if he bends in its direction:

> [...] has this Pulcinella any connexion with the 'cock type' which we have met with in classic mime? [...]The name [...] is not by any means unique [...] an Ioan

Pulcinella [is documented] in 1484; and a Lucio Pulcinella in 1572. The name is one, therefore, which is borne by a number of real persons, not connected with the stage, from the thirteenth century to the sixteenth. [...] On the one hand we may suppose that a real Pulcinella gave his own surname to the type; but on the other – and this seems more probable – we might assume that a stock type gave rise to a family called after him. (Nicoll, 1931: 291–93)

Whatever the truth, the swazzle distorts the consonants of all but the most practised professor ('professor' is the accepted if ironic handle to the name of every British Punch player). For example, the distortion caused the original name of Punch's wife, Joan, to sound like 'Judy' rather than 'Joanie', and Judy she eventually became.

It is obviously impractical to perform with comic glove puppets to use dialogue that is recorded (as indeed I insist is the case with most types of puppet), since their talent and most interesting function lie in repartee and the reaction of an audience. Much of the value of folk puppetry depended and still depends on improvisation, the puppet characters ringing changes in the script at every show, perhaps relaying the latest tidings and local gossip to villagers, ridiculing authority and exchanging pleasantries and insults with members of the public. To this day in many regions where television has not yet changed the way of life – for example north-east Brazil where the resident folk characters are called the *mamulengo* – people crowd to the street shows to hear news of the malpractices and infidelities of the local women, the venal lawyer, the doctor, the arm of the law – spicy gossip and parochial politics collected in advance by the puppeteers and his assistants from the local squares and bars, to be relayed by the puppets during the show.[6]

In contrast with Guignol of France whose repertoire of stories is wide, the traditional English Punch show is somewhat formulaic, tailored to a 'family audience'. This is the present evolution of the once anarchic street show which is not often encountered on the streets these days but sometimes on the beach in summer and at children's parties all year round. Its old satirical concept found a kind of reincarnation in *Spitting Image*, an adult television programme started in Britain in 1984. It lampooned the famous and infamous and was so successful that it was reproduced in several other countries, including Russia (post-glasnost).

The puppets were of latex, mobile reincarnations of brilliant caricatures modelled by Roger Law and Peter Fluck of the many celebrities and political leaders of the 1980s and 90s. At first they were large, cumbersome hand puppets manipulated with a minimum of technical trickery in 'real-time' and sometimes even (for the sake of topicality) broadcast live, by hard-worked puppeteers hidden beneath the figures. (I was reliably told that the

---

[6] http://gobrazil.about.com/od/olinda/ss/Mamulengo-Museum-Olinda.htm, accessed Oct 2008.

studio unit would leave for a coffee break forgetting to tell the exhausted but invisible manipulators that they could release their vertical hold and 'stand down'). At first the puppets' mouths were imperfectly synchronized with the speech of the actors, some live, some recorded; but after a time technology allowed the speech to be transmitted electronically to the puppet's mouth by an off-screen speaker, a practice that has since been adapted for occasional use in the theatre.

The operation of any type of puppet's mouth to coincide with text or song is called 'lip-synch' or 'lip-sync' (lip-synchronization). It is difficult enough to do well even when the speech is produced by the operator of the puppet, and almost impossible to do well if a separated actor is giving the voice, live or recorded. At present the electronically activated lips, whose accuracy is more or less guaranteed, have gained an advantage, but it is a technique rarely employed by the masters of live lip-sync, the operators of the Muppet Show characters, especially Jim Henson who played 'Kermit', and Frank Oz who immortalized the character of 'Miss Piggy'.

The Muppet characters were (and are) an amalgam of the nether-rod and the clap-mouth puppet, with one arm of the puppeteer reaching above his head, the hand in the character's mouth, and the other hand manipulating with practised dexterity the slender rods which control the arms. As already told, they were usually voiced live by their manipulator who watched their own performance in strategically placed monitors in order to see exactly the action the spectators would see. The technical and performing skills needed were of a high order.

On stage too the technique has been employed many times. In cabaret (though he won fame on television), one of the greatest performers to use it was the late Wayland Flowers, an American puppeteer mentioned in the last chapter whose vocal and lip-sync artistry was superb. The experts show that merely to 'clap' the divided parts of the mouth together (four fingers in the top lip, thumb in the bottom) at random is no way to convince the audience of the puppet's authentic power of speech. In the best manipulator's hands the mouth's opening will (as far as possible) vary with each syllable, as the human mouth does, the timing will be exact, until, as with Oz, Henson, Flowers and others, the skill becomes instinctive.[7]

In theatre the glove or hand puppet, generally with no moving mouth, can play scenes that are anarchic, violent and lewd, like those of the comic anti-heroes; it can also play subtly and charmingly for a genteel audience or for children. It varies in height from a few inches to over a foot and needs action rather than long speeches, as an unabridged performance of a literary text will amply demonstrate. The Chinese performances prove that it is capable of a wide range of movement and characterization, only occasionally achieved in western shows. All glove puppets play in a variety of booths

---

[7] The reader may like to try it before a mirror, speaking and miming with a bare hand.

among miniature settings and props, natural communicators with the spectators or the presenter. The glove puppeteers have, until now, preferred to remain hidden, but often see the crowd to gauge its reactions through a camouflaged panel in the front of the booth.

SHADOWS AND SILHOUETTES

Shadow puppetry is normally thought of as an ancient and beautiful art form portrayed by refined, leather images or solid silhouettes, especially suited to poetry and metaphor. Surprisingly, the shadow puppet can be almost as effective as the glove puppet in comic and risqué imagery and dialogue: one has only to think of Karagöz of Turkey, regularly portrayed with a giant phallus. Shadow puppets are also capable of violence, as in the stylized battles waged in the stories of the Ramayana, produced throughout southeast Asia.

The animation of shadow figures is accomplished by rods attached to the puppets, operated from below or horizontally, and by various kinds of lighting thrown from behind onto some sort of receptor screen which is traditionally stretched on a frame, but these days may be unsecured, high, low, huge or miniature. The writer, designer and maker of puppets Tina Bicât wrote:

> Shadows have a particular magic. They are experts in the art of transformation. Hold a shadow puppet close to the screen and the picture it throws will be crisp and clear; move it away and the picture grows and blurs. A simple shadow puppet, such as a cardboard cutout of a man on a stick, is capable of many actions, all of which will be clearer if we see him in profile ... providing him with a moving joint worked by a rod will give him a much more active life. Images and colours can be overlaid. Having several different light sources adds to the possibilities. It is no problem for the shadow whale to swallow Jonah: the whale's shadow will eat him with ease. (Bicât, 2007: 41)

Shadow play goes well with stories like this, surreal tales and comic nursery poems like that of the old woman who swallowed – in succession – a fly, a spider, a cat and other indigestible and unlikely animals, eventually causing her death. Played with coloured shadows fixed to almost invisible rods the spectator sees the creatures disappear into the old woman's ever wider mouth. Shadows can evoke the ineffable: dreams, memories, horrors, ghosts, even abstract forms, more difficult to express in any other more concrete medium.

Traditions of shadow play are rooted in all the countries of Asia, near, middle and far, as many ancient documents testify. Performances are still relatively easy to find there. Günter Böhmer gives an elegant lesson in the genre:

> The puppet theatre which is found in many forms and in all parts of the world, reaches its highest degree of refinement in Asiatic shadow puppetry. Without

forfeiting its deep-rooted popular nature or losing anything of its contact with the public, in streets and marketplaces and even in the remotest villages, the Asiatic shadow theatre achieves an almost esoteric spirituality through the artistic stylization of its figures and the magic ceremonial of its presentation.

From the skins of goats, sheep, donkeys, camels or cattle are produced delicate transparent figures of parchment, scraped thin and coloured, or of roughly tanned stiff leather, in the latter case looking like outsize scissor cuts. Chiselled and punched out by untiring hands, there emerge from coarse materials noble and horrific forms, lineaments and ornamental designs superbly stamped, which for all their liveliness and profusion, are invariably simple to the point of abbreviation and disclose a sense of economy and restraint. Even the exotic baroque of the Wayang Kulit figures of Java and Bali, which are painted as well as perforated, is characterized by a formal arrangement, controlled down to the slightest detail.

Shadow puppetry is not concerned, as with marionettes, or hand or rod puppets, with three-dimensional bodies and a spatial stage, but with flat figures moving on a two-dimensional plane which, as a rule, the spectator does not see directly in front of him.

The eye observes only the shadows projected on a white linen or silk screen. As though coming from nowhere, they float nearer and assume contours and shapes, only to dissolve again and to return to the same nothingness. An atmosphere of strange restlessness and unreality is created by the fluctuating movement to and fro of shadows or coloured forms, which rapidly become tiny while consolidating into material shapes as they approach, but grow into ever larger and more ghostly forms as they retreat, before vanishing like apparitions.

The use of optical and illusionistic aids in shadow puppetry, astonishingly modern in effect, constitutes one of the most interesting chapters in the history of the theatre. At the same time it is the puppet itself, through its filigree beauty, its rare and vivid magic, which enriches the history of non-European art with such an impressive special contribution. Shadow puppetry recalls – if we think primarily of the Thailand Nang figures of pierced buffalo leather or the elegant Szetschuan figures cut from parchment and coloured – the stained glass windows, so severe in their magnificence, of western cathedrals and churches.

At the same time one must be careful not to regard as works of art in their own right objects which fascinate by their bizarre ornamentation. Their true nature, depending on illusion and hallucination, is revealed only in their movements, or to be more precise in the projection of those movements. If the old historic shadow play, inconceivable without the white screen and the effect of light, is regarded as an archaic pre-form of the cinema or even of the modern colour film, then the individual figure has merely the significance of a 'still' photograph. But this comparison also is imperfect since such an individual figure, removed from the continuity of the play, is no more than a sort of secret cipher, which anyone not familiar with the religious concepts of the east is unable to understand, and which even scholars can never unravel completely.

When Alexander von Bernus says of the shadow play that it reflects 'in its purest form the dematerialized world of waking dreams', he has in mind the magic area where the threshold between this and the next world is crossed by ghosts and demons, such as the clearly differentiated good and bad characters of the *Ramayana* and the *Mahabharata* legends. (Böhmer, 1971: 112–18)

Even in the Middle East, or wherever the Muslim religion is strict about the ban on portrayals of human or animal effigies, shadow play has been a part of the cultural landscape for centuries. Jurkowski's research on puppetry and its literary allusions reveals that

> The notion of God was actually introduced by the Arabs, whose poets and philosophers expressed Arab determinism. Birri, the Anatolian poet of the thirteenth century, wrote in his gazel:
>
> > Wise man seeking for Truth
> > Look up at the tent of the sky
> > Where the Great Showman of the world
> > Has long ago set up his Shadow Theatre.
> > Behind his screen he is giving a show
> > Played by the shadows of men and women of his creation.
>
> (quoted in Jurkowski, 1988: 2–3)

The difference in the style and scale of shadow figures in every country is marked. The Turkish Karagöz and the Greek Karaghiosis are not unlike Punch in their love of violence, their cheerful contempt for authority, their

Figure 3.5   Modern shadow theatre in *The Lost Moon* by Mandy Travis (2008). Operated before and behind the screen. The shadows in the picture are of Mandy's fingers with three-dimensional puppets made by Peter O'Rourke.
© Korrina Roeding.

crude pursuit of the female. These shadows are coloured, made of pierced hide or plastic, and can be giants or miniatures. Like most of the protagonists of traditional folk comedies they are loquacious to the extent that only native speakers can derive much from their situations and scrapes. Karagöz, Karaghiosis and their like bring argument and combat upon themselves and others and sometimes the foreigner longs to understand the demotic they speak; but in expert hands and with a modicum of visual aids the shows still give even the foreign spectators a large measure of enjoyment.

The Chinese are also famous for their shadow puppetry, as for their marionettes. Their shadows, small and delicate, can often rank as works of art, and are projected and operated with exquisite skill and control.

> The cultivation of puppeteering and especially manipulating skills is an outstanding feature of the history of the Chinese shadow theatre. Some of the movements produced on the screen reflect the high standards and results of the intense training the players have received in perfecting the techniques of manipulation. There are usually three rods attached to the flat figure one of which is connected to the neck while the other two are tied to the hands ... Sometimes the movements are complex requiring considerable practice and particularly if he [the rod controller] has to manipulate four figures in both hands. ... Expert performers are also adept in the technique of hurling arrows or spears from bows held and operated by soldiers ... a skilled manipulator wields as many as five rods in making a militant female soldier release a javelin while riding a horse. (Tilakasiri, 1999: 163)

One might be forgiven for wondering whether the twenty-first century will see a relaxation of this rigour, whether the teachers of the Chinese puppeteers will come to value innovation as much as the perfection of technical skill. In fact the tradition of shadow play is alive and well throughout Asia, with new ideas and technologies supplementing if not replacing old ways. Of the Indian shadows those from Karnataka are the most beautiful. Smaller than the shadow figures of Andhra Pradesh they are transparent and many-coloured. In Tilakasiri's words 'it is indeed a very artistic cut-out, duly decorated and presented by expert performers' (Tilakasiri, 1999: 46). Some of the oriental figures, for instance in Thailand and Cambodia, represent not just one character but a whole scene and setting, animated by dancer-puppeteers.

India gives confirmation of the universality of the comic anti-hero, whether shadow or glove puppet. There is more than one equivalent of Punch, an example being the clown trouble-maker *Killekyata*. In China there is the beloved and irrepressible Monkey-King, a demi-god with magic powers.

The anarchic humour of these comic heroes is everywhere an entertainment, an escape, in fact a social necessity, and part of the puppet's mission is to be a lively mouthpiece for people's protests against authority, sometimes even a catalyst for effective action.

Shadows, black or coloured, are made of a variety of materials: I've mentioned pierced hide, but one can add thin sheet-metal, parchment, wire, card and plastic, gels, soft and textured fabric, three-dimensional objects, and in the case of silhouette work human hands and bodies. The figures are brought to life through clever manipulation, speech, music and action and may have articulated joints or heads and complicated or simple mechanisms. Their motion can be slow or surprisingly sharp, as in the expert operation of a Javanese *dalang* (a solo puppeteer), or the witty cut-out silhouettes of the exceptionally gifted Australian Richard Bradshaw (1938–). The movement of shadows and silhouettes is less variable than with other types, though they are capable of a number of gestures via articulation points and hinges: a hinge in the middle of the back allows the figure to turn about-face quickly and easily. A range of illusions, transformations, suggestions of three-dimensionality, approaches and retreats, crowds and battles are all possible through the skill of the best shadow players. A shadow show will be performed by a group or a soloist, like Richard Bradshaw, who manages to produce in rapid succession thirty or forty vignettes in a single show: his figures, rear-operated, are neatly stacked in playing order on his left, and, having performed, are transferred to a reversed stack on his right. The *dalang* has an army of puppets ranged at floor level on either side of his crossed legs, their rods stuck – also in careful order – in a split banana tree trunk, ready to be grasped and moved into the light. Somehow the *dalang* finds it possible to handle a number of characters at a time while giving each one its unique voice.

Sources of light for throwing the shadows vary in sophistication and scale from a single oil lamp, a lit match, a fire, a hand-held torch, an anglepoise lamp, a powerful spotlight, projectors and so on. The Italian company Gioco Vita's interpretation of Debussy's *Boîte à Joujoux* (Box of Toys) ruptured all illusion and brought the performers in front of the screens, casting shadows behind them. The sources of light were on the floor or carried by the performers, sometimes while dancing, sometimes kneeling or even prone. The world of shadow puppetry was changed forever in the late twentieth century by the work of this company from Piacenza. Gioco Vita's[8] large-scale version of the Gilgamesh story introduced a strong dramatic force to a previously picture-book area of western puppetry. In most countries (though not in Thailand or Cambodia) the shadows were confined to a stretched, immobile screen. Gioco Vita introduced shadow performances that took the puppeteers and the spectators to the areas behind and in front of the screens, not often fixed or stretched but loose cloths or mobile transparent sheets that billowed and rolled, moved upwards and downwards, hung from the flies or were hand-held, often changing the configuration of the stage space.

Gilgamesh captured the potential for dynamism, colour and excitement in shadow play, abjuring the static and the merely illustrative in the same way as many performances in, for example, Indonesia. The characters, constantly changing scale, were gigantesque or small, in sharp or soft focus, with the

---

[8] Roman Paska (1995), in (no ed. given) *Teatro Gioco Vita, Un Mondo di Figure d'Ombra*. Piacenza, Italy, 27.

unseen puppeteers performing a choreographed dance, as it were, some-times reversing with their figures to the full depth of the backstage area, sometimes working close to the screens. The design of the puppets was for some years the work of Emmanuele Luzzati (1921–2007), an artist of high repute. Once more the point is made: great puppetry usually arises from a theatre served by fine artists.

In a booklet produced by Gioco Vita Roman Paska, American puppeteer-director, wrote:

> After seeing Teatro Gioco Vita I see shadows everywhere. Like signs from an invis-ible world, apparitions from a world of internal light. Gioco Vita's shadows fill a space between perceived and unperceivable truths; and therein lies the poetry of their theatre. [...] Gioco Vita have taken me into Plato's cavern, into a metaphys-ical space, into the theatre of light.[9] (Paska, 1995)

New technologies are continually affecting the way shadow puppetry is produced. It is an aspect of theatre, of lighting design and of scenographic aesthetics that has probably always existed and now draws its own aficiona-dos, its festivals and literature, not to mention its dedicated performers. To this day it holds mystery and illusion for the uninitiated spectator. David Currell's richly illustrated book on shadows opens with the words

> The shadow has given inspiration to many writers, among them Edgar Allen Poe (*Shadows*), Hans Christian Andersen (*The Shadow*), Oscar Wilde (*The Fisherman and his Soul*) and Johann Wolfgang von Goethe, whose fascination with the phenomenon of coloured shadows informed his *Theory of Colour* and whose liter-ary work used the shadow as a strong image. (Currell, 2007: 7)

HUMANETTES

The *humanette* is a curious kind of puppet, part human (the manipulator's head and sometimes hands) and part puppet (body, arms and legs). Currell writes:

> There are many variations on the humanette: it may be used in 'black art' [black theatre] presentations with the operator's body remaining in darkness, or on a table top with the operator hidden under a dark cape. [...] The stuffed puppet body either hangs from the operator's neck or is attached to the backcloth. Sometimes [...] the legs are moved by the operator's own hands. Alternatively a large curtain ring may be fastened from a cord running from each shoulder to the knee. By slipping a finger into the ring and raising the hand, the leg can be moved.
> The humanette can be extremely funny. (Currell, 1974: 169)

---

[9] Roman Paska (1995), in (no ed. given) *TEATRO GIOCO VITA Un Mondo di Figure d'Ombra*, Piacenza, Italy: Gioco Vita, 27.

Figure 3.6 'Humanette' puppet
'Clementine' made and performed by
Mark Mander.

Reproduced by permission of Mark Mander
and Christophe Cohen.

I confess to a love of the humanette, a
label that is surely ripe for change.
The appearance of the performer's
face crowned with a hat, wig or other
headgear and attached to a miniature
body manipulated from the back of
the playboard by short rods (usually),
or with the puppeteer's hands
protruding through the sleeves of the
puppet's dress, is irresistibly funny.
The humour lies in the contrast
between the scale and expression of
the human face and hands with the
tiny body and limbs which seem to act
independently. Its use is doubly limited, because it is at home only in
comedy and because up to now no one (as far as I know) has moved the
figure around the stage other than behind a linear screen or in a booth, to
hide the trunk and legs of the puppeteer.

There was a version of the *Pied Piper of Hamelin* by the Italian company
Teatro Briciole for which the set was a courtyard within the four high walls
of a castle. Into it the spectators were herded, and the 'gates' closed.
Humanette characters appeared above the walls, on the ramparts as it were,
and were able to move all around the perimeter with the hidden operators
lending them voice and action. The effect was comically incongruous and
the show was a classic example of commedia-flavoured farce, a staple of
puppetry. The humanette has played well in cabaret and in short sketches,
but perhaps it has dramaturgic potential yet to be explored.

TOY OR PAPER THEATRE

The list of classic techniques is not yet complete: the toy or paper theatre,
with its miniature proscenium stages, is played by cut-out cardboard figures
(three to five inches high) slotted into wooden stands. The stands are
attached to lateral wires which the generally solo player slides from side to
side of the elaborately painted sets, giving limited movement to the hardly
articulated characters. Miniature lighting, lightweight music (some use a
musical box) and special effects can enhance the experience. The player is

usually visible above the stage, accentuating the scale of the performance. Born in the nineteenth century in several European countries but especially popular in England and Denmark, the toy theatre provided challenging family entertainment, keeping older children occupied for hours in constructing, rehearsing and performing the pieces. Now it can be found skilfully played by professionals or semi-professionals in intimate venues. The twenty-first century exponents form a loose association for the preservation and development of the genre and have established festivals of toy theatre in several countries, including Denmark, France, Germany and the United States. As it always did, the repertory parodies period melodramas of the nineteenth century. Toy theatre lends itself to scenographic extravagance and transformation, parody, wit and declamation. G.K. Chesterton wrote:

> It is a stage unsuited for psychological realism; the cardboard characters cannot analyse each other with any effect. But it is a stage almost divinely suited for making surroundings, for making that situation and background which belongs peculiarly to romance. (quoted in Baldwin, 1992: 148)

The genre was parodied in the groundbreaking British production *Shockheaded Peter*[10] for which the set, built to recall a toy theatre but on a scale to accommodate small humans and large puppets, itself amounted to an animated object, which was puppetesque if not actually a puppet.

MODEL THEATRE

This differs from toy theatre in that the small figures are three-dimensional and operated from above, like rod marionettes, or from behind, with short rods. The miniature sets and figures are always, I find, beguiling. They do not play a special repertory and are capable of a range of production styles. The surviving exponents of the box or cabinet theatre shows, all springing from the eastern European Nativity tradition, for example vertep, batleyka and szopka, may be said to perform Model Theatre shows. The repertory need not be tied to humour or period, but in fact Model Theatre is rarely seen nowadays, regrettably for the miniaturists among us.

'BLACK LIGHT' AND 'BLACK THEATRE'

Clever lighting designers producing precisely focused lighting make the 'Black Light' and 'Black Theatre' techniques a modern approach to a purely

---

[10] Production by Cultural Industry and the West Yorkshire Playhouse 1998, directed and designed by Phelim McDermott and Julian Crouch.

illusionist theatre. The two are not to be confused: 'Black Light' is a form of puppetry that, until you understand the simple technology of its production, seems to be a form of magic, since it shows moving shapes of intense colours and variety of movement apparently unconnected to any human operator. In fact the 'magic' is caused by the use of ultraviolet lighting in front of figures and objects painted or clothed in fluorescent colours, operated by puppeteers entirely enveloped in black material, moving against a black background. The UV lighting can render the performers totally invisible.

A superb exponent of this technique is an American company called Momix which uses a play of light and projected forms on dancers' bodies. The illusions are, when first seen, amazing, but only in the shows of Momix and the original Black Theatre of Prague have I not found a full-length show using the technique wearisome, suitable only for the lightest and briefest of entertainments. Watching it for more than a few minutes can make the eyes hurt. Used sparingly Black Light has its dramatic usefulness, especially for scenes where disembodied things apparently defy gravity.

'Black Theatre' on the other hand is the current description of performances lit from either side of the scenic space, casting a corridor of illumination – 'white light' – in which the puppets perform while the puppeteers attempt to remain behind the lit area, more or less unseen, ghostly shapes that occasionally spill into view. The manipulators dressed and masked in black stand behind their figures, using rear rods to effect the movement. The difficulty – in the shows I have seen – lies in the lack of depth of the acting space, and the enforced linearity of the action (though linearity is nothing abnormal in puppet theatre), but technical advances will doubtless overcome the problem. The contrast of the stygian darkness of the framing with the shifting lighting on the characters of the action makes for suitable stagings of supernatural, sinister and horror themes, as frequently exploited by the Corsario company from Valladolid in Spain. The deliberately sensational *Vampyria* (2001) and *Aullidos* (which translates as 'Howls', 2008) were violent and explicitly sexual spectacles in which four-foot high, rear-rod puppets were manipulated with, as it were, no holds barred.

'TABLETOP', 'BUNRAKU-STYLE', OR 'REAR-ROD'

As a worthy culmination of this section comes the type and technique of puppet currently favoured with more attention than any other, most of all in the west. It is variously referred to as 'tabletop', 'Bunraku-style' or 'rear-rod'. The figures are moved from behind by means of rods long or short and by one to three operators using collaborative, synergistic skills to effect the puppets' gestures and manoeuvre them through the scenic space. I call them 'rear-rod' puppets since both of the other current names, 'tabletop' and 'bunraku' are misleading: 'tabletop' because there is frequently no table, and 'bunraku' because the style is normally far removed from the aesthetic of the Bunraku-za, the National Theatre of Osaka, where the name originates.

The staging may indeed be a tabletop (as in the widely travelled *The Miser* by Tabola Rassa of France/Spain or a Liebe Wetzel show from the United States), but the characters are manipulated on a variety of surfaces, on the ground or through empty space as though the puppet's feet were touching an invisible floor.

All the Japanese companies operating the rear-rod technique are playing in the widely-practised genre that has come to be known for centuries as *ningyo joruri* – in essence a form of storytelling with music which in some way or another is common to puppets the world over. In many Japanese joruri performances the storyteller chants the text, seated next to the musician who accompanies him on a stringed instrument called the samisen or shamisen. Both are seated on a dais, normally on the audience's right, overlooking the action.

Few western puppeteers can aspire to the heights of precision and control possessed by the Osaka troupe. Neither do the other Japanese companies that play in the *ningyo joruri* style, with the default accompaniment of a storyteller/chanter and musician, but with figures that are less refined and manipulation less precise. The companies were and still are to be seen in temple courtyards as well as touring theatres. The island of Awaji boasts its own highly regarded joruri troupe and is a sort of homeland for many of these groups.

> Awaji was considered the 'island of the puppets' for several centuries not simply because there were numerous professional theatres and ritual performers on the island, but because people on Awaji took an avid interest in joruri recitation, puppet manipulation, and even puppet kashira [the heads of the figures] creation. (Law, 1997: 250)

Another form of joruri transforms and subverts the stately form of the Bunraku through a related technique called *kuruma-ningyo*, in which the large puppets are held in front of the puppeteer who is seated on a wheeled stool. There is no screen, so the performers are able to use the depth of the stage and can move around with speed and – occasionally – abandon. The puppet's legs are those of the puppeteer, its feet attached to his, and the puppet's head is also attached to either side of the operator's head by wires, so that his every nod or shake is copied and the puppeteer's hands are freed to operate the rest of the figure. This ingenious technique has been imitated outside Japan, notably in the abbreviated version of *Hamlet* written by Tom Stoppard in 1979 and played by a Croatian company over a number of years. The grotesque puppets were by the designer Zlatko Bourek. Comedy, aggression and fast action suit the *kuruma-ningyo* well – in marked contrast to the Bunraku of Osaka who are more used to playing in operatic tragedy.

The present popularity of the rear-rod puppet comes from its relative ease

Figure 3.7   Sketch of a Barry Smith puppet in the technique of Bunraku-za, with three puppeteers operating behind a metre-high figure whose physicality is transformed with each change of mask. *Pierrot in Five Masks* by the Barry Smith Theatre of Puppets (1980s).

© Barry Smith. Reproduced by permission of Puppet Centre Trust.

of operation, that is when it is not played in the highly skilled manner of the Bunraku-za with three operators to a puppet. The technique is applied with a limitless variety of materials and a range of control mechanisms, from the simple rod in the back of the head and/or the body managed by a single puppeteer, to a complicated arrangement of levers and strings which can bring about, for example, a change of facial expression, or an artificial hand able to grasp and grip.

For obvious logistical reasons it is almost impossible for puppeteers using the rear-rod method to be in a booth or behind a screen, although they may mask the upper body with material or lighting or, as with the Vietnamese Water Puppets, they may operate figures on long horizontal rods through gaps beneath a backcloth. Puppeteers and backcloth stand in shallow water (as though in a paddy field, since the show's provenance was a fertility ritual), and the rods, also immersed, lie under the water with mechanisms that allow the puppets magically to rise above the surface to perform. The mechanisms are a close secret and the technique is so far unique to the water puppet troupes.

For most operators of rear-rod figures visibility affords them freedom and almost infinite dramaturgical and staging choices. The puppeteer is able to plot unconfined movement over various configurations of the playing area, depending on the scenography. A visible puppeteer may be 'neutralized' by hood, mask or veil, or they may be dressed so as to echo the aesthetic of the scenography or to relate to the costume of a character or to represent a controlling force, as in more than one production of Büchner's *Woyzeck* played by puppeteers in uniform, metaphoric reminders of the central character's subjugation to authority.

A related technique with figures and objects operated from behind is the simple '*hands-on*' method, meaning the manipulation of the object or figure directly on the body of the puppet with the bare or gloved hands of the puppeteer but with no other control except possibly a short rod to the back of the head. The wish of the modern producer to avoid pretence or illusion is thus expressed by avoiding any manufactured or mechanical intervention between the animated and the animator.

If the uncovering of the hidden operator owes much to the Brechtian ideology, to reveal the mechanics of theatre and remove illusion, then the loss of screen and booth that has ensued in the puppet theatre must give rise to the need for a new breed of puppeteer – one as skilled in acting as in animating.

The changes in puppet playing and aesthetics also derive from the widespread use of the rear-rod figure that has brought the manipulators onto the open stage, obliging them to reveal their strength and weakness as actors as well as manipulators. It is a development of the practice of the string marionettists who have for many decades played on an open stage in variety and cabaret, interacting with their puppet – and secondly of the Japanese joruri theatre, perhaps the most influential of all. Now any player, even shadow puppeteers, may perform undisguised. Roland Barthes' explication of the new situation is given in an essay 'On Bunraku' reproduced in full in Chapter 6 on the aesthetics of puppetry.

This is not to say that hidden manipulators have had their day: it is not so and probably never will be. However sophisticated the spectators, whatever the fashion of contemporary theatre, the performance of the 'autonomous' puppet still induces wonder, whenever one is played with skill and conviction by the best puppeteers.

Other practices and ancient techniques of operation exist: for instance the puppet hung from a padded ring worn on the head of the puppeteer, freeing his hands to manipulate the puppet by rods or strings – a practice found in India, in the Karnataka region. Then again, a puppet's legs can be attached to the legs or feet of the puppeteer, so that their movements coincide pleasingly; or a supple puppeteer may bend double, operating the puppet through a cloak which covers his or her back; bare or costumed hands may play together as characters, usually to great comic effect. All these methods are employed, and there are still others: mouth puppets, finger puppets, body puppets, the list is open-ended. Of the classic types, however, I have included the marionette (worked from above), the rod puppet (worked from below), the shadows and the rear-rods (worked from behind) and of course the hand/glove puppet, warmed by the blood of its operator.

The fashion for the marionette gave way to the fashion for the nether-rod, the nether-rod to the rear-rod (the 'table-top' or 'bunraku') which presently seems a fixture, in competition only with the advance of new technologies. On the other hand, so to speak, the glove puppet and the shadow have no truck with fashion and are perennial.

In the next chapter some of the practicalities and complications of staging a production with puppets will be tackled.

FURTHER READING

Blackham, Olive (1960) *Shadow Puppets*, New York: Harper and Bros.

Currell, David (1999) *Puppets and Puppet Theatre*, Marlborough: Crowood Press.

Fettig, Hansjürgen (1997) *Rod Puppets and Table-top Puppets: A Handbook of Design and Technique*, English version by Rene Baker, Bicester: DaSilva Puppet Books.

Hadamowsky, Franz (1956) *Richard Teschner und Sein Figurenspiegel*, Vienna: Eduard Wancura Verlag.

Kott, Jan (1984) *The Theatre of Essence*, Evanston, IL: Northwestern University Press.

Venu, G. (1990) *Tolpava Koothu, Shadow Puppets of Kerala*, New Delhi: Sangeet Natak Akademi.

Wright, John (1951) *Your Puppetry*, UK: Sylvan Press.

Chapter

4 *In Performance*

The chapter provides a perspective on current practice, modes and methods of working with puppets found effective by practitioners and producers. To start with, the creation of a show involves the interaction of every one of these, even more than for a straight play, a fact underlined by Peter J. Wilson, a gifted director-performer-puppeteer who has enjoyed international success as much as in his native Australia. In *The Space Between*, a book written with Geoffrey Milne, he insists that in any production with puppetry 'collaboration is vital: among the design team itself, and also with the writer, director, composer, performers and puppeteers. Everything depends on everything else' (Wilson and Milne, 2004: 105).

Wilson was a founder member of the avant-garde Handspan company of Melbourne, for which he performed and directed. The company existed from 1977 to 2002 and was a world leader in innovative, multimedia theatre, touring all over the world. Since its closure Wilson has created several shows which have combined the traditional arts of east and west with present-day technologies and themes, the most high-profile of these being *The Theft of Sita*, an east-west fusion of traditional and modern shadow play and music from Indonesian gamelan instruments, played on an open stage by puppeteers on wheeled stools.

Although collaboration is vital it may be useful and interesting to describe separately the contribution to a production with puppets of each performance discipline, since the staging of puppetry makes particular demands on all of them. The work of the director, dramaturg and designer inevitably overlap, as in the human theatre, but their decisions and solutions will always affect the performer-puppeteers. Conversely, the practical needs of the puppet operators and their puppets will affect and modify the work of the others at every turn. The complications of the process go some way to explaining the predilection of many puppeteers to undertake a whole show independently, exerting complete control; although recently, for more than one reason, the one-person production is less commonly seen. Higher audience expectations are forcing all but the most prodigious of the puppeteers to recognize the limits of their talents and to delegate at least one or two components of their work to better-qualified specialists, for instance, to an experienced sound designer or dramaturg. This is not to

Figure 4.1 Three visible, costumed puppeteers with 'Margarete' from Gounod's *Faust*, a puppet with long rear-rods. Pastel sketch by Stefan Fichert of the Puppet Players, Gauting, (directors Stefan Fichert and Susanne Forster) realized at the Munich State Opera House (2008) in collaboration with the composer Hans Werne Henze and the director David Pountney.

Reproduced by permission of Stefan Fichert.

deny that some shows played by only one *performer*, though perhaps supported by a small production team, still rank among the best on the international circuits. The all-rounder wishing to be a jack-of-all-trades (and occasionally, surprisingly, master of most) can still be found. Such puppeteers are most satisfied when producing a show where they have themselves adapted or written, designed, constructed, determined the sound and lighting, arranged the staging – and performed.

From the preparation of a puppeteer we can return to the preparation of a production: 'In the Heart of the Beast' is a community group based in Minnesota, USA. Here is their method, not unusual in any form of devised theatre, of preparing a new production:

> Each show begins with some essential core of an idea. We almost never begin with a formal script, but rather with the raw tools of our work: idea, image, gesture, puppet, word, music. Sometimes early ideas demand research involving anything from live interviews, trips to the library, journeys to other regions, images from dreams, group discussions. Though there are common techniques and skills we all use to develop new work, each artist creates in his or her own way. I am always surrounded by image flashes that move between my thinking head and my dreaming heart. When I have gathered my early ideas, I call my co-workers together with sticks, cardboard boxes, cloth, tape and odd assortments of instruments to 'brainstorm in action' according to the working threads of the core images ... From the spin of the fabric, the click of the tongue, the odd gait of a box moved across the floor, I catch the poetic glimpses from which I plan the puppet design and draw a structured storyboard. This storyboard then becomes my map for the layering of puppets, sound, words, light and paint.
>
> [...] In puppet theatre, the visual language of the piece is intrinsically important, structuring the narrative in a similar way as a script might work in non-puppet theatres. (Spieler, 1999: 43–44)

WRITING

Writing for puppet play is an art that differs widely from writing for the drama. A group or company having chosen a theme or an existing play-text, the 'writer' must try to imagine the work, or the parts of the work relating to puppets, in pictures rather than in words. Whatever is committed to paper might be in the form of a storyboard with captions instead of or in addition to a typescript: it can appear more like a scenario than a play. Among his or her basic resources the creator of a modern work for figure or object play will need an acquaintance with the visual arts and a sensibility to the puppet's need for movement and action. Any verbal text will consist of narration, sung or spoken, or of dialogues for the puppet characters, but a writer has to bear in mind that the puppets' voices will be supplied by a performer, visible or invisible, and the words will appear to issue from a face that will not change expression (even if lighting and the imagination of the spectator can to varying degrees effect this change). If a verbal text is offered to the company the words will often be extensively cut in rehearsal, sometimes hard for a writer to accept. Treasured prose becomes superfluous when made redundant by illustrative action and/or the soundscape. Thus the literary playwright will consider the acquisition of a new competence, the turning of ideas into images, as for the scenario of a film, with which a puppet piece has much in common. There is much of the cinematic in puppetry, as there is much of puppetry and the puppetesque in cinema.[1]

The making of the production *War Horse*, a London success being re-staged in other cities including New York, well illustrates my point about the methodology of writing for puppets, and for other categories of visual theatre. Basil Jones, co-founder of Handspring, the company responsible for the puppetry in the show, wrote:

> In 2006, Handspring was commissioned to design and make nine life-size horses for the National Theatre's production of *War Horse*, in London. The idea was to make a theatrical interpretation of Michael Morpurgo's novel of the same name.
>
> For many reasons, this would be a challenging adaptation. For one thing the novel, the central character and narrator is a horse. This horse, Joey, goes to war alongside the British army and it is through Joey's eyes that we experience the horrors of combat. The horse's voice – producing a kind of 'equine reportage' – is a powerful narrative device in the novel, though one that we realised would not work on stage. So, the decision was made to keep the horse silent in its theatrical incarnation. This presented the playwright with a problem. How does one 'author' a character who plays the leading role in the drama, but who doesn't speak and is not even a person? (see Jones, 2009: 259–60)

---

[1] A 2009 doctoral thesis by the English researcher T. Butler Garrett on the subject of *Visual Theatre*, persuasively traces its contemporary manifestation through the influences of puppetry and the cinema.

Figure 4.2   'Theatre with puppets'. From the long-running Royal National Theatre production of Michael Morpurgo's *War Horse*, premiered in 2007. Puppets designed and crafted by Adrian Kohler of the Handspring Puppet Company, Cape Town. The visible puppeteer is Craig Leo; two others are partly hidden underneath the horse.
© Simon Annand.

Clearly the horse would have to be 'articulate' in languages that were not verbal, which is where the puppeteers came in. Jones goes on to explain that the role had to function on two levels: first and most fundamentally, that the puppets had to be designed with the broadest possible range of semiotic possibilities; and second, that the next level of signification had to be realized through a process of improvisation in the rehearsal studio. Movement sequences were developed in which the horses interacted with each other and with humans; episodes initiated by a number of people including the two directors, a choreographer, the two Handspring masters, the puppet 'captain', and the puppeteers themselves. There was

> a level of co-ordination far beyond what a scriptwriter could predict. Thus we came to realise that *authoring* a role for the horses functioned at levels that didn't have much to do with the original script author. [...] the scriptwriter effectively played the role of onlooker [describing] the various sequences, and those that were approved by the director were [...] incorporated into the working script used to rehearse the play.
>
> For example: *This is a big moment for Joey – the first time we've seen him alone with another horse since he was separated from his mother. He and Topthorn*

> *cautiously explore each other … They test each other … They compete … They play … They become friends. [...] (see Jones, 2009: 259–60)*

Jones continues his explication, in an essay that I find reaches towards the essence of puppetry in performance, by suggesting that there are many such sequences to be found in the final text which are essentially verbal descriptions of the most successful physical improvisations generated during workshops and rehearsals incorporated into what began as a 'visual' text.[2] He says:

> This was a different script fundamentally from the one published. [...] By convention the written text is considered to be the play's witness 'of record'. In the past, if one was thinking of producing a play, one went to a bookshop to buy a 'copy' of that play, not to a video store. So, even though in actuality a play may have been embodied in several parallel texts, (which encompass the verbal, the visual, the haptic and the aural), the *written* version of these texts claims supremacy because of the way that, historically and even today, a text enters the public domain through print. [...] No doubt studies of early plays exist which attempt to determine what actually happened on stage that was not about words and how the hierarchy between the verbal/visual/haptic/aural has changed over time. Traces of such archives do exist, for instance in travellers' diaries of performances they have observed. Prompt books can give some suggestion of a performed event, but even these survive as textual versions of the event itself. (see Jones, 2009: 259–60)

Mervyn Millar has since this show's inception in 2007 become associate director of the puppetry and is also the writer commissioned by the Royal National Theatre, the show's producer, to document its preparation resulting in a book *The Horse's Mouth*.[3] In it he insists on the important relationship of the playwright to the ultimate performance text even though the scenes featuring the horses were extensively altered, retaining little of the original script.

> Workshopping is a rich way of generating and developing material for a script, but it's nothing without the gaps between the workshops. [The writer and the puppet-maker] need to take away what they've learnt and apply themselves to their work, rewriting and replanning the shapes and details of the script and puppets respectively. Moments or ideas that seemed ingenious in the heady community of the workshop room can seem limp when examined more closely. And it takes time and thought to make the strong choices for the story structure and aesthetic. (Millar, 2007: 35)

This is not to imply that the playwright and/or dramaturg are not vitally necessary for visual forms of theatre. Millar goes on to quote Nicholas Hytner, director of the RNT, in words that seem to me crucial to the making

---

[2] The stage directions are a substitute for, and actually *become*, the text.
[3] See also the National Theatre's excellent DVD *The Making of War Horse*.

of a puppet production: 'no amount of brilliant visual and physical work will cover up for a slack narrative, or a narrative that isn't emotionally involving'. Even if it is not a spoken narrative.

Dialogue and narrative are usually a problem for the self-sufficient puppeteer. Of all the aptitudes possessed by even the most gifted, that of wordsmith or dramaturg is the most rare. There are exceptions: Violet Philpott was a wonderful spinner of children's tales written expressly for puppet play, and Dennis Silk's piquant, eccentric writing is part of the pleasure to be got from his works, some of which are in published form (Silk, 1996). There is more to be found about this aspect of modern puppetry in the next chapter on Dramaturgy.

Another way for a writer to present a piece for a puppet production was adopted by Howard Barker, the playwright whose performing company is The Wrestling School. He has up to now offered two plays to the Movingstage Marionette company without any restrictions on their adaptation. The plays were not specifically intended for puppets but were full of potential for a visual piece of theatre. The final performance texts differed from the play texts, of course, but the dialogue retained was in the playwright's own words, his particular poetic. Barker explained his point of view:

> I understand the importance of fine art elements in puppetry, but this does not seem more critical than on the live stage. But as for movement, yes, I knew at once here was a clear distinction from stage practice, as well as in the extent to which the director/operator possesses absolute control of the creation of mood. Those constraints of speech – the puppet cannot articulate – did not seem a reason to *reduce* speech, however. The speech and the demonstration of movement in the body of the puppet gave precisely that detail and excess I aspire to. To speak melancholy and to express melancholy simultaneously in the body – how many actors can do that? Very few. (see Francis, 1999: 38)

Figure 4.3 'What puppets?' Two invisible puppeteers operating a character startled in the middle of his lunch. *Picnic Man* was a Central School of Speech and Drama Postgraduate Diploma in Puppetry project by students under the direction of Gavin Glover of Faulty Optic. 1993.
© CSSD.

Both plays by Barker, *All He Fears* (1994) and *The Swing at Night* (2001) were later published as originally written, so there is no printed record of the marionette versions.

Every year scores of new productions with puppets are created, but few works that might serve as production models are reproduced, since anything published usually appears only in words. Since the value and meaning of the dramaturgy are often conveyed in the scenography and the soundscape as much as in the dialogue, any published text is an inadequate record. Writers who have written successfully for figures and objects will have cultivated a sensibility to puppetry's aesthetics as well as, *pace* Howard Barker, an awareness of the practicalities of staging a performer-puppet co-existence and the consequences of using different control techniques.

Claire Voisard, a Canadian writer who has specialized in writing for puppets, wrestled with the problem of matching the writing to the technique and type:

> Writing for puppets? What puppets? Given the diversity of styles, some traditional, some modern, that this art form offers, this is the principal question that haunts me right through my writing process. What is the ideal type of puppet that will best serve the text, that will best establish communication with the public and arouse in them the emotions that are worthy of this 'theatrical magic'?
>
> It is easily discovered that two glove puppets will hold a dialogue different from that held by two string marionettes. The physique of the first is characterised by short arms and an absence of legs. It is the manipulator's hand, the suppleness of his wrist and the oscillations of his forearm that effect the illusion of life. This often results in rapid staccato movements, which of course influences their speech and makes one opt for a dialogue of riposte, of cut and thrust. The string marionette however is different … It may take a somewhat realistic form, and its physique may even have human proportions. It is suspended by threads which are strung to a control held by the puppeteer. To properly master the tension of the threads, slow, majestic, realistic movement is built into its form. This type of puppet is suited to the interpretation of long tirades.
>
> True, these are extreme examples of the classic forms of the profession. But I think that it reveals a problematic that we find over and over again in the work of research and innovation in puppet theatre, both in the traditional and the avant-garde. In the form on the one hand, the potential movement of the puppet on the other, lie the characteristics that the writer ignores at her peril. S/he has to bear in mind the style of the puppet taking a role in the show's delivery, exhibit great humility from the first rehearsals, and often accept certain modifications of the text solely to serve the group's vision of the show. (see Voisard, 1989: 108–9)

Challenging though the discipline may be, puppetry needs empathetic writers with new ideas. Good writing, in words or otherwise, is never redundant, for puppets as much as for any other kind of actor.

DIRECTING PUPPETS

Only a relatively small number of theatre directors are yet experienced with puppetry, and little has been written to support and guide either on the theory or the practice. Some of the most distinguished of contemporary theatre-makers are among those who have employed puppets, for example Peter Brook, Antoine Vitez, Robert Wilson, Robert Lepage, Lee Breuer, Anthony Minghella and Tom Morris. In most cases, they have also employed a specialist puppeteer as consultant or director of the puppet action for the work in preparation. Marianne Elliott, a director working with puppets for the first time in 2007, declared herself 'fascinated' by the differences between directing puppets and actors:

> 'With the puppet', she notes, 'you just want it to reflect certain feelings, so there's no psychology behind it – well, I'm sure there is, but doesn't feel like it. If you move the hand a little bit on Emilie [a puppet child character], or move the head a little bit, it means something. And all you've done is move the head. You could never say to an actor: "just move your head to the left!" You could never do that'. [...] small movements of a puppet, or changes of posture, carry a great deal of meaning. (Millar, 2007: 87).

Suddenly the old-fashioned idea of 'blocking' becomes intensely relevant, not necessarily to plan the moves of the actors on the stage but to plan in detail the physical gestures, rhythms and movements of puppet and puppeteer (when visible). When these are imprecise, as explained in a former chapter, the effect is unfocused and unconvincing.

One of the first things a director new to puppetry has to learn is the extraordinary effect of the smallest gesture of the puppet on an audience. Basil Jones of the Handspring Puppet Company has researched the phenomenon:

> I see this research as being important for puppetry, because it serves to vindicate an experience that we have as puppeteers, namely that if we treat the audience as possessing extreme perception, and we ensure that therefore everything that the puppet does will be finely apprehended by our audience, then we will indeed engage our audience's deeper, 'animal' brain. By providing the audience with highly refined and skilled puppet manipulation, we encourage them to see and hear, and most essentially, feel (and I mean this in the haptic sense) the performance with what amounts to extreme perception. How else do you explain the fact that even from the back row of an auditorium the audience is able to perceive the tiny movements a puppeteer makes when he 'breathes' the puppet? Or the fact that an audience is able to perceive the angle of a puppet's head and feel sure that it is looking into the eyes of another puppet across the stage? (see Jones, 2009: 257)

The amount of time that needs to be set aside for rehearsing the puppetry in a show would be difficult to afford by an average company, but extra time with the director in the rehearsal room pays evident dividends in the realization of the puppetry's potential.

For *War Horse*, Handspring's Basil Jones and Adrian Kohler (the latter being the maker of the puppets) were engaged to direct the puppetry as a complement to the two directors of the whole production. The actors and puppeteers who were to operate or interact with the horses were separated for intensive sessions during the last hour of every rehearsal day, adding finesse to what had been found during the day's work with the complete cast. The extra time ensured that the puppeteers, already well trained before rehearsals began, were thoroughly familiar with the puppets' emotional role, as well as their weight, manoeuvrability and controls (Millar, 2007: 61). Since it is the performance of the horses that audiences remember as the highest achievement of *War Horse,* this proved an ideal way of working, but, it must be admitted, expensive and time-consuming, to be compared only with the production of the *Lion King* a few years before when an entire theatre was hired for the rehearsals.

In the preparation by smaller groups of less well-financed shows, the rehearsals proper start after a period of initial experiment and improvisation, and it quickly becomes clear to a sensitive director that the puppet characters will destroy their own illusion if not as strictly controlled as dancers in a ballet. Vague 'wafting' in the playing space, inexact gesturing and poor lip-synchronization (if the figure has a moving mouth), whether the puppet is on the operator's hand or at the end of a rod or string, almost immediately ruptures belief in its life. Similarly, if the manipulator is allowed to be even minimally unfocused, it becomes clear to the spectator that the object has been deprived of *anima*. The point was perfectly made in a Royal Shakespeare Company's production of *A Midsummer Night's Dream* (2005) in which the fairies were figures operated on rods held above their heads by actors among whom were only two or three puppeteers. Some of the fairies were vaguely waved in the air while a few were moved with more exact delicacy and transmitted energy: the latter seemed alive, the former were merely flapping dolls on sticks.

Sue Buckmaster has made a formidable reputation for herself, first as puppet-maker, then as artistic leader of the Theatre-Rites company. In her early career she made and provided productions with her crafted figures, but soon realized that most actors and directors didn't know what to do with the puppets that she provided:

> So I started to make it a policy to help direct companies to use the puppets I'd made. I wouldn't charge for the extra work at that point, it was all part of the making fee …
>
> At the time [the 1980s and 90s] there was no such thing as a puppet director for the actor's theatre. I realised, through my work with my own company, and through my freelance contacts, that I was discovering more and more about the potential of the actor and puppet relationship on stage. Gradually directing

puppets became more important to me than just making puppets. It was important that I spent time in the rehearsal room because I kept seeing people making
the same mistakes; like assuming that the puppet didn't need to arrive in rehearsal
until the last minute. I always say that a puppet is like an actor, you should have
them there from day one.

[...] generally they [the companies] didn't realise the skill involved in operating
a puppet effectively. They needed some very basic training, and more often than
not had not given themselves enough time. When a director instructs an actor to
move on stage, she or he can instantly do as asked. However, although it takes
time to rehearse actors, it takes ten times as long to rehearse a puppet, because
in order for a puppet to move, the puppeteer's movements have to have been
precisely choreographed. (Buckmaster, 2000: 14)

Specialist puppeteer-directors undoubtedly optimize the impact of the
puppetry, assisting the actor-manipulators and the overall director who may
not have worked with the medium before. Simon McBurney, director of
Complicite who has in fact often used the animation of objects to electrifying
effect, engaged Mark Down, director of the puppet-led company Blind
Summit, for a large-scale production, *Shun-kin* (2008–9), in which the central,
eponymous character was a puppet, to be operated by actors. Down kept a
diary of rehearsals:

I sit and watch the actors play. I give almost no instructions. Eventually something
odd and interesting happens ... and I say 'let's go with that'.
There's a hundred thousand ways to solve a problem. Working in collaboration
you find ways you might not have found on your own.
You have to hold your own and be prepared to argue your case with Simon. [...]
Two people, two heads, two ideas on how to do everything! But in many ways it
is easy having a director and a puppet director work together. ... I'm able to say,
'you look after the story and I'll look after the puppetry'. (Down, 2009: 9)

Tim Carroll directed three productions of music theatre using puppets, the
last in 2007 at London's Queen Elizabeth Hall, all confirming his belief that
puppets were 'his favourite performers'. The first time he used them, for
Purcell's *Acis and Galatea*, having imagined he was merely solving a problem
of scale, he substituted Acis with a puppet merely as 'a witty solution' and
the result 'bowled him over'. Working on the scene when the giant
Polyphemus crushes Acis under a rock,

[they] laid the puppet face down and pinned him to the ground with something
heavy. As soon as the performer [the puppet operator] lifted his [the puppet's]
head we were watching someone struggling against death. [... W]hen he was
dead [Galatea] slowly laid her head on his neck. At the end we looked at each
other in shock. None of us had bargained for such an intense experience. [...]

[It's] not because they do what they're told; it's because, like all good actors,
they make everyone around them raise their game ... A puppet is a kind of idea
and therefore pure. If it is to live it demands absolute clarity of intention in its

movement; simple, direct communication of text; and total imaginative commitment from its audience. (Carroll, 2007. Copyright Guardian News and Media Ltd 2007)

A puppet company with its own house style and *modus operandi* may call for another kind of directorial input where the director's role is almost functional, less creative; their role in the process perhaps better provided by a dramaturg. On their arrival in the rehearsal room the work may already be in progress, the story and the design determined, the puppets and sets made. In this situation the company is looking not for a conceptual artist but for an expert 'outsider's eye' who will absorb the group's intentions and assist in their realization. For the director of any production with animated objects it is an exacting but rewarding experience, responding to time and attention beyond the norm for human actors.

DESIGN AND MAKING

It has been called a designer's theatre, not only because the scenographer can design the sets but also the cast – that is, the puppets. ... 'the design itself in fact participates in the actual telling of the story' (Wilson and Milne, 2004: 105).

It is thus a favoured medium for the designers, when they find themselves a leading member of the production team, and is part of the conceptualizing process. There are almost unlimited opportunities for the proposal of imaginative, unrealistic ideas and their ingenious solutions. This may be witnessed in the work of, for example, Julian Crouch, William Kentridge and the Quay Brothers, and in productions by great specialist puppet companies rooted in fine art, like the Little Angel, Faulty Optic, Gioco Vita and scores of others. Each of the three named companies has a unique stylistic: the first, the Little Angel, based in a small theatre in London, produces work that is richly sensuous, a fusion of atmospheric lighting, music, colourful settings and luxurious costumes, superb manipulation of exquisitely-made puppets interpreting literary texts, with an aesthetic neither wholly traditional nor Modernist that has attracted spectators for half a century. Faulty Optic, a touring company with a sharply contrasting aesthetic uses found objects, grotesque puppets, dark themes, black humour, machines and micro-technology: the manipulation and timing of the two or three puppeteers half-hidden at the back of the settings is always impeccable. Gioco Vita is an Italian light-and-shadow group that revolutionized shadow puppetry in breaking with the fixed screen; their productions are on a large scale and the performers trained in movement and dance, appearing behind and in front of the projected images.

'*Material theatre*' is a term for a show using a manufactured or natural fabric or substance as metaphor for a theme: Barbara Mélois of France has made whole productions in miniature in which the stage and scenery, the clothes of the performer and even the figures are designed and made in a single material, which has been aluminium foil, transparent sticky tape or tissue paper.

Farm implements and country materials have depicted the background to more than one rural story, with scenography and puppets made of sackcloth, wheat, plants and seeds. In other contexts pliant textiles or harsh metallic shapes will signify atmosphere and affect the action of a theme, the difference from human theatre being that the characters are made of the same materials.

Until recently a puppeteer responsible for crafting the puppets for a show was considered and credited only as 'puppet-maker'; the 'designer-puppeteer' is a relatively new concept, though they may well build the puppets too. The designer-puppeteer may work alone, or in tandem with the overall scenic designer where a company can afford both. In the latter case the design concept must be united, extending to the figures or objects to be animated. If this seems an obvious precept it is often not obvious at all to a production team new to puppetry, who may be aware only of the hired-in puppeteer as a supplementary maker, with no input to the design.

In all the work of Julie Taymor one may perceive the eye and the sensibility of the puppeteer, even if a puppet *per se* is not present. She is a high-profile example of a director-designer able to take responsibility for the whole scenographic concept of a major stage production, as is evident in *The Lion King,* for which there was close collaboration between her and the maker Michael Curry who was able to realize her ideas. The same puppetesque sensibility is apparent in the writing and practice of Tina Bicât, a versatile set and costume designer:

> Anything, in the world of visual theatre, can acquire a character. One of the great arts of designing such productions is the ability to see everyday objects with an innocent eye, an eye that can look into the cupboard and see a vacuum-cleaner monster, a despairing lover in a jacket on a coat hook, and the comic and varied creatures, or perhaps the collection of emotions, that can hop or creep out of the basket of hats and gloves. A walk on a street can reveal a hidden message in a half-unstuck poster hanging one-eyed from a billboard, or sinister intent in the single black umbrella in the bobbing sea of colours at the station exit, an umbrella that could, perhaps, kill or flirt, peck or cause a caressing draft on a cheek [...] In many cases these found objects will need adaptation, redesigning and remaking in order that they can be animated in performance, but this will come later. The recognition of the possibilities of these objects is as much of a creative act as is their transformation into stageworthy items. (Bicât, 2007: 91–2)

Bicât's book is a useful and generously illustrated resource for professionals at an early or intermediate level of experience.

The pleasure of designing for puppetry is complicated by that most unavoidable of considerations: how will the physical presence of the puppet operators affect the staging? Are they to be hidden or in view? Are they to operate from below the puppets or from above? From the rear? Should they be costumed as acting characters or as neutral acolytes of the puppets? Veiled, masked, barefaced; wearing gloves or with bare hands? The famous Soviet producer-director Obraztsov (1901–1992) writes in *My Profession:*

> [The designer] must imagine not only the puppets' movements in space, but also the workings of the 'mechanism' which controls them. This mechanism is the actor […] If the designer only thinks about the production's external appearance without its constructive features, he cannot be a designer for the puppet theatre, in which construction not only influences the artistic image, but often determines it. (Obraztsov, 1981: 233)

STREET THEATRE

The scenography of giant puppets and street puppet theatre is another matter altogether. Street theatre attracts crowds and the media, and is part of the indigenous culture – ritualistic, celebratory, processional, political – of many countries, none more than Catalunya, where the 'gigantes' are seen in open air demonstrations of different kinds, always in energetic displays of activity and panache. Processional figures also need the talents of fine artists, sculptors on the grand scale to avoid a genre which if ill-designed and clumsily carried by self-conscious paraders can be embarrassing. However the traditions of many countries, notably Brazil, the Caribbean, and all of Spain, bring life and beauty in street culture and carnival. British companies such as Welfare State, Horse and Bamboo and Emergency Exit Arts employ sculptor-designers and makers specializing in this kind of puppetry. All are descendants of the legendary Bread and Puppet theatre of Vermont, USA, whose founder and director Peter Schumann is a sculptor by training.

Engineers of the Imagination, a book about the work of the radical company Welfare State International which became famous under the inspired direction of John and Sue Fox, has a chapter on street performance which begins:

> Welfare State learnt some of its craft on the streets. Getting out there, banging a drum, drawing a crowd and performing for them.
>
> From the earliest attempts in 1968 to more skilled and sophisticated recent work, certain things never change. With street theatre you are as good as the moment and no more. You have no reputation in the places you will normally work. Yours is not a theatre audience. They have never heard of you, and usually they were not intending to see a show. They have chanced upon you while they were out, as a rule, and if they don't like the show they can walk away. But if they love it they can forget the shopping, they are late back to work after lunch. They get lost in your dreams and share them for a few moments. There's an honesty in the contract between street theatre performer and audience. That's why it is a trade to work at and to be proud of. As performers you KNOW when it is working – you never get a bored, indulgent audience.

> Street theatre has been used as a powerful vehicle by several leading radical companies: San Francisco Mime Troupe gave birth to guerrilla theatre and were well-known for their anti-Vietnam war platform, Teatro Campesino raised consciousness among the Californian grape-pickers in their political struggle, Bread and Puppet developed their holy theatre and Odin Teatret from Denmark continue to present the same truly spectacular street pieces, sometimes for five or six years.
>
> The content does not have to be agit-prop. [...] The form can certainly show struggle and violence, but also the emotional world with hope and longing, humour and celebration, and most of all dreams, presented in a sensual way with dance, music, energy and colour. (Sue Fox in Coult and Kershaw, 1999: 31)

Animated effigies were a staple of the Welfare State shows, as were fire and pyrotechnics. *Engineers of the Imagination* is a lively textbook for creators of imaginative street theatre.

As memorable examples of the genre I recall the beauty, colour and giant-scale inventiveness of the puppetry in the opening ceremonies of the Olympic Games in Barcelona and Sydney. Similarly unforgettable was the enormous *Sultan's Elephant* (2005–6), a fabulously expensive piece of processional street theatre produced by a French company, Royal de Luxe. The tenuous story told of the visit from space of a time-travelling elephant as high as a castle, operated by complicated mechanisms and strong puppeteers, and its encounter with a young girl, a marionette as high as a house, mounted on a cart, operated by strings as thick as ropes. For the event city streets were cleared, even those of central London.

Clearly the range of scale to be observed in puppet productions, from the tiniest peep show to the gigantesque *Sultan's Elephant*, is extremely wide. In all of them the designer learns, practises, experiments and enjoys the role of central creative contributor to the process and the show.

Figure 4.4   A fine giant puppet, 'Johnny Appleseed' (1989), by the American company In the Heart of the Beast, from their book *Theatre of Wonder*, reproduced by kind permission of the company and the photographer. Designed and built by Greg Leierwood. The production was part of a Mayday festival with the theme *Voices of Trees*. © John Franzen.

STAGES AND OTHER PLAYING SPACES

The staging of puppets, as of all contemporary productions, is of necessity indeterminate: much depends on context and content which will determine the aesthetic, which will in turn suggest the materials, the type(s) of puppet, the human presence or absence, and the scale of the show. The space provided may force changes in any of these considerations. Studio theatres, usually an intimate black box with movable seating and staging, are the most common site for an indoor show; they can accommodate the end-on, the traverse or the in-the-round audience. Booth stages – as for the traditional Punch show – have severely limited sightlines. Marionette players have to be aware that it will be impossible for the spectator to see the puppet's feet or indeed anything on the stage floor unless the space is raked. A steep rake will on the other hand reveal a rod or hand puppeteer wishing to be hidden behind a head-high screen. Concealed operators need careful positioning if all the spectators are to share belief in the puppet's life. (Are such difficulties one more reason, albeit pragmatic, for the puppeteer to have emerged with some relief onto an open stage?)

One of the greatest *auteurs* of the puppet theatre was from the Netherlands: Henk Boerwinkel (1937–) is a sculptor, conceptualizer, designer, maker and performer for his company Figurentheater Triangel. His pioneering achievement was a show made with his wife Ans in 1963, which for years toured to countless international venues. It had more than one title but was in the end known as *Metamorphoses*. It was contained in a curtained booth, wider and deeper than the average glove puppet booth, hiding two operators able to manipulate the puppets from above, behind and underneath the stage frame. The programme consisted of a series of vignettes (the vignette form suits puppets well), each one a surreal metaphor, the style dark or darkly humorous. Perfection resided in the originality of the ideas together with the faultless manipulation, the expression of the puppet figures and the unity of aesthetic which amounted to a groundbreaking show.

The considerations of space for a puppet production are as varied as for theatre in general; the predilections and capabilities of the puppeteer and the dramaturgy will determine the choice – the possibilities are almost limitless. The glove puppet booth and the marionette bridge, the shadow screen and even the table-top have long ago become only a small proportion of the performance spaces occupied by the puppet.

LIGHTING DESIGN

Lighting is as important for the staging of puppets as for theatre in general, and can assist the puppeteer in enhancing the figures' appearance of life and movement. Some techniques – such as shadow play – depend heavily on the dynamics of light. David Currell's book *Puppets and Puppet Theatre* (Currell, 1999) devotes twenty pages to the subject, although the advance of the technologies of stage lighting means some of the solutions described are already superseded for the modern professional. Currell points out that 'the size of most puppets creates problems of visibility and they can be difficult to distinguish from the scenery' and suggests that puppets 'should be lit separately from the sets whenever possible'; he advises directors to 'avoid very dimly lit scenes; puppets often require more light than human theatre for a comparable scene' (Currell, 1999: 134). Writing about shadow puppetry Tina Bicât advises:

> Creating the right light for shadow play is a matter of angles and precision and juggling the available space with the position of the actor or object combined with the brightness of the light. None of the careful work on character or story, making the puppets and learning to animate them will be of any use to the audience unless the lighting and the position of animators and puppets are right. [...] There will need to be enough rehearsal time in performance conditions to make sure every moment throws good shadows onto the screen.
>
> Once you start to play with a light source, a blank wall, some paper and scissors, the possibilities start unfolding. Look at the way light changes when it passes through water, bubble wrap or coloured cellophane, and the variations in the shadow of a two-dimensional object when seen from different angles. The magic of changing shadows is simple physics but which holds all the possibilities of scale and surprise. (Bicât, 2007: 42):

Lighting for shadow play holds considerable potential for experiment, having moved on from the traditional single light source (an oil lamp or a naked electric bulb) to a range of light sources that can pull audience focus and affect mood. There is no need nowadays, as has been noted, to confine the figures (which may be black or coloured) to the rear of a fixed, stretched screen.

Among the techniques specific to puppetry, already listed in this chapter, are lighting for 'black light' theatre (with ultra-violet lamps) and for 'black theatre', the casting of a corridor of white light thrown from each side of the acting area. For both types of lighting the puppeteers are dressed from head to toe in black, and next to invisible.

The use of special lighting effects and projections – even the potential for 'animated light' – is developing fast. A recent development is the so-called 'animated gobo', producing an effect of lighting in motion. A production of *Peter Pan*, in which the fairy Tinkerbell was a pinpoint of light that raced all over the stage and even above and below the proscenium opening, was a successful example of a low-tech solution.

Most puppet productions are including projections of one sort or another in the scenography. From an aesthetic point of view, the integration of the two-dimensional with the three-dimensional is still problematic, the stage illusion is easily ruptured, although the rupture can serve a dramaturgical purpose.

The puppeteer's love affair with technology and 'new media' may be merely fashionable or, as I believe, will prove an enduring one. In the meantime many small touring groups make fine work with the simplest lighting arrangements, though few now have to make do with the two stands on either side of the playing area with any change in the basic state of illumination operated by the soloist's foot, which was for so long the standard kit of the touring show.

SOUND DESIGN

Because of the close relationship of the puppetesque to the cinematic, creative and inventive sound and music are of greater significance than in human theatre, requiring a finely-tuned sensibility.

The first principle lies in the integration of the music and sound with the poetic and the scale of the piece. Ideally both music and sound effects will be live, specially designed and sensitively woven into the action. A performance can be enhanced or deadened by sound that has no regard for the scale and style of the production. For instance, a full symphony orchestra will crush a toy theatre show with density and emotional weight, just as a musical box will diminish the impact of a grand dramatic work. The most effective aesthetically is undoubtedly an original soundscape performed by one or more live musicians with 'found sound' effects. Tina Bicât again:

> The use of a soundscape to support the emotional interior lives of the characters is often very effective, although this is no more a rule than any other rule in this lawless genre. These composers [or sound designers] have an ear for the unusual, for example the plastic drinks bottle that makes a sinister crackle and the human qualities in the sound of instruments. They understand that an oboe is more prone to constipation than a trumpet and a flute more virginal than a cello. (Bicât, 2007: 45)

PUPPETEER AND ACTOR

As explained in the first chapter, today's practice provides employment for two types of professional puppeteers: those who hire out their skills where they may, finding opportunities to work with a variety of producers, and those in an established company. All are self-trained or the product of a school or an apprenticeship. (It's worth remembering that at the beginning of the twentieth century the training of the professional actor was like this, until their vocational education was provided by private academies and, later, by the tertiary education sector. The puppeteer seems to be following in the actor's footsteps).

The would-be puppeteer and those performers who wish or need to learn the skills of animation can attend material and object workshops, where unselfconscious play and improvisation with objects are taught. They can work alongside a designer on styles, materials and the choices of control for manipulation of the figures; or with a mentor, perhaps a writer/dramaturg, on ways of shaping a rehearsal-text, and to be an 'outside eye'. Provision of formal training is still sporadic, but like everything else in puppetry its growth is steady, not to be compared with what little was available in 1990 (except in eastern Europe).

Théâtre du Soleil, a company based in a one-time munitions factory on the edge of Paris, has included puppetry and the puppetesque in its productions since its inception in 1964. Hélène Cixous, author of the scripts for two productions, *L'histoire terrible mais inachevée de Norodom Sihanouk, roi du Cambodge* (*The Terrible but Unfinished History of Norodom Sihanouk, King of Cambodia*, 1985) and *Tambours sur la Digue* (*Drums on the Dyke*, 1999), has written an account of the *modus operandi* of Ariane Mnouchkine, the artistic director. Cixous addresses the director and writer as well as the performer:

> Be two-in-one. One, but inhabited. Make the move, design it. A puppet comes in. Stop. Move on. Do not jerk. Proceed carefully, bring dance-like precision. A puppet that does ten things at once boils over and ceases to be a puppet.
>
> Be two. It is just like writing. The puppet writes with moments, clear pauses, (invisible) blanks, separating and connecting at regular points the sentences, the strokes, the leaps of passion, defining a space whence the cry, the crisis, the outburst will suddenly spring, separating, cutting, perfectly ordering, before suddenly the flash, the lightning explodes out of the tension, like the spring of the *Shite* in Noh Theatre. Like the spring that slowly gathers force in the body of the cat, unleashed only when it is fully coiled. (Cixous, 2000: 20)

Unlike actors, puppeteers are never required to be simply interpreters of a text with a single role to play. They are a breed of practitioner who may be part creator, part technician, part manipulator, part ventriloquist, part double, and only part actor – and that with several roles to inhabit. The puppet operators will be visible, in all probability, so that their physicality as they operate their puppet character becomes part of the scenography, as their puppet is by its nature. Until late in the twentieth century the expression of the puppeteer's face and body usually went unseen, but today the demands are more complicated. Added to the aesthetic considerations of their normal or assumed physical presence, the manipulator of the puppet or object is often required to play a role other than their puppet's, to interact with other characters (human and material) on the stage *on equal terms*. Here lies part of the rationale of the east European schools which were founded for the 'actor-puppeteer', separate from the designer-builder-puppeteer.

My observation of the vocational puppeteer reveals one capable, without consciousness or the imposition of his or her own personality, of transferring vitality into a figure or object, revealing its peculiar personality, physicality and vocality. In performance these puppeteers appear 'neutral', sometimes expressionless, sometimes reflecting the emotion of the character they manipulate, but only as a *reflection*, not as a personal reaction.

In contrast, the actor turned puppet operator, or the trained 'actor-puppeteers', show how difficult and sometimes impossible it is to withdraw themselves, to effect the magic transfer into the puppet. They *act*, and the puppet dies. You may observe the same phenomenon in a number of recent productions where actors animating figures or objects are engaged.

Thus contemporary puppetry is confronted with a more or less serious dichotomy. If the dramaturgy calls for – for any number of reasons – puppetry performed by visible performers who are also required to act, the director's choice is most likely to fall on trained *actors* who, the director imagines, will have little trouble moving and speaking for a puppet, in preference to experienced puppeteers with little or no acting training. In answering the question *What Makes a Good Puppeteer?* at a symposium on the state of the art in 2000, the directors Julian Crouch and Phelim McDermott of Improbable Theatre, a company which gives puppetry a high profile in its work, agreed that this was a contentious question which they were interested in posing:

> We would propose that it is related to the questions: what makes a good performer, a good improviser, a good show? There is, of course, no simple reply. We would suggest that the reason it feels difficult to answer is because it's not necessarily to do with how good they are in terms of their skills as a puppeteer.
>
> What we mean by this is that often when we have worked with trained puppeteers the biggest stumbling block to creating a great ensemble or a complete show has been those very skills which trained puppeteers have. Often with performers in our shows what we are looking for is what we would call 'metaskills' – these are feeling skills and attitudes which lie beneath any technical skills a performer may have as a puppeteer, improviser or actor. Often these qualities seem to be paradoxical.
>
> The first of these is confidence and humility. We must be committed to truly learning our craft and brave enough to stand in front of the audience, but must have the humility to realise as yet we know nothing. It is our ability to be invisible with humility that makes it possible to reveal ourselves to an audience. The next is precision and carelessness: we have to know that certain things just seem to work if they are done 'just so', and this is very clear when working with puppets. However the great puppeteer knows that the gold lies in the mistakes, in the involuntary movements. This is the beautiful relationship between chaos and order. It is the alchemy of our profession. Next, the performer needs to be aware of rules but possess the courage to break them ... The rules are very important but remember that puppets love breaking rules. Finally the performer needs to have total belief and detached awareness. To make a puppet 'live', it needs total belief and focus from the puppeteer. Each move must be felt. It is real. (see Dean, 2000: 13)

These and many other distinguished directors of shows even now on the road have preferred the trained actor (or dancer) to the trained puppeteer. The result can be an unhappy one, aesthetically and practically: when the actor forgets to project into the puppet and it becomes a mere prop. Sue Buckmaster of Theatre-Rites says:

> I was concerned that actors rarely knew how to project any emotion through the puppets. Actors are trained to be present, to be the focus. Asking them not to be the focus is often a difficult thing for them to achieve. Some actors just can't work with puppets effectively, because they're such good actors you can't help looking at them. That's their skill [...] Whereas other actors naturally 'slip away' [...] and find it easy to send the energy down the arm and into the puppet [...] Having myself trained as an actor, I knew when I came to direct puppetry what was needed – very specific direction for the puppet. As a director I talk directly to the puppet, I don't talk to the puppeteer. I'll talk directly to the piece of wood or cloth, which forces the puppeteer to work harder. This is the only way for the puppet to come truly to life. I always say, if the fire alarm goes off, the puppet should be the first one to run. This is a true indication that the puppeteer is working properly through a puppet. (see Dean, 2000: 15)

As the availability of education and training for puppetry improves, the question 'who is training the trainers?' will arise until a greater body of relevant practitioners, theorists and 'practical academics' has been formed. Rene Baker trained herself mainly from several years of working with good directors, performing and making traditional and avant-garde puppet theatre, recording her own learning as she went. Now she has developed a rigorous methodology and has become an inspirational teacher, in demand all over Europe. She teaches the 'fusion' of the performer (of any discipline) with the artificial actor, the performing object. Her work is 'about directing energy, learning to give presence and focus either to an external object or to the actor, or both'. For the conference 'Theatre Materials/Material Theatres' (2008), she ran a workshop for actors and puppeteers which she called *From Prop to Protagonist*. The first workshop exercise was called 'Animating a Shoe'. The participants were asked to pick up a shoe so that the spectator would focus only on the actor; next they were to pick up the shoe so that the spectator would be aware of both actor and shoe; lastly the shoe should be picked up so that the focus was only on the shoe, without hiding the actor.

> Students learn to shift back and forth between having a vibrant physical presence as an actor and then neutralising their body in order to project energy through their hands and give presence to the object. (see Margolies, 2009: 52)

One might call it the most important lesson the performer has to learn; for many actors it is difficult. As an observer you may see actors whose gaze is tightly concentrated on their puppet, usually the back of the puppet's head, but without any effect of its animation. The figure remains an effigy, and it is the actor, expressing their own presence and the puppet's 'absence', who draws the eye.

At the Edinburgh festival in 2008, in which I counted at least fifty productions using puppetry, there was an interesting example of an actor playing as a part-puppet. The manipulation and lip-synching of a speaking latex head worn on the head of the performer were impressive; his torso was covered by a shirt/apron hung loosely from a shoulder crosspiece. The actor's right arm and his trousered legs were unmasked. There was no coordination of the two halves, puppet and human: the voice and bearing of the head were those of an old man, as the author intended, while the lower half, especially the flailing right arm, was that of a young, undisciplined actor. Belief in the character was impossible, since only the head was 'inhabited'.

A visible operator may wear a veil or a hood to neutralize his or her presence, to symbolize an absence; more often the puppeteer's face is uncovered, when the spectator may observe how some performers are able to transfer emotion to the character they hold while their own visage remains impassive; others will betray emotion, but ideally there is no self-awareness.

You may imagine therefore how difficult it is for the vocational puppeteers, absorbed by the figure they carry, to change role, gesture and function when required to play another character, puppet or human. If they are required to perform as a human actor, they must re-invest, re-centre themselves in their own physicality or in that of the character they are playing. If the transfer is to another object to be animated, the effort of the change and the more or less instant projection into a new role demands considerable energy, imagination and skill.

The animation of any object not manufactured or intended for the stage calls for equal artistry: the intention may be to convince spectators of the life in a teapot or a broom, to turn a fish head into Red Riding Hood's predator; to give a suitcase speech and thought, make a chair dance, an Alka Seltzer kill itself for love. This form of performance weaves the remembered and retained fantasy of a child with the expressivity of a master communicator. The object will only be inhabited through the total conviction of the puppeteer, and his or her complete familiarity with its tactility: its size and weight, its rigidity or flexibility, its every edge, angle and change of texture: there can be no fumbling. Its recognition by the hand of the manipulator almost makes it an extension of their body.

To be a performer-puppeteer is not easy, but the once isolated puppeteers now recognize that they are creatures of the theatre at least as much as creatures of the fine arts and crafts. They see that the intrusion of puppets into the human theatre is not via a one-way street: the human theatre-makers are in turn bringing new opportunities to puppetry.

FURTHER READING

Blackham, Olive (1948) *Puppets into Actors*, London: W. Taylor.
Butler, R. (2003) *The Art of Darkness. Staging the Philip Pullman Trilogy*, London: Oberon Books.

Currell, David (1999) *Puppets and Puppet Theatre*, Marlborough: Crowood Press.

Dean, Anthony (ed.) (2000) *Puppetry into Performance, A User's Guide.* Colloquium Papers and Interviews, London: Central School of Speech and Drama.

Lee, Miles (1958) *Puppet Theatre Production and Manipulation*, London: Faber and Faber.

Millar, Mervyn (2007) *The Horse's Mouth, Staging Morpurgo's 'War Horse'*, London: Oberon.

Sheehy, Colleen (ed.) (1999) *Theatre of Wonder: Twenty-five Years. In the Heart of the Beast*, Minneapolis, MN: University of Minnesota Press.

Voisard, Claire (1989) 'Écrire pour la Marionnette', *Cahiers de Théâtre Jeu*, 51, 108.

Walton, J.M. (ed.) (1983) *Craig on Theatre*, (containing Gentlemen, the Marionette! 1912) London: Methuen.

Chapter 5 *Dramaturgy*

In this chapter 'dramaturgy' refers to two things: theatre works scripted for and performed by puppets, or by human performers and puppets, and the staged interpretation of those works, the performance-text. The following pages give examples of recent productions that have perceived the potential for puppetry in an idea, a story, a poem, a painting, and have developed the idea successfully and specifically for the genre. Taken all together, an explication, an idea, of what makes for sympathetic subject matter and 'writing' should emerge. In this lies the essence of the work: not in the script-writing but in the idea. The terms 'writer' and 'writing', as explained in the chapter on puppetry in performance carry a meaning somewhat different from that normally understood in the preparation of a rehearsal text.

PUPPET PRODUCTION SCRIPTS

The examination of a body of texts or scripts for puppet productions is almost impossible since examples published in English since 1990 are hard to find. There are a number of explanations for this, the first being that a *post-production* script for puppets consisting only of the show's spoken element will be the barest bones of the staged performance-text – a skeleton to be fleshed out by means of the creative input of an artistic team wishing to reproduce the show.

Contrast the situation of the Modernist era, roughly 1890–1935, the period covered by Harold B. Segel in *Pinocchio's Progeny* (Segel, 1995), when theatre artists manifested an unprecedented attachment to puppets, at the time preferred to actors who were found not only egocentric but incapable of portraying the spiritual and hieratic qualities of their characters. Segel's book, exclusively concerned with the Modernist playwrights, is a comprehensive review of their plays and music theatre pieces principally intended for puppet play. The themes concern the spiritual, the religious, death and dark forces, magic and madness: then as now all valid vehicles for puppets. The authors were of high distinction and included Lorca, Maeterlinck, Büchner, Poe, Wyspianski, Jarry, Claudel, Schnitzler, Ghelderode, Benavente, Valle-Inclan and Čapek. Their plays are published, although almost none of the Modernist pieces can claim to be part of the repertoire of a modern company (but most of the themes certainly can). It is interesting to note the change in the accessibility of a repertory for puppets between then and now, even though there are good reasons for the change.

Edward Gordon Craig (1872–1966), inventor of the notorious, inconsistent and misleading concept of the Über-marionette, claimed understanding of the exigencies of the genre before anyone else. In an essay written in 1918 and signed by 'Tom Fool' he wrote:

> Perhaps one of the chief distinctions between a Drama for Marionnettes [sic; he means all kinds of puppet] and a Proper Drama is this […] that whereas a Proper Drama has to be vague and roundabout in its movements, a Marionnette Drama had always better be direct and rapid and even obvious […] A Marionnette is not at all clever – not subtle. He must fit the character like a hand fits a glove, or all is undone. Therefore when we make a character in one of our Dramas we make the Marionnette to fit it. And so it comes about that a Marionnette does not play a number of parts, he plays only one … that is himself. This is different from the actor who plays many parts and must therefore pretend. The Marionnette never pretends … (Craig, 1918: 38)

Before the second half of the twentieth century scripting for puppets was not much different from scripting for the human performer, whom the puppets strove to imitate. They appeared to speak lines, to dance, and sing arias. Only the 'trick marionettes' or *fantoccini* were *sui generis*.

Neither the Modernists nor the 'popular' puppeteers, have much in common with the twenty-first century repertoire which has evolved a discrete language for puppet theatre, searching for suitable and original ideas to exploit its hyper-real potential. Meanwhile the theatre mainstream has adopted puppetry as a genre suited to a 'visual theatre', although the label poses problems, seeming to exclude as it does the sound and music components so intrinsic to puppet theatre. Artaud was not the only thinker to prefer the term 'total theatre':

> Practically speaking we want to bring back the idea of total theatre, where theatre will recapture from cinema, music-hall, the circus and life itself, those things that always belonged to it. This division between analytical theatre and a world of movement seems stupid to us […] Thus on the one hand we have the magnitude and scale of a show aimed at the whole anatomy, and on the other an intensive mustering of objects, gestures and signs used in a new spirit. The reduced role given to understanding leads to drastic curtailment of the script, while the active role given to dark poetic feeling necessitates tangible signs. Words mean little to the mind; expanded areas and objects speak out. New imagery speaks, even if composed in words. But spatial thundering images replete with sound also speak, if we become versed in arranging a sufficient interjection of spatial areas furnished with silence and stillness.
>
> We expect to stage a show based on these principles, where these direct active means are wholly used. Therefore such a show, unafraid of exploring the limits of our nervous sensibility, uses rhythm, sound, words, resounding with song, whose

nature and startling combinations are part of an unrevealed technique. (Artaud, 1933: 66–7)

Similarly Tadeusz Kantor regarded his painting and theatre work as a 'total activity'. Quoted in the preface of Michael Kobialka's collection of Kantor's writings, *A Journey Through Other Spaces*, he insists that 'one must embrace Art to understand the essence of theatre. The growing "professionalism" of theatre destroys its essence, marking its "separateness". Theatre does not have its own, single unique source. [Its sources] are in literature, drama, the visual arts, music and architecture' (Kantor, 1993: xvi).

While the pursuit of a visual theatre certainly enabled puppetry to gain a place at the mainstream table, it may have contributed to the reluctance of playwrights to contribute to the new genre in that it was, and to an extent still is, uncharted territory for the dedicated wordsmith. In the event they need not have worried, or not over-much. Although puppetry has become a predominantly plastic medium in the last hundred or so years, speech and song show no sign of disappearing as an element of the productions. The playwright needs only to understand the conception of a text through images, and the frequent redundancy of words.

Few writers of note have contributed original work to the puppets' repertory of the last thirty years, although some well-known names have been successfully commissioned by puppet companies: in Britain they include Angela Carter, Adrian Mitchell and Wendy Cope. All have responded to a medium which transcends the limitations of the actors' physical form, giving them the freedom to ignore practical limitations of gravity, of size and scale, and to give free rein to ideas of staging the surreal and the fantastic in the telling of a story.

Henryk Jurkowski compiled a selection of plays for puppets, published over a period of four centuries, up to the mid-1900s (Jurkowski, 1991), including Cervantes and Ben Jonson in the seventeenth century, Henry Fielding and Samuel Foote in the eighteenth, Maurice Sand and Lemercier de Neuville in the nineteenth, and Lorca and Ghelderode in the early twentieth.

Jurkowski's introduction to his collection of authors gives one explanation for the rarity of accessible texts for puppet play both in the distant past and the present:

The reason is found in the difference between the puppet and the actor. [...] The actor needs a script; the puppet can do without. This explains the absence of dramatic texts written for the theatre of puppets. [...] No need whatever for a script where a simple story, written or otherwise, will serve as model. [...] Thus if any scenario did exist, it had to be very short and very like the art of the mimes [...] The script only appeared at the last moment when there had to be some fixed record of the action so that it might be recalled and repeated [...]

[After a report by Athéneé in the third century A.D.] we have to wait more than ten centuries to find the first preserved texts. And if we look at other cultures, it appears that Asiatic puppets, according to the most ancient reports, were only recently aware of developed dramatic forms. The scenarios of the Indian and Chinese theatre emanate from their great national epic poems – Mahabharata, Ramayana, Voyage to the West, the Romance of the Three Kingdoms. The Japanese Joruri or the Indonesian Lakoon have conserved the epic character of their shows until now, underlining the fact that the text was recited by a performer-chanter who, in the Indonesian dramas, is at the same time the animator of the puppets. (Jurkowski, 1991: 3–4, trans. PF)

To Jurkowski's explanation must be added another: the current dramaturgy favoured by vocational puppeteers is often an expression of a personal vision or conviction, articulated almost entirely in action, movement and sound, that is difficult to commit to paper. These artists do not conceive of the use of their shows by others, as the performance-text that their spectators witness is dependent on a synthesis of theatre-making techniques that is wholly authored by the puppeteer. Examples are many: soloists like Stephen Mottram who explores 'the basic mysteries of life' such as the growth of a child in the womb; the German Ilka Schönbein, her slight body the site of her dramaturgy, manipulated and transformed; Hoichi Okamoto who drew on many Japanese theatre styles 'as a result of my vision of the relationship between a man and the puppet on his hand'; Neville Tranter, Australian purveyor of grand guignol, a clever actor-manipulator who portrays the villainous and the depraved; the Catalan Joan Baixas, first and last a performance artist, exciting the spectator through his interaction and transformations with palette of sand, glue, paint and canvas; partnerships like the British Faulty Optic, portraying a dark but comic vision of a world peopled by the deformed and the desperate; a group from Argentina, El Periférico de Objetos, whose themes are sinister, surreal and intellectual; Hotel Modern, German artists of the miniature whose themes can be cruel and disturbing. Of all these groups none, I believe, has created a show intended for re-enaction by others – none has published a script.

A small survey of practitioners, asked whether or in what way they recorded their work, elicited the following comments, spoken in 2010:

Tam-Tam Objektentheater of the Netherlands: *Although we have quite precise scenarios for our performances (as you might suspect) they would be more or less unreadable for other performers. We give our objects names ... and use descriptions of the scenes that are very subjective and only useful to us I fear.*

Although we have been asked to publish our plays, we did not feel like it. I think because it is such a personal kind of art, where not only the scenario but also the way we perform it is a totally personal expression of the way we interpret life around us. It's just like with movies: You couldn't have a Jacques Tati or Buster Keaton movie done by someone else and still be just as good ... don't you think so?

And also the 'live' element of the performances is pretty hard to catch in writing and even on video ...

We always tell audiences that ask us for a DVD, CD or booklet that they should remember very well what they saw, heard and felt during the performance as that is all they are going to get. It is something like a perfume: you cannot catch that in writing or on DVD …

Meg Amsden of Nutmeg Puppet Theatre: *As to my performance texts, I do draw storyboards, but after devising and before rehearsals proper start, so they are sometimes superseded. We also have scripts and the actors write in their own directions. I've never really considered other companies performing my shows because they are so particular as to time and place and require such specific staging/puppets.*

Sue Buckmaster of Theatre-Rites: *Regarding Scripts and my work … In my earlier work I would often have an A4 of writing which got shaped into the show. Later work has taken the form of storyboarding cards which get mixed up and placed in different order to work out the dramaturgy alongside the visual story of the object/s.*

Some of the shows have been audio described for those who are blind. All of the shows have been videoed for record. We refer to these if we recreate it. We have an uncut version for this purpose and a four minute version for promotional purposes.

There has never been a need for a script.

The work of all these artists may be available for others to view on a screen but almost impossible for them to replicate on a stage. Nor are the performance-texts of larger-scale companies with a strong artistic leadership and a recognizable style, such as Sandglass of Vermont and Tübingen of Germany, two out of the dozens to be found throughout western countries. They may record their work for their own rehearsal and revival purposes, but up to now their work is inaccessible, other than in photographs or videoed versions of productions which would be difficult to use as a production text for logistic, artistic and copyright reasons.

There are exceptions: in 1999 the playwright Marion Baraitser edited two issues of the *Contemporary Theatre Review*, slim paperbacks in which were printed a single work of each of four living 'authors', all useful as an illustration of a modern dramaturgy for puppet and object play. *Nuptial Night* by Johanna Enckell of Finland, has a cast of actors, puppets (including a Parrot and the parrot's Soul), a mask and a number of bowler hats. In the style of the surreal world of Magritte the set is a room with a staircase but without an exit, the central character being a pregnant woman and her visualized fantasies and insecurities. Enckell describes how in her early career she had been constrained by Finnish theatre custom to work for a literary world of realism reinforced by Stanislavski's acting methods, she finally left to join the puppet theatre of Michael Meschke in Stockholm, Sweden:

Suddenly, I found myself in an atmosphere nourished by a theatre language familiar to me, where Artaud was understood and Ubu Roi played triumphantly with Meschke. I began to write for puppet theatre which seemed to me a more free expression than writing for actors. With Gösta Kjellin (also influenced by Michael Meschke) I finished my puppet pieces for children and adults – *Noah's Hat, Mother Blue* and others. I also wrote for actors' theatre but directors tended to radically suppress the puppet section of a piece. This finally pushed me into making my own productions. However there were two directors who completely understood my combination of actors and animation – Eric Bass, an artist much appreciated by puppeteers, and Anita Blom, actress and director. (see Enckell, 1999: 57–8)

A sad morality tale *Odd if You Dare* by the British Doo-cot group (Nenagh Watson and Rachael Field) is included in the Baraitser anthologies, printed in the form of an essay, with directions for its staging. It is one of the very few that offer an opportunity for a medium of expression other than puppets – for instance it could be performed by actors trained in mime and capable of manipulating scenic objects.

I have already referred to Howard Barker and his two plays (and an opera) that have been performed by puppets. In *All He Fears*, written in poetic dialogue, the soundscape is a vital part of the dramaturgy (wind, violin, screaming, explosion, rattling) underscoring the disturbed state of mind of the main character. A director might imagine the protagonist played by a human surrounded by puppets, the characters symbols of human emotions, jealousy and cruelty, love and infidelity. There is a speaking Rat, for example, symbolizing Fear and Death. The dialogue is significant and an essential element, as might be imagined from this author/poet, but lends itself to illustration and scenographic engineering appropriate to a puppet interpretation. In an interview Barker was asked to explain how he had come to write for the medium:

> I am a poet and an artist, I require language as the primary resource of my existence. On the other hand, I have an interest in the context in which the speech is delivered. [...] The visual image is critical, as a counterpoint and enhancement of the verbal content of a scene. [...] I have written for theatre, radio, film, and opera. I consider that a poet who has a voice, and has refined that voice over a number of years, can employ it across all media. On the other hand I was aware that puppetry conventionally discards density of language. I thought of it [All He Fears] primarily as a poem, but I wished to ignore all problems that would arise in the staging of this poem. I ignore all problems of staging a play also. The achievement frequently comes out of overcoming these problems. I had seen no puppetry. When I began writing for theatre I had seen virtually no theatre either.
>
> [...] Of course I would write again for puppets. I have a constant reservoir of half-formed notions for texts that have no particular locus. I would agree that on the whole, the freedom of the puppet stage would or should stimulate better stage writing. But I have never lacked those elements in my stage work. Again, I think the freedom of imagination – its promiscuity – should be a tool for any stage writer. It is only the fatuous domination of naturalism that has separated out these media, and I have never written naturalistically. [...] What puppetry lent me in this instance was a purity of expression that came from the very non-humanity of the 'performer'. When a puppet *contemplates* for example, the element of mimicry of human contemplation lends a huge emotional injection [...] one is faintly *charmed* [...] and yet this charm, born of intense mimesis, is also *frightening*. (see Francis, 1999: 37–9)

Of Baraitser's small collection the Handspring Company's *Faustus in Africa* (1995), produced in collaboration with Lesego Rampolokeng and the artist William Kentridge, is nearest in appearance (on the page) to a conventional playscript. This adaptation of a frequently staged theme for the puppet theatre was written in South Africa's apartheid era and mounted with a cast of life-size, jaggedly carved wooden figures that included a terrifying Hyena, designed and crafted by Adrian Kohler, who with Basil Jones is a founder-director of Handspring. Kentridge's animated charcoal sketches together with a haunting score served as background to the action. Kentridge, who worked with Handspring on several productions, wrote:

> The principle behind all the work whether on text, image or puppet, was to see if, in the process of working, of drawing, carving and rehearsing, a coherence and meaning can be made, rather than an established polemic be illustrated. (see Kentridge, 1999: 46)

Faustus in Africa toured to many countries, as did the company's *Woyzeck on the High Veld,* with the same Kentridge-Handspring aesthetic and collaboration. Its theme of tyranny and exploitation of the poor and uneducated found resonance in audiences wherever it was played. Even if most of the characters were human, their archetypal depiction was more powerful and affecting than that of any human actor. Woyzeck himself, his head bandaged and an expression of anguish and incomprehension carved into his face, was especially moving. Puppets do victimhood well.

Another in the *Contemporary Theatre Review* collection is by Dennis Silk, English/Israeli surrealist poet, actor and puppeteer, here writing for his own company 'Thing Theatre'. *The Head or Watch it, Kid!* features a severed head which speaks most of the dialogue in its attempt to find a home within or on the bodies of other characters. Like Enckell's piece it is short and impossible to stage except with puppet figures and objects. In the essay printed with the play is a sort of manifesto:

> The marionette is a poet from Peru who got education. He comes from a long way off to talk to us. He talks of bread and trousers and the crease in a shirt. Because he is safe among things, because he is himself a thing, a 'thing thing', he allows himself our town-talk. He kneels to talk to dis-membered man. He doesn't have the impediments of an actor. An actor's body is so untalented. It doesn't have doors, it doesn't take in pain, it can't play us the world-tooth rending and shredding. The marionette – because it is a thing and yet a man – because it is this poet from Peru – plays us this mastication of things, and of ourselves. The marionette is shredded over the suburbs. He plays us the world-breakfast. His well-jointed body speaks for us. He uses the nearest grammar to hand. 'I simply couldn't contain myself', he says. And comes apart at the joints. 'Pull yourself together', he's admonished. His scattered parts do their best to come together. 'I couldn't keep my eyes off her', he confesses. She removes his eyes with distaste from her private parts. (Silk, 1999: 76)

The most important collection of the work for objects and puppets by Dennis Silk was published in America near the end of his life in a volume of plays and essays, *William the Wonder-Kid* (Silk, 1996). The plays are offered for performance, but have yet to be staged in Britain.

An American magazine, *Play A Journal of Plays* [sic] (Hurlin, 2004), holds eight short pieces and extracts by distinguished *auteurs* for animated object play, all with little or no dialogue, a mixture of picture and text, the pieces clearly not intended for production by others. Other twenty-first century puppet scenarios, published in languages other than English, certainly exist but they are rare.

Notable exceptions are the six plays by the writer-actor-puppeteer Ronnie Burkett, published between 2002 and 2009. Each contains a stream of dialogue, with detailed stage directions. They seem to offer a substantial addition to the contemporary dramaturgy for puppets, but in fact the plays are tailored for solo performance by Burkett himself, and until the time of writing had not been performed by anyone else. In each play the author/puppeteer appears alone with a large number of string marionettes to each of which he gives a distinct voice and physicality while manipulating the characters and delivering their lines. The plays, always for sophisticated adults, have won awards for the quality of the writing and their unconventional, not to say shocking, themes. The range of subject matter encompasses the relationships of various inmates of an internment camp in Czechoslovakia (*Tinka's New Dress*, premiered 1994); the existential state of a group of people waiting for release from an institution gradually revealed as an anteroom of death (*Happy*, premiered 2000); a grand guignol piece inhabited by a cast of grotesques in which Burkett plays Jesus (*Street of Blood*, premiered 1998); the pursuit and objectification of beauty, European decadence in the *belle époque* (*Provenance*, premiered 2003); the innocence and insouciance of a mentally disabled boy for several days unaware of his mother's demise in her bedroom (*10 Days on Earth*, premiered 2006); and the biography of an ageing cruise cabaret puppeteer at the nadir of his career (*Billy Twinkle*, premiered 2009). A seventh is in preparation. As produced and performed by the prodigious Burkett, the plays have ingenious and elaborate settings with a strong element of camp, glitter and attack in the presentation, cynicism contrasted with innocence underlying the content. A perceptive overview of his work, by Beccy Smith, stated:

> His characters are often damaged, fragile individuals but his approach is unashamedly melodramatic, running us through a flamboyant barrage of emotions as he unlocks their tales. His is theatre on an epic canvas, and always with issues to explore – identity, sexuality and the power of art to change the world and our experience of life. (Smith, 2007)

An extract from *Billy Twinkle* gives an idea of the style of this 2008 production. It depends on a striking contrast between the despair of a washed-up puppeteer wanting to end his life and the ghost of his mentor Sid, who

Figure 5.1 Ronnie Burkett's *Billy Twinkle* (2009). The characters are 'Billy' and 'Sid' designed, made and performed by Burkett.

© Ronnie Burkett Theatre of Marionettes.

intervenes in the unlikely guise of a glove puppet. The setting is a cabaret stage on a ship, the décor and puppet action glitzy and gaudy, the dialogue overwrought but comic in its satirical depiction of an empty world and an anti-hero too conscious of its emptiness. The puppeteer appears as human and as puppet at different stages of his life, from childhood when he discovers his vocation and Sid becomes his mentor, to adolescence when he recognizes his homosexuality, to ripe middle age when all the spirits of his past come to haunt him.

There are scenes which human actors could play, but the ghosts from Billy's past, would be difficult to portray as effectively as in Burkett's hands.

Billy Twinkle by Ronnie Burkett
The following extract is taken from the middle of the play, which has no division into Acts.

Enter **BILLY** *middle-aged*, with the spirit of Sid his old mentor, a glove puppet

BILLY: I need a drink.
SID: Say, are you still doing that drunken society dame number? Hilarious! I loved that routine.
BILLY: You hated that routine.
SID: Did not!
BILLY: Did so!
SID: Let's see it again.
BILLY: No.
SID: Hit it boys!

Without warning, the lavish intro to the Billy Twinkle show theme music begins. The Mylar backdrop for Billy's act is drawn closed in front of the marionette stage and lighting becomes showbiz theatrical again. Sid is hung behind the leaning rail, and Billy rushes down the stairs and puts on his tuxedo jacket.

A marionette-scale table is set CS. It is circular and covered with a damask tablecloth. Sitting on the table is a full wineglass with a straw. The glass is fixed to a rig, which, when operated by a foot pedal, causes the liquid to 'disappear' underneath.

Billy takes the marionette of Biddy Bantam Brewster from under the stairs. She is a strongly caricatured society dame wearing an outrageous chartreuse green velvet gown festooned with chiffon rosettes. As the music ends, Billy sweeps Biddy onto the main playing area of the deck. She plays directly to the audience.

BIDDY: Hello! Hello! Hello! And welcome to this, another afternoon recital of 'Wine, Woman and Song'. I, your hostess, Biddy Bantam Brewster, am of course the woman who will serenade you with song, while you, dear gathered friends and lovers of music, enjoy the complimentary wine, provided this afternoon by the lovely people at Dirtroad Estates Winery and Feedlot, conveniently located near the civic dump off Highway 71.
BIDDY 'drinks'.

Oh my, that's quite nice! A good week, that. A subtle hint of pork mixed with the stronger notes of the grape. [...]
[At the end of her act] she drinks again and burps.
Awkward silence.

SID, 63: It was good.
BILLY, 25: Thanks.
SID, 63: Yes. Good.
BILLY, 25: But?
SID, 63: No buts. No.

Awkward silence, again.
Although, I wonder how many times we have to see a puppeteer doing a drag act with a comic opera singer. There's nothing new there, Billy.

BILLY, 25: How many times do we have to see Shakepeare, Sid? Nothing new there either, but people still do it.
SID, 63: Touché! Even if you disregard that the magic lies in the personal interpretation of those timeless words. But I'm interrupting your rehearsal, which no doubt you need.

Sid turns and starts to leave.

BILLY, 25: Hey Sid ... do you wanna watch? I'd really like your opinion.
SID, 63: I'm flattered, Billy. Although, inane cabaret turns have never been my forte; no, that is more your dominion. I really don't see what help I could be.
BILLY, 25: It's Shakespeare.
SID, 63: You're doing a Shakespeare?
BILLY, 25: Do you mind?
SID, 63: Mind? Billy, I have waited years to hear you say this. At times, I thought I never would. There were moments when I despaired over having wasted my time on you. What took you so long to submit to my influence, to hear the Bard's whispers, to see the light? But now, at last!

He hugs Billy enthusiastically.
'Bless thee, Bottom, bless thee! Thou art translated'.
True, by the time I was 25, I'd already done four substantial productions, but better late than never. Alright, let's see what you've got. Show me your stuff, kid.

Billy runs offstage. Music begins. The red velvet curtain is closed and the lighting shifts to a more theatrical pool CS.

Billy reappears; a duplicate of the Billy marionette at age 25, and he has in his hands two marionettes. They are somewhat larger than the small puppets used in the scenes of Billy at ages twelve and fifteen.

Petruchio, renamed Petrooster for this version, has the head of a rooster and a humanesque body. Petrooster is in brightly coloured Elizabethan garb, with his muscular legs encased in tights and a very noticeable codpiece. Kate, renamed for this interpretation as Cowtrina is, indeed, a cow, anthropomorphized to the point of standing on two legs in cloven high heel hooves. A pink udder juts out from her faux-Elizabethan gown. [The show is a seriously unfunny travesty of the original, which Sid interrupts].

[…] Sid interrupts the show.

SID, 63: And I can bear no more! Billy, please. Stop. I beg of you.

The performance stops, and the marionettes of Petrooster and Cowtrina droop lifelessly in Billy's hands.

BILLY, 25: *What's wrong, Sid?*
SID, 63: *I have a question, sir.*
BILLY, 25: *Okay.*
SID, 63: *Tell me, was it your intention to have the Bard roll over in his grave so you could fuck him up the ass?*
BILLY, 25: *What are you talking about?*
SID, 63: *I'm talking about the bullshit you were just doing with that pig and chicken.*
BILLY, 25: *It's not a pig, Sid, it's a cow. It's* The Taming of the Moo.
SID, 63: *Oh Christ!*
BILLY, 25: *[…] Admit it, Sid. You didn't like it because it had a cow and a rooster, that's all. Why do you hate animal puppets so much, Sid? It's like a sickness with you.*
SID, 63: *Your puppets are supposed to be reinventions of self. To edify, to exalt, and yes, to mock and even condemn our graceless state. But is this how you want to be seen? As livestock?*
BILLY, 25: *Who says they're reinventions of me or you, Sid? They're characters, that's all.*
SID, 63: *And if that's all you invest in them, sir, cleverness and parody, well, then that's all the audience will take away. Unless of course the point is not the text or the characters at all, Billy. Yes, of course, there's no need for more of you in the words or the characters because that would mean we'd stop looking at you.*
BILLY, 25: *It's called open manipulation, Sid.*
SID, 63: *You're visible simply for the sake of being seen, prettyboy! Your focus is nowhere near the puppets at all; standing above them, mugging and posturing like a powdered vaudevillian playing God. We don't need you to be God. We don't want you to be God. There's already a god onstage, and it's not you. It's the goddamn puppet!*
BILLY, 25: *You tell me I'm not God, but I'm supposed to manipulate Him? Which is more arrogant, Sid?*
SID, 63: *Arrogance is to have the ability and not use it. To create something that breathes; that truly lives inside your audience, long after the puppet stops twitching.*
BILLY, 25: *They're not alive, Sid. They're puppets. And the audience leaves. They go home, without you.* (Burkett, 2009: 47–59)

The play continues in this vein, with Burkett playing all the parts, summoning up a different voice for each character. All his shows are technically a tour de force, unlikely to be achieved by any other puppeteer.

The straining of an artist after innovation and originality affects the creator of object and puppet theatre as strongly as in any other medium, maintaining a powerful dynamic, where the adult is catered for at least as much as the child. A growing trend in contemporary puppet theatre must be remarked upon. It is a trend, which some find exciting and others hard to stomach, that concerns the depiction of dark, buried areas of the human psyche where such matters as torture, psychopathy, extreme sexual eccentricities like necrophilia and so on are graphically enacted. Some are mediated by the matter-of-fact presence of human performers operating the puppets, resulting paradoxically in an intensification of the horrors practised on the puppets, which in performance are difficult if not impossible to regard as insentient objects. The spectator invests in these creatures; the imagination cannot sleep. From the impassivity of the creator/performers it seems they are unaffected by the performance, although in fact his or her imagination must plumb depths of suffering to produce and perform such a piece repeatedly. Sometimes the process rebounds, as in the case of a Scottish puppeteer, Richard Medrington, who created a show called *The Interrogation* about a Romanian dissident. According to the man's story, he had helped other dissidents escape from Romania to the West, but was betrayed, imprisoned and tortured for four years, before managing to escape from a prison hospital. After three years on the run he reached the West himself and lived in Spain and England where he died in about 2000. In an email Medrington continued:

My play featured scenes of torture and interrogation which would have been very difficult to replicate using actors (though they were not particularly graphic – no blood and guts, just threat mainly). People commented on how helpless the rag doll puppet seemed – at the mercy of the human interrogator (played by me – it was a mixed cast!) Andy Cannon [a children's theatre director and performer] said he wanted to run onto the stage and rescue the poor little guy. My friend John Fardell created an automaton – a figure that ran round and round in circles above a brutal clockwork mechanism. Zinnie Harris co-directed and we used some very powerful music by Dave Heath. It was performed for two weeks at the 2004 [Edinburgh festival] Fringe and was well reviewed, but the audiences were small and it didn't lead to any bookings. Not a very popular subject I suppose.

As things turned out I'm glad I didn't get to perform it again. I totally believed in the story and felt compelled to tell the tale of this man, who died in abject poverty, alone in the dark basement of an old people's home.

Actually building and performing the show was deeply traumatic – by the end of the run I felt like I was the one alone in the basement. I went into a kind of depression and went to live in Canada for three months – just needing to escape!

I'm not sure I would take on a purely adult puppet show again. I like performing for adult audiences (in many ways they are much easier to please) – but I can't help feeling that puppets aren't very happy things when you give them material that can't be seen by children. Maybe there is something particularly evil about a toy gone bad. (see Medrington, personal email to PF dated October 2010)

In 2004 the use of puppets in a cruel theatre was still rare, or at least underground, but it is certainly finding bookings now, on the western theatre festival circuit.

PLAYSCRIPTS FOR CHILDREN

Moving to the other end of the innocence/experience/sophistication spectrum the theatre-maker hoping to find an audience for a kids' show, will discover it is easy to misjudge the expectations and reactions of the young. In the middle years of the twentieth century dozens of books of playscripts intended for children were produced, most of them heavy with dialogue. Most lacked any sensibility to puppetry aesthetics, any knowledge of techniques or any relevance to the tastes of a modern child. Only a very few, such as those by A.R. (Panto) Philpott, Violet Phelan Philpott, the Czech Jan Malik and the Pole Jan Wilkowski, all writing successful and *original* stories, would be useful today.

Children seem to respond best to stories peopled with characters painted with broad brush strokes, recognized from the child's own experience as good or bad, funny or serious. In performance the best shows are full of visual invention; they boast scenography that is colourful, given to transformation and changes of scale; action that is flowing and engaging, well filled with surprises. They allow for the keen eyes and intelligence of children accustomed to the production values of television and cinema. For the very youngest a slow, quiet rhythm works well, and even two-year olds appreciate a scenario that reflects their own concerns and is spiced with physicalized, non-violent humour. I witnessed a French company able to keep a score of toddlers enthralled with a piece about a lost *doudou*, (pacifier or dummy), and another which held a larger audience of under-fives rapt with a long and quiet piece about a charmed tree. Noisy stimulation and 'audience participation' are no longer the norm for the younger ones.

Theatre-Rites, the company led by Sue Buckmaster, already mentioned, can boast a number of well-reviewed and (now) well-subsidized productions for children. She embeds in the dramaturgy a subliminal educational and ethical content conveyed in colours, material, shapes, music and lively action, or for the youngest through dreamy atmosphere and gentle adventure. A production that will always stay with those who saw it, *The Lost and Moated Land* (1998), from a poem by Robert Graves, was designed by the extraordinary installation artist Sophia Clist who transformed a small studio into a world of conical shapes of all sizes, in pastel colours and soft materials, the whole played in the round and enhanced by subtle lighting. This was an exemplary piece of theatre for the young, with as much care for production values as for any adult work.

Figure 5.2 Theatre-Rites' *The Lost and Moated Land* (1999), a memorable production for children. Directors Penny Bernand and Sue Buckmaster. Scenography Sophia Clist. Players Adam Bennett, Zannie Fraser and Lynette Clarke.

© Andy Rumball.

The hero, a soft-bodied baby, goes on a quest for his lost star, stolen by a giant bird with a conical beak and guarded by a villainous dragon made of conical segments. The puppeteers were dressed to merge with the aesthetic of the piece, gracefully operating the puppets in cone-shaped garments. Every aspect was produced with care and intelligence to please the youngest children.

Popular illustrated publications for children have become a favourite resource for puppeteers, familiar titles serving to attract sizeable family and school audiences. The adaptor-dramaturg is an important element in the success or failure of this kind of show. If the aesthetic of the book illustrations has not been captured the children are disappointed; if the spectator does not know the original and the show's dramaturgy is unclear, both adult and child are disappointed (one should not have to buy the book in order to make sense of the show). If on the other hand the adaptation of the story is faithful, and the scenography reflects the book's illustrations, the result can be a commercial triumph. Perennial productions of the *Charlie and Lola* and *Gruffalo* stories are cases in point. Another is a 2009 production of Roald Dahl's *The Giraffe, the Pelly and Me*, by the Little Angel Theatre of London, satisfactorily fulfilling all the criteria of excellence for a puppet-led production: the story was perfect for puppets because the protagonists were caricatured animals and humans; the designs were kinetic, puppetesque adaptations of the book's illustrations by Quentin Blake, with sets that were almost puppets in themselves, in a continuous state of transformation. A house was taken to pieces and restored again; a towering backcloth depicting a mansion became a screen for shadow play. In every aspect a high level of craftsmanship and a unity of aesthetic in support of the spirit of the story, thanks to the scenographer and director Peter O'Rourke.

The methodology for the making of the show was interesting and instructive. O'Rourke, who sees 'everything through the eyes of the medium, a dance of shapes moving through space', worked closely with the writer and the composer before rehearsals, when a 'provisional logic' was put in place, rough notes to reflect his ideas on pace and mood. Room for creativity was left for rehearsal room ideas, questions held in the air to be resolved with the performers. The stylistic of surreal humour, invention and colour were perfectly integrated in design, music and dialogue. The performers measured up to the style and the spirit: four talented puppeteer-actors played in full view, manipulating, singing, playing instruments and rearranging the décor.

As usual, there are no plans to publish any version of the performance text which exists only in copious notes and sketches.

Figure 5.3 'A dance of shapes'. *The Giraffe, the Pelly and Me* (2008) designed and directed by Peter O'Rourke for the Little Angel Theatre from the story by Roald Dahl. The scenography was as animated as the puppets.
© Peter O'Rourke

To recapitulate, since the 1990s productions by professional puppeteers and theatre-makers employing puppetry have surpassed anything seen before in richness and variety of forms, themes and ingenuity of presentation. This incontrovertible renewal of the art form can be largely attributed to its closer ties with the 'human' stage, which have brought an injection of new dramaturgical life springing from a fresh approach by mainstream artists and theatre-makers trained to stage productions that rely on content as much as form, on adult audiences more than children. They have provided a necessary balance to puppet performance that formerly paid too little regard to dramatic values and relied too much on the visual arts and crafts. Both are of course intrinsic and essential to puppetry, babies never to be thrown out with the bathwater. Because of the growing numbers of practitioners with little puppetry technique, the problem of balance (of content and form) has not yet been solved. But it is difficult to exaggerate the extent of the progress.

A major contributor to the puppetry renewal, propelling it into the postmodern era, was the DRAK company of Eastern Bohemia (in what is now the Czech Republic). Its artistic director from 1971, Josef Krofta, was educated and for a time practised as a director of actors' theatre, but fell foul of the Communist authorities and was no longer allowed to work in that sphere. Puppets not being rigorously supervised, he was able to accept an offer from Jan Dvořák, in charge of the already well-respected DRAK theatre in the small town of Hradec Králové, some distance from Prague. Krofta applied his knowledge of actors' theatre to the new company and astonished the international puppetry world with his earliest productions, their impact attributable to a revolutionary aesthetic that had nothing to do with the Moscow model. DRAK's originality was perceived in the staging, the vitality and versatility of the performers in view with their puppets, but especially in Krofta's choice and treatment of a variety of stories from *Cinderella* to *Til Eulenspiegl*, from *The Three Golden Hairs* to *Kalevala*, in which scenography, music, humour and the puppetry were smoothly blended, pleasing adults as much as children.

One of his experiments, darker in tone than the popular family productions, was a version of the episode in *Don Quijote de la Mancha* known as the *Retablo de Maese Pedro* or *Master Peter's Puppet Show*. Krofta's 1976 adaptation was in conceptual and interpretative terms well ahead of its time:

> This was a Don Quixote both grotesque and romantic. His grotesqueness was evident in his exaggerated features and the naivety which was emphasised by the contrast to the selfish and cynical world that surrounded him. His romanticism was seen in his spontaneity, which never allowed him to measure his forces against his intentions. It was stressed in the scene in which Don Quixote (played by an actor) as a chained prisoner, tries to bring help to the two lovers (puppets of 'Don Gayferos' and 'Melisandra') threatened by the Moors [...]
>
> The show manifested some of Krofta's personal feelings about the human condition in relationship to its dreams of freedom and the free expression of feeling. In

addition, the production contained many formal artistic experiments, of which the most significant was the 'atomisation' of the scenic situation. It was Luigi Pirandello who showed the division between actor and character: here Krofta went further, following certain artists from the time of the Avant Garde. He showed that reality functions in a state of dispersion or atomisation, and that it is for the spectators to reconstruct this reality in their imagination.

A good example of this was in the scene of Don Quixote's punishment. The audience saw an actor beating an empty bench, another in the costume of Don Quixote reacting as though he were receiving the beating, a manipulator holding the puppet of Quixote and actually breaking its limbs, another actor who cried as if suffering great pain. Atomisation of the action was the basis of the intended image for the spectator to reconstruct. This was a new approach, possible only in a multi-media form of theatre. (Jurkowski, 1998: 320)

The DRAK company were masters at adapting texts where the presence of the puppets alongside the performers always had dramaturgical validity. The subjects were never uniform in mood, the dark alternating with the light. *Dragon, (The Song of Life,* 1976) from a story by Evgeny Schwartz, told of a village tyrannized by a dragon-monster who annually demands tribute in the form of a local virgin. The village is saved by Lancelot who kills the 'dragon' and rescues the girl. Villain and hero were played by humans, the villagers by puppets, a telling metaphor. The reference to Nazi tyranny was overt in the costume of the 'Dragon', the intended reference to Soviet tyranny rather less so.

The Krofta stamp was evident in all DRAK's work until his retirement a few years ago. His version of Pinocchio (2000) was widely acclaimed, and in 2001 a rough and unsentimental version of the Romeo and Juliet story showed the star-crossed lovers as puppets manipulated literally and metaphorically by their human families.

Although I am referring here to productions made before the period under review in this book, the 1990s and onwards, the phenomenon of DRAK and its worldwide successes is included because the company made a direct contribution to the acceptance of puppetry by modern mainstream audiences.

The puppets in DRAK's shows were commonly rod marionettes held in front of the actor-puppeteer, sometimes with no rear controls other than the performer's hands. This 'hands-on' technique is used with increasing frequency and has its dramaturgical uses, for example where the character has literally to be broken apart and then reassembled. The figure can be held as though it is a portrait of the alter ego of the human character, as in a production of Strindberg's *Miss Julie* when the two lovers each carried their puppet double (which represented their inner self), visible only to the other. For the climactic love scene the puppets were thrown to the floor and dismembered, as metaphor of their passion, later to be put back together as the couple composed themselves. A version of *Hamlet* staged by the artist-director Julia Bardsley at the Young Vic in 1994 (with a question mark after the title) was set in a circus arena. Every character except Hamlet and Horatio (the only two innocent of duplicity) carried a puppet as their public face. In both shows the dramatic effect was powerful, the puppets a valid, metaphoric extension of the characters. The puppet operators were in both required to be actors as well as manipulators. Paul Taylor, theatre critic of the Independent newspaper with a keen eye for the semiotics of theatre, wrote of *Hamlet?*:

> To reinforce this sense of a world haunted by doppelgangers, the characters carry puppets, each bearing an uncanny, stylised likeness to themselves. This produces some bizarre correspondences: the puppet of the ghost, which Boyd Clack's Claudius is hypnotised by the conjuror into manipulating, looks uncannily like the usurper himself, while the bagful of marionettes that stand in for the troupe of travelling players are identikit versions of the members of the Danish Royal Family whose parts they take in [the scene known as] 'The Mousetrap'. In a decidedly creepy touch, the Player King, a scaled-down facsimile of Hamlet, is found nestling, like a barrier to incest, between the Claudius and Gertrude puppets. (Taylor, 1994)

For some it 'worked' triumphantly. Most of the critics, unused to looking for the dramaturgy in the visuals, could not read it, and perhaps for that reason condemned it.

DEVISED AND MIXED MEDIA PRODUCTIONS

In the fourth chapter I pointed out that performances, including those with animated forms, are devised by an ensemble, with the puppetry only one discipline among many. Devised theatre is no longer new, as it was even at the end of the last century and the creation of a show through the interaction and collaboration of a company is commonly practised. If a show is to be based on a text, even a Shakespearean or other classic text, the conventional recipe of a prepared script handed to the actors at the first rehearsal together with a model set design and a preliminary blocking of the moves will gener-ally not obtain. Set, costume, script, sound and movement will emerge from improvisation and 'work-shopping' (experimental explorations) by the whole group. When puppets are involved the theme of the performance will have been examined for its potential for metaphor, symbol, metonymy, metamorphosis and logistics of the staging.

The absence – hitherto – of a methodology for preparing a show, devised or otherwise, that mixes puppetry with other disciplines can be a problem, particularly in getting the dramaturgy right. Audience dissatisfaction is most often attributable to flaws in the coherence of the final performance-text. For example, the sense of the story can be lost in symbols and metaphors too recondite for the average spectator to read; or a folk tale told without reference to its inner, original meaning can be simply vacuous; or there is an absence of internal logic in the unfolding of the action; for example, a never-to-be-forgotten production of Peter Pan (it shall remain anonymous) wherein the crocodile *roared*; or a Pinocchio only too visibly 'under control', although the dialogue had just emphasized the puppet's freedom from control.

Useful strategies exist for the integration of puppetry into a devised show, though they do not yet amount to a methodology. One strategy lies in periods of group improvisation with one or more objects or practice figures, another is to examine the emerging performance-text for metaphor, symbol and action beyond the physical capability of the human performer. A devised piece describing the solitude of a woman building a metaphorical barrier between herself and society, decided to use real stones for the 'barrier'. A puppet-maker in the group brought into the rehearsal room a four-inch cube of polystyrene sponge, a maquette painted to look like stone. She (Eve Ravenscroft) 'unfolded' it so that it opened into the form of a homunculus with legs and arms; then she closed it so that it became again an apparently inert cube. The group immediately adopted the idea of the stone man as Carrier of the symbolic stones. A much larger version of the puppet was attached to the feet and body of the puppeteer – a ghostly presence which stacked up the stones around the performing area, then retired to become a 'block' again. The effect of the 'Stone Man' and its repeated metamorphosis from block to humanoid was striking, adding an element of the uncanny, of spirit materialized, to the production. The genius of the puppeteer whose idea it was had also made possible its dramaturgical and practical application.

Writers are by nature a source of original ideas for every genre of performance and visual and puppet theatre are no exception. A student playwright not previously acquainted with puppetry when asked to produce the outline of a piece for puppets wrote a sketch set in a maternity ward where a group of half-a-dozen mothers (masked humans) admire each others' new-born babies (swaddled puppets). The babies converse with each other as adults, recalling the delights of the spirit life they led before they were born. They warn each other not to drink from their mother's breast, or their otherworldly memories will be blotted out forever and they will descend into normal human infantilism. One by one they are clamped to the nipple, and in spite of resistance, each in turn is subsumed into the human condition, their paradise forgotten. The writer was able to apply his imagination to an unaccustomed area of performance, perfectly capturing the quality of the medium.

Normally one encounters puppet shows, other than street demonstrations, in studios and other small performing spaces, but in the last twenty years productions for large theatres have proved puppetry's potential for commercial success. For example *The Lion King*, *Avenue Q* and *War Horse* have all enjoyed long runs in London and on Broadway. The basis of their success is in large part a dramaturgy that satisfactorily answers the question 'why use puppetry?' They feature caricature and satire *(Avenue Q)*, anthro-pomorphism, daemons and other fantasticks *(His Dark Materials)* life-size horses (not anthropomorphized) in a cruel theatre of war *(War Horse)*, the sensuality of the gods *(Venus and Adonis)*, the political initiation of the young Gandhi surrounded by dreams of giant spirits *(Satyagraha,* an opera by Philip Glass). All juxtapose puppets and humans; most rely on the use of puppetry as metaphor; all contribute to an understanding of its potential and the rationale for its presence.

The Lion King has proved one of the popular successes of the decade, in several countries. The designer-director Julie Taymor was allowed a rela-tively free hand in the adaptation for the stage of one of Disney's sentimen-tal films, also titled *The Lion King*. Taymor returned the story to its African setting, introducing a sub-Saharan aesthetic in the music and the design. Most of the costumes were body-masks and body puppets, finely engineered and constructed to reveal the operator. The whole production betrayed the puppeteer that Taymor originally was, with an imagination unmatched for visual invention. For example, for the opening of the show a shimmering cloth, lying on the stage like a golden lake, rose slowly to dominate the action as the rising sun, its light attracting a procession of stylized animals (costumes and masks worn by puppeteers and dancers) which converged from the corners of the auditorium.

The Théâtre du Soleil of France led by Ariane Mnouchkine was an early example of a critically admired company working collaboratively on devised performance-texts, in which the animated object and the puppet were recurring elements; they have used them to show physical differences of scale and thereby metaphorical questions of status. In *Tambours sur la Digue (Drums on the Dyke)* the performers behaved and moved both as manipulators and as Bunraku puppets. Likewise the work of English company Complicite, created with the group members, is based on visual and auditory transformations – stimuli for a devised text which tells stories through moving images and scenic metaphors, words and music. The modus operandi of the company has for some years been regarded by other professionals as an inspirational model of contemporary theatre-making.

Complicite (pronounced *Complicitay)* uses the medium theatrically, with transformations that objectify humans or humanize objects, for example, a collapsed chair morphs into a walking skeleton (in *Mnemonic)*, a pillow into a child *(Caucasian Chalk Circle)*, books into birds *(Street of Crocodiles)*. These and a widening pool of comparable companies are turning to puppetry for the expression of the otherwise inexpressible, and for its dramatic impact.

Validity for the use of puppetry in a mid-scale, mixed-media production for adults is illustrated by *The Tale of Teeka*, premiered in 1994 and devised and produced by the French-Canadian Deux Mondes company. It presented, through scenographic metaphor and an actor's spoken commentary, the story of a boy submitted to serial abuse (beatings) by his parents. To the surprise of Deux Mondes, which had conceived it primarily for psychologists and educationists, the show was a critical success and toured for several years to theatre audiences in America and Europe. Some spectators received it as a touching tale of the relationship between a damaged boy and a goose (*Teeka*), but most detected the signifiers and symptoms of domestic violence in the imagery. Any intended utilitarian purpose for the show was transcended by its aesthetic and dramaturgical integrity.

The setting was the wide horizon of a Canadian farm in which were two buildings: a realistic wooden barn and a larger, steel-clad house without windows, metaphorical prison of the boy and location of the violence he endured, wishfully subsumed and transformed in his imagination as a play-ground jungle of dangerous adventure. The opening thunderstorm, another metaphor for the rage in the house, revealed the boy straddling the roof, shouting defiance and invoking the protection of his jungle god. The next scene found him seated outside the barn, one arm in a sling. His parents have gone to market, and he is accompanied only by his adult self, an actor unseen by the boy, the narrator revealing his memories. On his arm he wears the head and crop of a goose, a puppet which timidly interacts with the boy.

The goose, Teeka, is the only puppet, realized in accordance with the boy's perceptions: graduating from hand puppet, to toy, a plaything on wheels, then as a realistic bird. It is an escapee from the barn where the parents breed geese for their feathers and meat. For a few hours, the boy and goose form a tentative, delicate, unsentimental friendship. The boy's instinct is to torment the bird as he has been tormented, but soon realizes this will lose him his playmate. He carries the goose into the house whose steel walls open to show the fantasy world of his bedroom, the 'jungle'. They interact happily until the boy's exuberance ends in a burst goose-feather pillow, when for the first time he realizes Teeka's inevitable destiny, soon to be added to his own punishment. The parents return (one sees only the truck's headlights) and the boy prepares for his beating, first 'saving' Teeka by wringing the creature's neck. The ending is softened by the narrator, the boy grown-up, apparently freed from the cycle of violence into which he almost fell.

An original idea was given time and care in its preparation and perform-ance that would be difficult to fault. The writing was concise and graceful, the direction took advantage of every opportunity to create strong images, the acting and the manipulation restrained and convincing. The production served as evidence of the value of puppetry as effective and affecting element of a drama.

The dramaturgy of *shadow theatre* has been similarly enriched by the new attitudes, the application of new technologies and the talent of artists not necessarily puppeteers. When the Meiningen theatre in 1998 staged a version of Andersen's *Constant Tin Soldier* (1998) it was played in a vast circular white tent magically inflated from the sheets of Andersen's deathbed. In the tent images were thrown from a central projector (operated by the actor playing Andersen), while two or three other projectors were manned by operators placed invisibly outside the structure. The immersive effects produced in the changes of scale and perspective were overwhelming; the tiny tin soldier was swept away from his beloved doll dancer by what seemed like rushing waters advancing across the walls of the tent. The Andersen tale had been adapted with exceptional skill and an original use of shadow puppetry.

The Theft of Sita, a modernized episode from the Ramayana, was another large-scale shadow show that toured the world. It was an extended metaphor for the evils of tyranny and the destruction of the environment (in this case the forests of Indonesia), explicitly blamed on the then president Suharto.

> *The Theft of Sita* told the story of the Ramayana from the perspective of two comic Wayang Kulit characters, *punkawan* servant clowns [...] while progressively moving the action to contemporary Indonesia. The demons [...] representing greed, the destruction of the natural environment and political corruption, were transposed to the modern world. Using hundreds of puppets, traditional and newly created, *Sita* combined the beauty of a popular Indonesian shadow play with contemporary politics, fart jokes and slapstick humour. The spiritually sublime was to meet 'the Simpsons on Speed', in [the director Nigel] Jamieson's own words.
>
> At the outset, a [...] crocodile stalks a duck, a buck mounts a doe, humans live like gods. King Rama and his wife Sita are seen leading an idyllic existence in the pristine forest until an evil spirit, the demon Rawanna, kidnaps the beautiful Sita – embodiment of the natural environment.
>
> The tranquil old world then shifts to the modern industrial world. Giant animated logging-machine beasts rampage through the forest, wood-chip factories (for toilet paper) spoil the beauty of the landscape, while rice terraces are drained dry of water for tourists' white-water rafting. (Fenton and Neal, 2005: 186)

Presented in both New York and London in 2001, the show's example of cross-cultural collaboration was uplifting. Its staging, with no fixed shadow screen and many lighting sources, transformations of the scenery and the archetypes of the puppet characters, was made possible through the techniques of puppetry. The gamelan (orchestra) played indigenous music that elided into a modern beat with the temporal change in the story. The production was a mixture of western and eastern styles, a collaboration of artists from Australia and Indonesia.

On examination the most avant-garde productions of puppet companies point to some continuity of traditional dramaturgies: this is most obvious in the fare presented to young audiences which still consists largely of folk and fairy tales, myths and legends, adaptations of familiar literature. Adult audiences, even if offered more adventurous themes, may find in them a residue of many of the old categories, such as parody, satire, ribaldry, explicit sex and violence. Punch may be perceived in any modern Ubu, Pierrot in an African Woyzeck, Maria Marten in an Indonesian Sita.

To conclude: the new dramaturgical resources for puppetry have resulted in a growth of attention from the arts establishment and many true artists which in turn has made for a more discerning public. The genre has now largely escaped the confines of the traditional puppet theatre repertory, and shows itself in many artistic modes, from mimesis to symbolism, from object play to installation art.

Puppets can represent gods and devils, purity and pornography, symbols and portraits, slapstick and tragedy, the tyrant and the victim. Their relationship to text, Jurkowski believes, has gone through three phases: dumbshow or pantomime, narration and finally drama and poetry.

All these relationships persist, but the dramaturgical field has been thrown wide open by the new expressive resources of theatre: inter-disciplinarity, inter-textuality (the languages of other disciplines), the staging of work in spaces not intended for performance and perhaps the most challenging and insistent: the evolving language of the technologies of light, sound and projected image.

Most actors ask, when they get a script, 'how good is the part?' and only then 'how good is the play?' For the puppet the first question must be about the play: the vehicle must be right, worthy of the puppet's genius and its genus. It needs to feel at home on the stage: the spectator needs to feel it is at home. Fortunately it is comfortable in many kinds of home, as I have tried to illustrate.

FURTHER READING

Arnott, P. (1964) *Plays Without People: Puppetry in Serious Drama*, Bloomington, IN: Indiana University Press.

Artaud, Antonin ([1933] 1970) *The Theatre and its Double*, trans. Victor Corti. London: Calder and Boyars.

Barker, Howard (1993) *All He Fears*, London: John Calder.

Barker, Howard (2001) *The Swing at Night*, London: John Calder.

Batchelder, M. and Comer, V.L. (1959) *Puppets and Plays*, London: Faber and Faber.

Bensky, Roger-Daniel (1969) *Structures textuelles de la Marionnette de Langue Francaise*, Paris: Editions A-G Nizet.

Besnier, Patrick (2007) *Alfred Jarry*, Paris: Cultures France.

Burkett, Ronnie (2002) *Tinka's New Dress, Street of Blood, Happy*, Canada: River Books.

Burkett, Ronnie (2005) *Provenance*, Toronto: Playwrights Canada Press.

Burkett, Ronnie (2006) *10 Days on Earth*, Toronto: Playwrights Canada Press.

Burkett, Ronnie (2009) *Billy Twinkle*, Toronto: Playwrights Canada Press.

Dvořák, Jan (ed.) (2001) *DRAK. A Plague O' Both Your Houses!!!* Prague: Japan Foundation.

Eruli, B. (ed.) (1995) 'Ecritures et Dramaturgies' in *PUCK: La marionnette et les autres arts*, no.8, Charleville-Mèzières: Editions Institut International de la Marionnette.

Sherzer, D. and Sherzer, J. (1987) *Humor and Comedy in Puppetry: Celebration in Popular Culture*, Bowling Green, OH: Bowling Green State University Popular Press.

Tribble, Keith (ed.) (2002) *Marionette Theater of the Symbolist Era*, Lewiston, NY: Edwin Mellen Press.

6 *Aesthetics*

This chapter presents some theories of the aesthetics of puppetry. It consists of essays by five of the art form's most respected commentators: Kleist on the Romantic conception of the puppet; Henryk Jurkowski on puppetry's aesthetics at the start of the twenty-first century; Roland Barthes on the Bunraku theatre; Roman Paska on illusionism and primitivism; and Brunella Eruli on the contemporary uses of puppets in theatre.

The poet and playwright Heinrich Von Kleist (1777–1811) was the first of the Romantics to bring the aesthetics of a puppet performance to the attention of an educated public, and one of the first to endow the puppet figure with sentiment, praising it as a performer without the ego or self-consciousness of the human. Nearly a century later Edward Gordon Craig and the Modernists followed Kleist in turning to the puppet as the ideal 'impersonal' actor. Kleist wrote 'On the Marionette Theatre' the year before he killed himself at the age of 34. The essay continues to resonate, giving rise to a surprising number of interpretations of the essay's meaning and significance. Here is one of its many translations into English.

6.1   ON THE MARIONETTE THEATRE
Heinrich Von Kleist
Translated by Christopher Halsall

While I was spending the winter of 1801 in M–, I met Mr. C. in a park one evening. He had recently become principal dancer at the Opera in the town, and was enjoying an extraordinary success with the public.

I told him that I had been astonished to see that he had, on several occasions, visited the puppet theatre which had been set up, and which was entertaining the common people with short dramatic burlesques interspersed with songs and dances.

He assured me that the pantomimes of these puppets gave him much pleasure and stated emphatically that any dancer who wished to improve his art could learn a great deal from them.

From the manner in which he made this statement, it seemed to me that it was more than a casual remark. I sat down beside him to question him more closely on his reasons for making such a strange assertion.

He asked me whether I had not myself found the dancing movements of some of the puppets very graceful, especially the smaller ones.

I could not deny it. One group of four peasants, dancing a *ronde* to a fast rhythm, could not have been painted better by Teniers. I enquired about the mechanism of these figures. How was it possible without countless strings to move each limb and extremity in time with the movements or the dance?

He replied that I should not imagine that each limb had to be operated separately by the puppeteer at each moment of the dance. Each movement, he said, had a centre of gravity: it sufficed to control the one in the centre of the figure. The limbs, which were no more than pendulums, followed mechanically of their own accord without any prompting.

He added that this movement was very simple. Whenever the centre of gravity was moved in a straight line, the limbs described curves. Often, even if simply shaken at random, the whole puppet would fall into a kind of rhythmic movement similar to dance.

This observation seemed to me to throw some light on the pleasure he claimed to have found in the puppet theatre. I still did not begin to realise the conclusions he would later draw from it.

I asked him whether he thought that the person who controlled the puppets ought to be a dancer himself or at least have some idea of what constituted beauty in dancing.

He answered that an activity might be mechanically simple, but this did not mean that it could be carried out without any sensibility. The line which the centre of gravity must describe was indeed simple and, as he believed, in most cases straight. In cases where it was curved, the curve seemed to be of the first or, at the most, of the second order. Even in this case it was just an ellipse, a form which was the natural movement of the human body (owing to its joints): it did not therefore demand any great skill from the puppeteer.

On the other hand, this line was something very mysterious, for it was no less than the path of the dancer's soul, and he doubted that it could be found except by the puppeteer transposing himself into the centre of gravity of the marionette: in other words, by dancing.

I answered that the business had always been presented to me as something rather spiritless, rather like turning the handle of a barrel-organ.

'Not at all', he replied, 'The movements of the fingers are related to the movements of the puppet rather as numbers are related to their logarithms, or the asymptote to the hyperbole'.

However, he believed that even this last fragment of spirit of which he had spoken could be removed from the marionettes and that their dance could be completely transferred to the realm of mechanics by means of a crank, just as I had thought.

I expressed my astonishment that he should deem this art form, invented for the masses, worthy of his attention. It was not simply that he considered it capable of higher development: he seemed to positively concern himself with it.

He smiled and said that he felt able to state that if a craftsman were to build a marionette according to his plans, he would be able to make this marionette perform a dance that no other skilled dancer of the day, not excepting even Vestris, would be able to match.

'Have you', he asked, (since I looked down in silence) 'have you heard of the mechanical legs which English craftsmen build for those unfortunates who have lost their own?'

I said that I had never seen such things. 'A pity', he replied, 'for when I tell you that these unfortunates dance on them, I almost fear you will not believe me. I say "dance": their movements are admittedly restricted, but those they are capable of having a composure, lightness and grace which must astonish the thoughtful observer'.

I said, jokingly, that here was the man for him. The artist who could build such remarkable legs would certainly be able to construct a whole marionette in accordance with his plans.

It was his turn to look down a little awkwardly. 'What are these plans with which you propose to challenge craftsmanship?' I asked.

'Nothing', he answered, 'except that which is there already: balance, mobility, lightness – but all to a higher degree – and especially a more natural arrangement of the centres of gravity'. 'And the advantage which this puppet would have over living dancers?' 'The advantage? Firstly, a negative one, my good friend: that a puppet does not give itself airs and graces. Affectation appears, as you know, when the soul ("*vis motrix*") is elsewhere than at the centre of gravity of a movement. Since the puppeteer has only that single point under his control, through the string, [PF – rod?] all the other limbs are as they should be: dead, mere pendulums which simply obey the law of gravity, an excellent characteristic which one seeks in vain in most of our dancers'.

'Look at P–', he continued, 'when she plays Daphne pursued by Apollo and is looking around for him: her soul is in her lower vertebrae, she bends as if she would break, like a naiad of the school of Bernini. Look at young F– as Paris, standing between the three goddesses and handing Venus the apple: his entire soul (a dreadful sight!) is lodged in his elbow'.

'Such blunders', he added finally, 'are inevitable since we ate of the Tree of Knowledge. But Paradise is barred, and the cherub behind us. We must travel to the other side of the world to see if it is open again at the back gate'.

I laughed, 'At any rate', I thought, 'the spirit cannot err where it is not present'. Yet I noticed that he had more to say and begged him to continue.

'In addition', he went on, 'these puppets have the advantage that they are not subject to gravity. They know nothing of the weight of matter, that characteristic most inimical to dance, since the force which raises them into the air is greater than that which shackles them to the earth. What would our dear G– give to be sixty pounds lighter or to have that force come to her aid in entrechats and pirouettes? Puppets, like elves, need the ground only to brush against and to give their limbs new impetus through a momentary check. We need it to rest upon and to recover from the exertions of the dance: a moment which is obviously not a dance itself and with which nothing can be done except to make it as inconspicuous as possible'.

I said that, despite the skill with which he argued his paradox, he would never bring me to believe that there could be more grace in a jointed marionette than in the form of the human body.

He asserted that it was impossible for a human being even to match the marionette in this respect. Only a god could treat matter in such a way and this was the point where the two ends of the circular world joined together.

I was more and more astonished and did not know how to answer such strange arguments. It seemed, he said, taking a pinch of snuff, that I had not studied the first Book of Moses, chapter three, with sufficient attention. He who did not know this first period of human development was poorly equipped to discuss those following, and especially the most recent.

I said that I knew very well the damage which self-consciousness causes to the natural grace of man. A young man of my acquaintance had, before my very eyes, lost his innocence through a simple observation. Afterwards, he had never been able to regain the paradise of that innocence, in spite of all imaginable efforts. He asked me what had happened.

'About three years ago', I replied, 'I was bathing with a young man whose physical appearance was of remarkable grace. He was, I believe, in his sixteenth year or thereabouts; the first traces of vanity, called forth by women's favour, could be faintly perceived. It chanced that we had recently seen in Paris the statue of a youth removing a splinter from his foot. The cast of the statue is well known and is in most German collections. A glance in a mirror, in the instant he set his foot on the stool to dry it, reminded him of this statue. He smiled and told me of his discovery. Indeed, at the same moment I had made the same discovery, but either to test the Grace who attended him or to counter his vanity somewhat, I laughed and answered that he was seeing phantoms. He blushed and lifted his foot a second time to show me but the attempt, as might easily have been predicted, failed. Mystified, he lifted his foot a third and a fourth time. He lifted it ten times more. In vain! He was unable to reproduce the movement and the movements he did make were so comical that I held back my laughter only with difficulty!

'From this day, from this moment, an inconceivable change came over the young man. He began to stand in front of the mirror all day and, one after the other, his charms left him. An invisible, mysterious force seemed to settle upon the free play of his movements like an iron net. When a year had passed, no trace was still to be found of the agreeable nature which had previously delighted those around him. There is someone living yet who was a witness to that strange and unlucky occurrence and can confirm my account word for word'.

'Here I must tell you another story', said Mr. C. amiably, 'whose relevance you will readily understand'.

'During my journey to Russia, I found myself on an estate of Lord G–, a Livonian nobleman, whose sons were at that time assiduously practising fencing. The elder son, who had just returned from university, saw himself as a virtuoso and one morning when I was in his room he offered me a rapier. We fenced. It became clear that I was his superior, passion began to distract him and almost every thrust of mine struck home. Finally, his rapier flew into a corner. Half joking, half in wounded pride, he said as he picked up his rapier that he had met his master, but that everything in the world did likewise and he would at once lead me to mine. The brothers burst out laughing, crying, "Come, come! Down to the woodshed!" With this they took me by the hand and led me to a bear which their father, Lord G–, was having raised in the courtyard.

'As I stepped before it much astonished, the bear reared up on its hind legs and leaned against the post it was chained to, with its right paw raised. It looked me straight in the eye: this was its *en garde*. I wondered if I might be dreaming, seeing such an opponent before me. "Try a thrust", said Lord G–, "and see if you can teach him anything!" I had recovered a little from my astonishment and I attacked the bear with my rapier. He made a short movement with his paw and parried the thrust. I tried to distract him by feints. The bear did not move. Once again I attacked him with speed and skill. I would infallibly have scored a hit on a man's breast. The bear made a short movement with his paw and parried the thrust. Now I was in the position of the young G–. The bear's composure robbed me of my own. I alternated thrusts and feints; sweat dripped from me. In vain! It was not simply that the bear parried all my thrusts like the world's finest swordsman, but he was not taken in at all by feints – a thing no swordsman in the world can match. He stood, looking into my eyes as if he could read my soul, his paw raised in readiness and, if my thrusts were not in earnest, he did not move.

'Do you believe this story?' 'Absolutely', I cried in approval, 'I would believe it, from a total stranger: all the more from you!'

'Now, my excellent friend', said Mr. C, 'you know everything you need to understand me. We see in the organic world that the more the powers of thought become dark and feeble, the more grace shines majestically through.

'But like the intersection of two lines on one side of a point, which after passing through infinity suddenly finds itself repeated on the other side, or like the image formed by a concave mirror which, after receding to infinity, suddenly reappears close to us, so grace returns after understanding has passed through infinity. It thus appears in those human forms which either have no consciousness at all, or have an infinite one: in the marionette and in the god'.

'So therefore', I said in some confusion, 'we should eat once more of the Tree of Knowledge in order to return to innocence?'

'Certainly', he answered. 'And that is the last chapter of the history of the world'. (Kleist, [1810] 1983: 3–4).

* * *

Henryk Jurkowski's writings have punctuated this book. His wide-ranging essay on the aesthetics of puppetry at the beginning of the twenty-first century summed up the state of the art, and remains valid. This version was published in *Puppetry into Performance. A User's Guide* (2000), one of an occasional ongoing series of User's Guides edited by Professor Anthony Dean, this one following a Symposium with the same title held at London's Theatre Museum.

6.2   PUPPETRY AESTHETICS AT THE START OF THE TWENTY-FIRST
       CENTURY
       Henryk Jurkowski

The word aesthetics, in the general sense, refers to a system of views on the nature of beauty, which is combined with views on the processes of artistic creation. In colloquial language we often use this term to label the activities of an individual artist or group of artists. The word 'aesthetics' is applied to achievements which have specific features, different from earlier or contemporary artistic works (individual or generic).

Artists and writers such as Foote, Kleist, and Craig, and German and American theoreticians (Buschmeyer, Eichler, Bensky, and Tillis) have all offered their views on the puppet and the puppet theatre. But few developed a complete aesthetic system. Eminent puppet artists such as Sergei Obraztsov and Michael Meschke have left us reports on their artistic activities, suggesting that their experiences might have a universal aesthetic importance. In this article I will try to tell how these enunciated and particular views stand in relation to the present situation of puppet theatre.

Between sacred object and artefact

It seems that one of the basic aesthetic questions refers to the nature of the puppet, whether as an actor, a performer, or simply as a stage character. For hundreds of years audiences and also many puppeteers retained the conviction that puppets had a sacred or magic nature. No wonder, since the puppet originated in the moveable idol or ritual figure. The popular puppeteers believed in its magic life even in the nineteenth century. In many countries outside Europe this belief has lasted till today. Nevertheless, the first written comments referring to the nature of the puppet underlined its artificiality. A puppet is an artificial actor – so declared Ben Jonson, Alain-Rene Lesage and Samuel Foote. We might assume that most European artists of the Renaissance and Enlightenment periods decided once and for all to acknowledge the puppet as a secular actor. However, such a statement would be too great a simplification.

It was Romanticism that renewed the irrational root of the puppet, evidenced in the essay *On the Marionette* by Heinrich von Kleist. It is not important that Kleist considered the puppet as a mechanical actor with its centre of gravity as a sort of dispatcher of the puppet's self-dependent motion. The important point was that Kleist analysed the marionette's values in relation to the human and in relation to God. The marionette, unconscious of its life, was for Kleist the antithesis of God, who possesses full, absolute consciousness. In spite of that fact the marionette, uncontaminated by our limited human self-consciousness, could retain a gleam of divine harmony and beauty.

Modernists bent their steps in the same direction. We must leave aside the practical reason for their interest in puppets. For us it is their way of thinking that is important. Edward Gordon Craig may serve as a good example. Like many other artists of his time, he considered theatre art as a field of human creativity that had no obligation to imitate life. Thus a theatre production was an artefact, an artificial human production. Craig considered puppets to be artefacts also. Introducing what he believed to be necessary changes within the contemporary drama, he placed his trust in the Ubermarionette. The huge, hieratic figures from the banks of the river Ganges, as images of the gods, were his inspiration. The modernist super-puppet and its associate – the puppet – were thus born within a context of transcendence.

I believe that the twentieth century thesis, claiming the puppet as theatrical subject, originated from the same tradition of thinking. The puppet as substitute for the actor was equipped with an apparent personality. Thus it was entrusted with the function of a stage character: and thus it became 'a subject'. Among puppetry scholars, the German theoretician Lothar Buschmeyer was the principal advocate of this generally accepted belief. In my opinion the puppet as a theatre subject cannot be anything but a remnant of the belief in its spirituality which survived in Europe even into the middle of the twentieth century.

Starting from this time the puppeteers identified with the modernist thesis that a theatre show is an artificial product of the human. Any instrument including the puppet was also an artefact. Arm in arm with the vanguard artists, puppeteers went even further. They started to show audiences the process of creation of their productions. The puppet player appeared on the stage and his story was unfolded together with the display of all its theatrical secrets. Thus it was quite natural that the puppet in the hands of a visible puppeteer completely lost its subjective qualities and slowly

returned to its natural status as an object.

This evolution towards profanity in every field of art leads us, step by step, to an entirely subjective expression. What kind of messages do we transport by means of our puppets, inanimate forms or objects. We can also reveal a certain reticence in the use of the very word 'puppet'. We prefer to speak about the theatre of figures or objects. Certainly in this way we want more or less consciously to walk away from the religious and traditional values of

Figure 6.1 Faulty Optic's Blue Face from *Tunnelvision* (1998). Their aesthetic consists of the grotesque, dark humour and cruelty.

Reproduced by permission of Liz Walker, Co-Founder of Faulty Optic.

puppet theatre, which is so much linked to art for children, according to existing superstitions.

The birth of the theatre of objects, collateral of the puppet theatre, was the consequence of this process. It is interesting that this notion of a 'theatre of objects' provoked the protest of Dennis Silk, Israeli poet and theoretician of puppetry. He is the founder of the notion of 'Thing Theatre'. His reservations about object theatre had as background the philosophic interpretation of the words 'thing' and 'object'. According to Silk's semantics a 'thing' means a product of nature (or creation), while 'object' means a human product. Silk wrote: 'In most of Europe and the States, Thing Theatre is called, I think inaccurately, Object Theatre, which presupposes a division between actor or performer, and prop. The word "prop" is the invention of an atheist. It is there to be changed into a thing by an attempt at connection, which at base is always religious, though its expression may be in farce. Perhaps the thing will lapse into an object but this is due to a failure of attention'.

Naturally this is not a suggestion for practising religion, but a problem of understanding the world, which is saturated with a certain spirituality, and, it follows, with sacredness in some sense. This issue has not held much significance for the European puppet theatre as a whole, neither has it become a subject of scientific deliberation among artists or scholars.

It was quite the opposite in the case of the dramatic theatre. Here the avant garde evinced a fascination for ancient forms of rituals. The vanguard artist found there a model for new theatre as a community of people, a community of coryphées (the actors) and participants of the ritual (the spectators). A certain impetus was given to theatre by researchers who in their investigations on religious and ancient cultures explained the sacredness of ritual as immanent for human nature. Philosophers and sociologists of our time have applied this idea to any ceremonial behaviour in political, cultural and civic life, discovering suddenly an existence of a 'profane sacredness'.

In fact the hallmark of avant garde drama is an aspiration to transcendence, to the spiritual in its widest sense. At the same time, along with antimaterialism and radical politics, Christianity is frequently rejected as the official organ of the social establishment, with the result that the 'holiness' of this theatre is unrecognisable by conventional religious standards or, when the links with religion are closest, is sacrilegious.

In the last twenty-five years the dramatic theatre has exploited these impulses towards the sacred and its achievements have been fully described and documented. The same cannot be claimed for puppet theatre, although it has strongly manifested interest in the avant garde. The exception is Peter Schumann and his Bread and Puppet Theatre. Spirituality and ritual have not become the subject of artistic or scholarly investigation within puppet theatre.

We may ask the question: why have puppeteers omitted this tendency towards transcendence? The answer is complex. We may find some explanation in the presence of ritualistic groups from Southeast Asia at certain world puppet festivals. Puppeteers have not turned towards ritual, because they have it within easy reach. What is more they classify Asian theatre as a traditional theatre, quite distinct from the consciously practised 'artistic' theatre in Europe.

While in past centuries the nature of the puppet in both its aspects, metaphorical and aesthetic, has provoked the interest of writers, the concept of puppet theatre's specificity has only recently appeared. Producers of the Baroque puppet opera or French puppet melodrama, or the puppet theatre of artistic salons, considered it to be a miniaturised art of drama. Accepting this definition other artists decided that puppet theatre might also be used as a deforming, satiric mirror both of theatre art and of life. They did not consider the possibility of the puppets' participation in other genres of spectacle, such as the imitation of variety shows or of circus. All their deliberations on the aesthetics of puppet theatre regarded this theatre as drama. The German philosophers pursued this way of thinking throughout their research. They applied phenomenological aesthetics to their analysis of the principles. They presumed that puppet theatre is a miniaturised dramatic art, which has a specific character. Its similarity to drama consists in the fact that the puppet, in the same way as the actor, represents a stage character. Thus the puppet is a theatrical subject. However they observed many differences, the most important being that the puppet as artefact has capacities distinct from those of the actor. Its material, construction and technique of manipulation limits its expression.

Buschmeyer believed that due to the nature of the puppet (a dead thing with the ambition to act on stage) it always seems grotesque and comical. However, he agreed that the will of the artist is able to change the natural expression and aesthetic function of the puppet, which may sometimes become tragic. This emphasis of the decisive role of the artist's will was announcing new features in the modern puppet theatre.

In spite of that, phenomenological aesthetics demands that the puppet display its 'puppet-ness', that is, its formal features. Advocates of 'puppet-ness' postulated the choice of puppet repertoire in accord with this criterion, the criterion of 'puppet-ness'. They did not allow for the mixing of the means of expression, i.e. the different kinds of puppet. They were partisans of a homogenised puppetry. Such was the way of thinking of most of the puppet theatre theoreticians. Petr Bogatyrev, the Russian semiotician, thought that puppet theatre differs from actor's theatre solely in the fact that the puppet replaces the actor. He stated in his conclusion: 'Actor's theatre and puppet theatre are two different but closely related semiotic systems of dramatic art'.

This principle dominated European puppetry for dozens of years, but at the end of a period this principle was abandoned to give way to many innovations. New artistic practices led directly to a theatre of visibly animated figures, and to a theatre of various means of expression. It was in the 1960s that the principle of homogeneity was broken. After that the actor entered the puppet stage not only as the puppet's visible manipulator but also as its partner. However, let us not cherish the illusion that the notion of specificity was then forgotten. This specificity has been regularly discussed until now. The language of the puppet has been discussed at several scientific sessions and also in some publications, in which eminent semioticians from the second half of the twentieth century have presented their studies.

The puppet theatre is a theatre art, the main and basic feature differentiating it from the live theatre being the fact that the speaking and performing object (the puppet) makes temporal use of physical sources of vocal and motor powers which are present outside the object. The relationships between the object (the puppet) and these power sources change all the time and the variations are of great semio-logical and aesthetical significance.

It is worth noting that in the 1970s we used to speak about the puppet as 'performing object', but meaning a theatrical subject. The objectification of the puppet was to take place some years later. The application of visible manipulation brought immediate comparison with the Japanese *ningyo joruri* (Bunraku) and also provoked some deliberation on the principles of Brecht's epic theatre.

In Germany this situation gave birth to the theory of puppetry as synergetic art by Konstanza Kavrakova-Lorenz [German academician, 1941–2005]. This theory, deal-ing with 'the mutual co-operation of two elements', may be regarded as a code for the theatre of visible manipulation.

It is right to say that the dynamic artistic work of practitioners has accelerated the appearance of theoretical comments. Multimedia theatre, theatre of objects, mate-rial theatre – all these new forms are attractive subjects for scholars and artists for description and for the research of their aesthetic values. An important conclusion that arose from these studies was that the new genres related to puppetry offered a new poetic language with an endless number of visible metaphors. It is to be regret-ted that few scholars have gone beyond the description of new phenomena. The only work of synthesis from that period is that of Steve Tillis, which is limited to the discussion of the 'classical' puppet theatre and puppet theatre in the first period of its atomisation. There is still much to do if we want the contemporary puppet theatre and its related genres to have commentaries more advanced than the description of the work. We need a kind of synthesis which will be possible only if preceded by detailed studies concerning their language, their presented world, their links with other arts and their sensibility towards social problems.

The question is urgent, in that the so-called puppet theatre is still boldly progress-ing along the road of alternative research. It disregards the law of the cyclic devel-opment of art, which implies a return to the starting point. It is still eager to discover new forms and new means of expression. Though it may follow the path of the historical vanguard, it is nonetheless true that this path is constantly complemented with ideas. Let us take the case of 'material theatre'. Having made several creative experiments with manufactured material, some of the 'material' artists then applied the term to the human being. They objectified the human body. Thus they went farther than the historical vanguard, which atomised the human body only in dramatic writing. In fact they used parts of the human body to create a new perform-ing entity. This has been the greatest novelty, although not the only one.

It is obvious that the material theatre has its diachronic context and is surrounded by many other sub-genres of the 'puppet theatre'. The programming team of the last [UNIMA] festival in Magdeburg (June 2000) took this as a basis for its courageous conclusion concerning the aesthetic of the contemporary puppet Theatre: 'In the juxtaposition of the remaining representatives of traditional forms of puppetry [...] with modern figure theatre productions [...] and the representatives of object theatre [...] it may become evident that there is no longer any formal specificity to puppet theatre ... like no other form of theatre, this theatre is sustained by the question of the distinction between body and material, the objects, the figures and the puppets. The potential perception of that space – as scenic archaeology, so to speak, of the boundary between body and material, between body and identity – makes possible one of the most interesting sensory experiences of thought provided by the puppet and figure theatre of the present day'.

Each declaration of this kind may become a sort of trap for its author. The authors of the above quotation stated that there is no longer a 'formal specificity', but then immediately added that within the contemporary puppet theatre the most important sphere is the 'space between various means of expression'. It really sounds like a new generic specificity of the contemporary puppet theatre, and thus its formal specificity. Besides, the observation is not a new one. Scholars have, since the 1960s, discussed the phenomenon of meanings generated within the space of a relationship. Scholars have also discussed the phenomenon of the birth of metaphors resulting from the juxtaposition of expression.

These 'Magdeburgers' went on to make a list of sub-genres of the present 'puppet theatre' such as traditional theatre, theatre of objects and material theatre. This fact means that they must also see the differences that exist between these genres. Many more of these sub-genres of 'puppet theatre' could be mentioned: the classic puppet theatre (not necessarily traditional, but homogeneous although with modern scenography), mask theatre, multimedia theatre, plastic theatre (taking inspiration from painting). Each of these sub-genres has its own specificity. In fact each of them is worth the profound analysis of its expressive and aesthetic power. Thus we are in a situation, when we can guess at the existence of many aesthetics – one for every sub-genre. If we embark on a new research programme we will surely discover new problems and questions.

To give a few examples, there is the question of inter-generic inspiration (between puppetry, fine art, music, circus or mime), cross-cultural inspiration (eg Africa, Asia), or the professionalism of performers. The performer's professionalism is also important for aesthetic studies. There are different types of professionalism. One promotes general capacities; another emphasises a narrow specialisation. The latter normally aims for a perfect performance. A Chinese glove puppet player trains his hands for many years and learns acrobatic puppet leaps for the performance of Peking opera. Thus his manipulation will be excellent. The European puppeteer often changes his scenic instruments; sometimes he acts as an actor, so he is unlikely to be so skilled. He does not look for that kind of perfection, because as we know from the Magdeburgers' declaration, he is not concerned with the direct expression of the performing object, he is concerned with what is happening 'in-between'.

This means that although we still derive pleasure from time to time from the performances of the classic puppet theatre, there are no longer many classical puppeteers, meaning those who work towards perfection in dealing with the instrument they operate. The traditional puppet player is replaced by artists with wide artistic interests. In fact these artists use a variety of instruments. Sometimes they themselves act on stage, sometimes they use masks, and sometimes they are

Figure 6.2 Poppentheater Damiet.
Theatre artist Damiet Van Dalsum's
Silver Bird, a marionette from *Mijn
Kleine Prins (My Little Prince)* (1998).
Reproduced by permission of Damiet van
Dalsum.

accompanied by a puppet. This is the
new professional situation, which has its
generic consequences.

The sub-genres of the puppet theatre
have an ephemeral life, dependent on
the preferences of the artist, who are not
only graduates of puppetry schools but
also drama and opera directors, even
painters applying puppetry in their
productions. In this situation I am taking
the liberty to formulate a 'negative' definition of the puppet theatre. I call this
definition negative because it implies
distrust in the durability of this kind of
theatre as a parallel to the drama theatre. I can sum up thus:

The contemporary puppet theatre exists thanks to the will of the theatre artist.
The artist introduces on stage various means of expression which he thinks necessary to achieve his artistic objective. Sometimes these means originate from the
world of the human, sometimes from the world of animated objects (puppets),
sometimes from the world of utilizable objects. Sometimes the artist mixes them in
one production. When the artist decides only to employ puppets the 'puppet
theatre' is allowed to exist. The artist may use puppets throughout a production, or
now and then, or only fleetingly (exceptionally). He may choose various conventions for his show – the mimetic theatre, the epic theatre, literary or visual theatre.
He is the demiurge of his artistic world and also its constant innovator.
(see Dean, 2000: 32–34)

*   *   *

The artists responsible for the *ningyo joruri* of Japan were originally story-
tellers who illustrated their stories with puppets and chanted narration. In
the nineteenth century Uemura Bunrakuken, as already related, brought
renewed dignity and refinement to the art of *ningyo joruri,* since when his
company has been the model for a style and technique of puppetry which in
many adapted and distorted forms is in use all over the world. Bunraku introduced the highly-trained manipulators and the exquisitely crafted puppets to
his performances. The critic and philosopher Roland Barthes interprets the
genre as another kind of model, theoretical rather than practical.

6.3   ON BUNRAKU
Roland Barthes
Translated by Sandy MacDonald

Bunraku puppets are up to three feet tall. They are little men or women with mobile limbs, hands, and mouth; each puppet is moved by three visible men, who surround it, support it and accompany it. The master puppeteer controls the puppet's upper body and right arm; his face is uncovered, smooth, light, impassive, cold as "a white onion freshly washed" (Basho). His two assistants are dressed in black; cloths cover their faces. One, gloved but with his thumb left uncovered, holds a large, stringed, scissor-like extension, with which he moves the puppet's left arm and hand; the other, crouching, supports the puppet's body and steadies its course. These men move along a shallow trench, which leaves their bodies visible. The scenery is behind them, as in the theatre. On a platform to one side are the musicians and narrators; their role is to express the text (the way one squeezes a fruit). This text is half-spoken, half-chanted; punctuated by the samisen players' loud plectrum beats, it is both restrained and flung, with violence and artifice. Sweating and still, the narrators are seated behind little lecterns on which is placed the large script they vocalize. One can perceive the vertical characters from afar when the narrators turn the pages of their librettos. Triangles of stiff cloth, attached to their shoulders like kites, frame their faces, which are prey to all the throes of their voices.

Bunraku thus uses three separate scripts and presents them simultaneously in three places in the spectacle: the puppet, the manipulator, the vociferator, the effected gesture, the effective gesture, the vocal gesture. Bunraku has *a limited* idea of the voice; it doesn't suppress it but assigns it a very definite, essentially vulgar function. In the voice of the narrator there converge: exaggerated declamation, the tremolo, the shrill feminine tone, broken pitches, weeping, paroxysms of anger, moaning, supplication, astonishment, indecent pathos – every emotional recipe, openly elaborated at the level of this internal, visceral body, whose larynx is the mediatory muscle. Also, this outbreak is given solely under the very code of outbreak: the voice moves only through some discontinuous signs of outburst. Thrust from an immobile body triangulated by its clothing, bound to the book which, from its lectern, guides it, and sharply hammered by the samisen player's slightly out of phase (and therefore impertinent) beats, the vocal substance remains written, discontinuous, coded, subjected to a certain irony (excluding from the word any caustic sense). Also, what the voice exteriorizes, finally, is not what it conveys ('feelings'), but itself, its own prostitution. The signifier, cunningly, only turns itself inside out like a glove.

Without being eliminated (which would be a way of censoring it, that is, designating its importance), the voice is thus put to one side (scenically, the narrators occupy a lateral platform). Bunraku gives the voice a balance, or better, a check: gesture. Gesture is double: emotive gesture at the puppet's level (people cry at the suicide of the puppet-lover), transitive act at the manipulators' level. In western theatre, the actor pretends to act but his acts are never anything but gestures; onstage, there is only theatre, and ashamed theatre at that. Bunraku, though (by definition), separates act from gesture: it shows the gesture, allows the act to be seen, exposes art and work simultaneously and reserves for each its own script. The voice (and there is then no risk in letting it attain the excessive regions of its gamut) – the voice is plated with a vast volume of silence, on which, with all the greater subtlety, other tracts, other scripts are inscribed. And here, an unparalleled effect is produced: distant from the voice and nearly without pantomime, these silent scripts – one transitive, the other gestural – produce an exaltation as unique, perhaps, as the intellectual hyper-esthesia attributed to certain drugs. Speech is not purified (Bunraku in no way strives for asceticism) but – if this can be said – is amassed next to the action; the sticky substances of western theatre are dissolved. Emotion no longer inundates, no longer submerges, it becomes reading material; stereotypes disappear, without, however, the spectacle resorting to originality, or 'felicity'. All of this achieves, of course, the *Verfremdungseffekt* advocated by Brecht. This distance, was reputed in the west to be impossible, pointless, or ridiculous and readily abandoned, although Brecht very specifically placed it at the center of revolutionary dramaturgy (and the following undoubtedly explains why) – Bunraku shows how this distance can work: through the discontinuity of the codes, through this censorship imposed on the performance's different tracts, so that the copy elaborated onstage is not destroyed, but as if broken, striated, saved from the metonymic contagion of voice and gesture, soul and body, which mires the western actor.

A total though divided spectacle, Bunraku of course excludes improvisation; to return to spontaneity would be to return to the stereotypes which constitute western 'profundity'. As Brecht saw, here reigns the *quotation* – the pinch of script, the fragment of code – because none of the promotives of the action can take on himself responsibility for something he never writes alone. As in the modern text the braiding of codes, references, detached statements, and anthological gestures multiplies the written line, not by virtue of some metaphysical appeal, but through a combinative activity which unfolds in the theatre's entire space. What is begun by one person is continued by another, without pause.

Animate/Inanimate

In dealing with a fundamental antinomy, the animate/inanimate, Bunraku muddies it, makes it fade, without benefiting either of its terms. In the west, the puppet (Punch, for example) is expected to offer the actor the mirror of his contrary; it animates the inanimate, but the better to show its degradation, the indignity of its inertia. A caricature of 'life', the puppet thereby affirms life's *moral* limits and presumes to confine beauty, truth, and emotion in the living body of the actor, who, however, makes of this body a lie. Bunraku, though, does not put its own stamp on the actor; it gets rid of him for us. How? Through a certain conception of the human body, which inanimate matter rules in Bunraku with infinitely more rigor and trembling than the animate body (endowed with a 'soul'). The western (naturalistic) actor is never beautiful; his body would be of a physiological, not plastic, essence. He is a collection of organs, a musculature of passions, whose every spring (voice, facial expressions, gestures) is subjected to a sort of gymnastic exercise. But by an absolutely bourgeois reversal, although the actor's body is constructed according to a division of passional elements, it borrows from physiology the alibi of an organic unity, that of 'life'; it is the actor who is a puppet here.

The basis of western theatre is, in fact, not so much the illusion of reality as the illusion of totality: periodically, from the Greek *choreia* to the bourgeois opera, lyrical art has been conceived as the simultaneity of several expressions (acted, sung, mimed) with a single, indivisible origin. This origin is the body, and the totality claimed is modelled on organic unity. The western spectacle is anthropomorphic; in it, gesture and speech (not to mention song) form but one fabric, conglomerated and lubricated like a single muscle which puts expression into play but never divides it. The unity of movement and voice produces *he who acts;* in other words, it is this unity which constitutes the 'person' of the personage; that is, the actor.

Actually, under his 'living' and 'natural' exterior, the western actor preserves the division of his body and, consequently, food for our phantasms: now the voice, then the look, now again the figure are eroticized, like so many pieces of the body, like so many fetishes. The western puppet, too (it's quite apparent in Punch), is a phantasmic subproduct: as a reduction, a grating reflection whose place in the human order is constantly recalled by a caricatured simulation, it lives not as a total body, totally trembling, but as a rigid part of the actor from whom it is derived; as an automaton, it is still a piece of movement, a jerk, a shove, the essence of discontinuity, a decomposed projection of the body's gestures; finally, as a puppet – reminiscent of a scrap of rag, of a genital dressing – it is quite the phallic 'little thing' *('das Kleine'),* fallen from the body to become a fetish.

It is very possible that the Japanese puppet retains something of this phantasmic origin, but the art of Bunraku imprints on it a different meaning. Bunraku does not aim to 'animate' an inanimate object so as to bring a piece of the body, a shred of man, to life, all the while keeping for it its vocation as a 'part'. It is not the simulation of the body which Bunraku seeks; it is – if this can be said – the body's tangible abstraction. Everything we attribute to the total body and which is withheld from western actors under the name of 'living' organic unit, the little man in Bunraku collects and states, without any lies. Fragility, discretion, sumptuousness, unparalleled nuance, the abandonment of all vulgarity, the melodic phrasing of gestures – in short, the very qualities ancient theology accorded to heavenly bodies, to wit, impassivity, clarity, agility, subtlety – this is what Bunraku accomplishes, this is how it converts the body-fetish into a body worthy of love, how it rejects the animate/inanimate antinomy and banishes the concept hidden by all animation, which is, quite simply, the 'soul'.

Inside/outside

The function of the western theatre of the last few centuries has been essentially to show what is said to be secret ('feelings', 'situations', 'conflicts'), while hiding the very artifice of the show (stage effects, painting, powder, light sources). The Italian-style stage is the space of this lie; everything takes place in an interior which is surreptitiously opened, surprised, spied upon, savoured by a spectator hidden in the shadow. This space is theological, a space of Guilt: on one side, under lights which he pretends to ignore, the actor (gesture and speech); on the other, in the darkness, the audience (conscience).

Bunraku does not directly subvert the relation of the seats to the stage. It changes most profoundly the motive link going from character to actor, which westerners conceive of as the expressive path of an interiority. In Bunraku the agents of the space are both visible and impassive. The men in black busy themselves about the puppet, but without any affectation of competence or discretion, or any advertising demagogue; quiet, rapid, elegant, their acts are eminently transitive, operative, colored by that mixture of force and subtlety which marks the Japanese gestuary and is like the aesthetic envelope of efficacy. The leader's head is uncovered; smooth, naked, without powder – this confers on him a civil (non-theatrical) cachet – his face is offered for the spectator's perusal. But what is carefully, preciously given to read is that there is nothing to read; one finds here this exemption of meaning which we in the west scarcely understand, since, for us, to attack meaning means to hide or invert it, but never to keep it away. Bunraku exposes the sources of theatre in their emptiness. What is expelled from the stage is hysteria – that is, theatre itself – and what replaces it is the action necessary to the production of the spectacle. Work substitutes for interiority.

It is thus vain to wonder whether the spectator can forget the presence of the manipulators. Bunraku practices neither the occultation nor emphatic manifestation of its springs; it rids the actor's animation of all sacral staleness and abolishes the metaphysical connection the west cannot keep from making between the soul and the body, cause and effect, motor and machine, agent and actor, destiny and man, God and creature. If the manipulator is not hidden, why – how? – do you want to make him a god? In Bunraku, the puppet is not controlled by strings. No more strings, therefore no more metaphors, no more destiny. The puppet no longer apes the creature, man is no longer a puppet in the hands of divinity, the *inside* no longer rules the *outside*. (Barthes, 1971: 76–79)

* * *

Roman Paska, puppeteer, director and academic, takes the discourse around the visible/invisible puppet operator further in an essay that conceives of the *hidden* puppeteer as part of the 'illusionistic' tradition of puppet theatre that wills its spectators to think of it as 'real' and, by contrast, the *acting* puppeteer in a theatre of revealed objects. He terms the producers of one as the 'illusionaries' and of the other as 'primitives'.

6.4 NOTES ON PUPPET PRIMITIVES AND THE FUTURE OF AN ILLUSION
Roman Paska

Having no interior life, the puppet is, strictly speaking, incapable of expression. Having nothing to express, it can express nothing. The mask of an actor or dancer conceals the density of humanity; the puppet, nothing but emptiness. Nothing.

What is the Nothing that hides behind the mask of the puppet? What is the puppet stripped bare?

The fascination of the puppet, its secret power of seduction, lies in what it hides, not what it expresses.

Narrative, mimesis, representation: all 'othodox' aspects of puppet theatre in the West. Little human simulacra illustrating human quirks through the imitation of human poses and gestures. Mimicry and parody as the twin peaks of the puppeteer's art.

The bright side of the picture has been the reasoned defense of puppetry on naturalistic principles: puppetry as a 'humanistic', socially redeemable practice because, through the representation of human foibles, the puppet holds the mirror up to man.

The shady side: the parodistic puppet shares its bed with trained monkeys, pigs, dogs, elephants, dancing bears and every other circus animal that relies on mimicry for theatrical effect.

Only the puppet is an *über*-monkey, being more high tech.

What is a *pure* art form?

Sooner or later during this century [the twentieth], all of the arts have submitted to the litmus test of modernism. Cinema, dance, painting; but the Theatre, handicapped by its inherited Wagnerian identity as a hybrid (therefore impure) form, has lagged behind in attracting critical favor. It only began to make headway with its eventual reduction to an empty-space, naked-actor theatre of essentials. (At about the same time, the puppet gave birth to the hand-mime).

Puppetry or puppet theatre? If puppetry can function as a performing art in various contexts (cinema, drama, cabaret, circus, television, performance art, avant garde theatre), what exactly is the meaning of the expression 'puppet theatre'?

Puppet theatre in the West has been largely dependent on (and derivative of) the dramatic actors' theatre. But apologists and defenders of the art who hope to legitimise puppetry *as theatre* by citing its similar nature as a composite theatrical form (using Craig's variation on Wagner's concept of the *Gesamtkunstwerk*), are only asking to board a sinking ship.

If puppetry is an art form in its own right (or at all) according to modernist criteria, it has to manifest qualities that distinguish it from the theatre in general – qualities both inherent and unique that define its essential 'puppetness'. (Even if the puppet itself is only implied or virtual, as in the hand-mime or object theatre).

The most visible sign of the puppet's ongoing relationship with the theatre in the West is its thirst for realism.

Realism in the theatre means the illusionistic tradition (referring to the illusion of reality or the real), a tradition that began with the development of perspective and the Italian proscenium stage, and exploded with the fusion of performance and photography in the cinema. The cinema promptly usurped the role of the theatre as the principal purveyor of illusory reality; since when the theatre has chosen to survive by letting go.

Recent trends in puppetry, like the 'theatre of objects' movement, represent the most recent in a series of efforts by puppeteers to liberate their art from mimetic narrative and the illusionistic tradition. But the majority of puppeteers, like the majority of actors, cling nostalgically to illusionism in character representation.

Puppet theatre followed the lead of dramatic theatre in moving away from exclusively proscenium-style presentations, even though the conventional hand-puppet or marionette booth was never illusionistic in the same sense as the actors' stage. In the puppet theatre the principal aim in concealing the mechanics of representation was to suggest a theatrical, not a dramatic reality – a 'real' stage with 'real' actors before any other reality. The spectator was never expected to lose himself in total empathy (Don Quixote's error was never the norm).

The only illusion consistently pursued in puppet theatre has been the illusion of the mechanical autonomy of the puppet object itself, an illusion typically thought of as encompassing the subordinate sense of the puppet as a real character. But character realization is dependent on the illusion of mechanical independence; the object must first 'become puppet' before it can start to become a character. The former is a performative function, implying a real transformation in the nature of the object; the latter is strictly symbolic. The object acquires puppetness in real time through its active use in performance – as opposed to the imaginary, narrative time in which the puppet takes on character value. The act of performance (implementation) marks the 'becoming puppet' of an object.

Like a fish out of water the puppet out of performance is a dead thing, a potential signifier only. As demonstrated most recently by the theatre of objects, the signifying properties of the puppet as a passive formal object or sculpture are ultimately unnecessary to the object's kinetic, signifying activity as a puppet actor in a performance context. The puppetness of an object is determined by use, not latency, and is a renewable, not a permanent, quality.

In the contemporary world of puppetry, puppeteers differ mainly in their attitude towards character. 'Illusionists' (or 'illusionaries') focus on *representation*, treating their puppets as independent characters; 'primitivists' ('primitives') focus on *presentation,* treating their puppets as interdependent objects (sacred or otherwise).

Like the illusionistic theatre, illusionistic puppetry has found its greatest potential for realization in the cinema, where the puppet can enjoy an ontological status equal to the objectified human actor. But in the cinema, with its aura of ambitiously heightened realism, the specificity of the puppet is often smothered by its frequency of exchange with mannequins, masks, automata, stop-action animation figures, dummies, robots, and other staples of the animation, fantasy and horror genres. In the service of a comprehensive cinematic illusion, the image of the puppet *character*, often created only in the cutting room as an assemblage of physically dissociated pieces, supersedes the value of the puppet as a discrete object or *thing.* (Compare this with the fabrication of a human character through the artificial combination of principal actor, body and stunt doubles, speaking voice, singing voice).

In this scenario, the integrity of the puppet-as-object completely succumbs to character representation, and may even cease to exist outside the illusion of continuity. The signifying puppet dematerializes into pure simulation.

Two conclusions:

- The future of illusionism in puppetry is linked to technological evolution in the cinema.
- The puppet-as-object in live performance still represents the 'zero degree' of puppetry (the point from which all reckoning begins).

In the interest of an illusion of total autonomy, illusionaries paradoxically tend to downplay or even negate the role of the puppeteer (the human part of the puppet actor). In illusionist theory, the puppeteer is often presented in strictly mechanistic terms as something more akin to a fork-lift driver than a performer – the motor force behind a well-programmed machine (logically expendable with advances in automation), rather than a performance motivator. Just a difference in function in design: while the fork-lift lifts, the puppet vehicle simulates sentient being.

Naturally, as a manipulated object, the puppet can only begin to approach real being by detaching itself from any external control. Its first task is therefore to capture the sense of naturalness implied by freedom of movement. For Kleist movement is natural when it is automatic; habitual but not willed. The natural is a mechanical response, and the puppet is perfectible because it has a memory but no will. In this line of thinking the mechanical and the natural are matching towards some sort of cybernetic union where mechanical perfection means not only the absolute reproduction of the real, but freedom from accident.

Puppet primitives on the other hand have little interest in mechanical perfection. If primitivist puppetry is humanistic, it isn't because it represents the human condition mimetically, but because it is produced by human beings. The core of the art is the confrontation or interaction between performer and object. The puppet seems to perform only because the puppeteer performs, and the fact that the puppeteer provides *all* of the energy expended in performance means that for any given performance object, there are as many performance variations as there are various performers. The puppet is no more mechanically perfectible than a guitar.

The open intervention of the human performer situates the primitivist performance squarely in the space of accident, utterly negating the possibility of a clockwork presentation. The live performance thrives on risk – the tension resulting from the struggle between the skill of the performer and the resistance of an object which, in practical terms, is hardly more dependable or reliable than the performer. The more 'dangerous' the object, the more engaging the performance, which partially explains the attraction of simply constructed figures or found objects for many contemporary performers.

Primitivism differs from illusionism in consciously directing audience focus back and forth between the outward sign and the inner process of simulation. And the primitive puppet is flagrantly exhibitionist in exposing its own emptiness as a vehicle for expression in performance.

In effect, puppet primitives let the puppet 'die' and, discarding the pretence of realism, take it for the inanimate object (dead thing) that it is. The dead thing can only be reborn as a puppet from one moment of performance to the next. While illusionists hope to produce an unbroken series of such moments so that the puppet seems always alive, primitives aim always for a series in which the illusion of being is consciously fragmented by the intrusion of awareness into the structural mechanics of animation, the real nature of the objects employed and the real time of theatrical activity. In the *pure* puppet performance, focus oscillates between the real time and nature of the puppet as an object, and the illusory time and nature of the puppet as a character sign. The puppet seems to *come* alive without pretending to *be* alive, with an effect closer to magic than technology.

Primitivism in puppetry has found its greatest potential for realization in the theatre of objects, with its tendency to foreground the human performer. The puppet itself is demystified (objectified) sometimes to the extent that it functions chiefly as an accessory or appendage to the performer – not a prop exactly, but an object whose potential for signification is just minimally transformed by use or context. In the theatre of objects puppetness is only ever a concept or a possibility. (But the object is a virtual puppet before it is anything else, which is why the theatre of objects is still puppet theatre). [...]

Primitivism has also discovered affinities with the cinema. But while illusionists continue to use the cinema as a realistic, representational medium, primitives exploit it as a presentational model for its inherently stylized, nonrealistic compositional structure based on montage and synchronization.

The overall synchronization of discrete elements (image, movement, sound) is a distinct aspect of puppet theatre in general; even traditional puppetry is close to cinema practice in this regard. But in the cinema of the late 1920s, with the addition of sound to moving images, synchronization, (the temporal equivalent of collage) was considered a novel, even surreal perceptual experience by audiences accustomed to the naturalistic theatre. Now synchronization triggers normative responses. While the cinema dictates current conventions of representational realism, the naturalistic theatre is considered less realistic (because less illusionistic) than cinema or television.

Logically this should mean that puppet theatre, where synchronization has always been the norm, would be more widely accepted and used as a vehicle for realism. In fact that's what is happening in the conjunction of illusionistic puppetry with the cinema. But the normalization of synchronization also accounts for the readiness of audiences to enter into relatively obscure primitivist puppet shows, with their tendency towards free association and apocalyptic imagery. The theatre of objects would be unthinkable in a world that had not already known the influence of cinema and television.

Conclusion? Two futures or one: primitive illusionaries singing the body electric; illusionary primitives speaking in tongues.
(see Kominz and Levenson, 1990: 37–42)

* * *

Brunella Eruli holds an honoured place in the contemporary development of puppetry both for her own writings and for her recognition of the need for academic analysis by semioticians and other commentators on the art form. She has edited one of its most valuable periodicals, *PUCK, la marionnette et les autres arts (PUCK, the puppet and the other arts)* since 1988. She is a Professor in the University of Siena.

6.5   THE USE OF PUPPETRY AND THE THEATRE OF OBJECTS IN THE
PERFORMING ARTS OF TODAY
Brunella Eruli

It seems that for some time the contemporary scene has been haunted by a ghost, the ghost of the puppet, which appears in different guises in pieces with quite diverse aesthetic values. This demonstrates the broad range of possible applications of a theatrical form that until now we were overly inclined to view as entrenched in its own tradition, or suitable only for the performance of an unvarying repertoire designed for children.

The avant garde movements of the twentieth century looked closely at the puppet. It had its moments of glory when Gordon Craig, the Futurists, Oskar Schlemmer and Meyerhold elevated its expressive potential. Later, it was eclipsed for some time. Its traditional image seemed incompatible with experimental theatre and its new face was not recognised in the installations of the visual artists and in their experiments with materials. However, in the theatre, the forms in Bread and Puppet, Kantor's manikins, and the actors of Foreman or Wilson all bear witness to a change that was taking place in the mind-set of creators.

Slowly but surely, the puppet was re-forging the links that had always tied it to other theatrical forms, and the ideas and efforts of creators at the very heart of puppet theatre led to the decompartmentalisation of the genre.

According to some, these experiments threatened to wrench the puppet away from its tradition, and therefore from its roots and soul. I believe that what actually happened was more or less the opposite.

A new generation of directors free of the old prejudices, such as Braunschweig, Roy Faudree, Lepage and Barberio Corsetti, along with writers such as Ceronetti, Kermann and Lemahieu and choreographers such as Maguy Marin, Decouflé, Jan Fabre and Josef Nadj, looked at the puppet and saw a vehicle for strong ideas and original perspectives on issues pervading contemporary theatre: the body, substance, voice, image, words, text.

The Argentinian company 'Periférico de Objetos' places the actor-puppeteers alongside dolls and filmed images, while the faerie universe of Julie Taymor and the Brazilians in 'XPTO' show that the puppet has stamped its mark on contemporary creation. The internationally successful 'Figurentheater' of Frank Soehnle (Germany) and the Handspring Puppet Company with William Kentridge (South Africa) mix different visual languages.

If modern puppet theatre is difficult to place in relation to its traditional image, then object theatre poses even knottier problems, first and foremost in terms of its relation to puppet theatre, with which it is associated. How can one define object theatre? Indeed, how can one define an object – in relation to whom or what should it be examined? At stake in these questions is a theatrical form in which the traditional roles of subject and object are reversed: the object is no longer a theatre accessory or a form expressing a plastic or aesthetic concept: instead it is the starting point for the question 'who is speaking and what are they speaking about?' In Alice in Wonderland, when Alice asks whether you can 'make words mean so many different things' Humpty Dumpty replies that the question is 'which is to be the master?' In this form of theatre, the object speaks its own language and shows that the subject's desire to be or conviction that it is at the centre of the piece (in Beckett's *Fin de Partie*, Ham is always asking if he is in the middle) is subject to the same restrictions as the objects. The discovery of a condition common to both subject and object removes the distinctions between verbal and visual language.

According to neurologists, words and images are dealt with by different sides of the brain, and words are incapable of containing or reproducing an unstable and contradictory reality, whereas images can synthesise its heterogeneous components.

Object theatre, in separating the form from the utilitarian function that has been assigned to the object by realist convention, recaptures the surrealist aesthetics behind collage and the unexpected or playful misappropriation of the object. The plastic element plays an important role in the dialogue that object or puppet theatre has initiated with other artistic forms. Peter Brook, Kantor and Wilson are proposing a 'plastic' theatre that acknowledges the poetry of the object or puppet while using video and images projected onto the stage, to remove the distinction between reality and simulacrum, reducing still further the distance between actor and puppet or object. This makes it difficult to distinguish between the genres, but that is in no way a bad thing. Puppet theatre, object theatre and also human theatre converge in the search for a language that goes beyond representational discourse and makes way for a metaphorical and emotional voice. It is perhaps no coincidence that Tristan Tzara said a cup could resemble a feeling.

Why do modern theatre directors show an interest in puppets? The presence of actors made of wood or light alongside actors made of flesh and bone provokes a deep questioning of the role of the actor.

Kleist's *Traité de Mannequins (On the Marionette Theatre)*, which fascinated Schulz and Kantor and is coming back into fashion, leads to a different perception of theatre, which becomes the place where the viewer gives substance to signs that are open to any interpretation.

Craig, Kantor and Foreman were quick to place puppet theatre alongside darkness and death. Removing the distinctions between truth and fiction, the real and the virtual, the human and the inanimate, they glimpsed the nebulous spaces where the puppet draws its energy.

The levelling of the traditional codes of puppetry has resulted in contemporary creators understanding all that the terse idiom of puppet gestures – that body that barely touches the ground, that theatrical object floating in a space where interior and exterior tend to merge together – could offer in terms of fertile ideas for the development of the contemporary actor. The gap between gestures and words is no longer considered the sign of a poor actor but now acts as an invitation to explore the shadows that exist at the heart of objects.

Using a language that is essentially visual and plastic, similar to that of the puppet, image theatre has identified the common elements of an expressive idiom the strength of which is to be found in a new way of exploiting the actor. The actor is no longer placed on the stage to confirm the existence of a reality and an identity that are stable from a material or physical point of view. The continuity implied by the representation of a character is removed by the presence of bodies that evolve on stage, oblivious to their own mysteriousness. These bodies are blind creatures inhabiting an unstable equilibrium, bodies in constant transformation, as seen in contemporary dance, expressing themselves through stylised gestures. These gestures, of which Wilson is fond, are sometimes carried out in slow motion, and at other times are repeated compulsively, demonstrating a complete irreconcilability with real life.

Whether the modern actor is a 'prepared object' as Kantor would have it; or a monster in a damaged body, the metaphorical incarnation of worldly imbalance, as portrayed by director Romeo Castellucci in the *Giulio Cesare* of Societas Raffaello Sanzio; or indeed one of Novarina's word-mills; whether he is a dancing body or the vehicle for naked text, the actor, like the puppet, is no more than a random presence, moving amongst impenetrable images. The actor's body, like that of the puppet, becomes the link in an imaginary chain, a monument erected on the stage, which acts as his plinth.

Even nudity does not make the body more true or real (like the naked body of the stranger in The Lady from the Sea by Ibsen, directed by Wilson, a body sculpted by light, transformed into an image without depth).

Unstable bodies, residing in a precarious equilibrium; repeated gestures in contemporary dance, challenging the body with imbalance; fragmented bodies projected onto a screen; or clones of reality captured on screens showing a different reality, parallel to the one we know: all of this indicates a partial presence, fragmented in time and space. The audience of Lee Breuer or Roy Faudree, Barberio Corsetti or Lepage, subject the image to the threat of the reality of the body. The actor is both present and absent from the stage since, just like a puppet, he becomes a presence that is distanced by its own image or Voice, which transfigures him. As long as the actor or dancer is touching the ground, he is not really in danger. While bodies distort themselves and cease to obey the logic of so-called 'natural' forms, the voice also takes root in mysterious territories and starts to speak another language, unknown but not foreign, which one can understand without knowing. After centuries of viewing the puppet condescendingly, as an incomplete actor, incapable of speech, the human actor has finally understood the importance of voice distortion, of being able to speak a text in the language of the birds or the gods, a text in which the voice constructs the images that are hidden in the shadow of the words.

Transformed into a screen, a receptor for the various projections that cross his surface, the actor has abandoned the rhythm of theatrical speech. He has learnt to utter silence, to find distorted sounds, he makes use of recordings of his voice and thus becomes that bit closer to a puppet, the mute actor whose voice always comes from another part of the stage, with an essence that springs from a different body and a different substance. Carmelo Bene's main contribution to contemporary theatre was his use of recorded voices, doctored voices and voices that mingle with the noises and even with the incidental sounds that are made on stage. It is surely no coincidence that he always showed a keen interest in the world of puppetry. Bene transformed the voice, bringing to it many layers of disparate and intermittent acoustic and emotional realities, creating a space that could not be controlled, belonging neither to the actor nor the character, but where the word could be conveyed.

This shift in the use of the actor's voice and body has introduced a new relationship with the next, which, as in Kantor's productions, becomes one element among others, or, as in Wilson's productions, an underlying text, conveyed by silence, gesture and image, as in puppet theatre. However, the reinvented voice of the contemporary scene seeks also to convey the original concept of the text, as part of performances that are concerts for voice and words.

The convergence of puppets and actors shows that theatre has embarked upon an arduous path towards *terra incognita* where the answers can be found for the fundamental questions it poses. The actor has set off with a stowaway on board, the secret companion that Conrad speaks of, a vehicle for his hidden self, and therefore that which is most necessary to his life: the puppet.

(see Waszkiel, Francis et al, 2000: 10–16)

FURTHER READING

Bell, John (ed.) (2000) *Puppets, Masks and Performing Objects,* Cambridge, MA: MIT Press.

Fisler, Ben (2002) 'Exposing Intercultural Gestation: A Study of the Engineering of non-Western Puppet, Mask, and Costume Traditions in The Lion King', in James Fisher (ed.), *The Puppetry Yearbook Vol. 5,* Lewiston, NY: Edwin Mellen Press, 33–61.

Green, T.A. and Pepicello, W.J. (1983) 'Semiotic Interrelationships in the Puppet Play' *Semiotica,* 47, 1/4.

Jurkowski, Henryk (1988) *Aspects of Puppet Theatre,* London: Puppet Centre Trust.

Kominz, L. and Levenson, M. (eds) (1990) *The Language of the Puppet,* USA: Tears of Joy Theatre.

Kott, Jan (1984) *The Theatre of Essence,* Evanston, IL: Northwestern University Press.

Meschke, Michael (1992) *In Search of Aesthetics for the Puppet Theatre.* New Delhi, India: Indira Gandhi National Centre for the Arts.

Tribble, Keith (ed.) (2002) *Marionette Theater of the Symbolist Era,* Lewiston, NY: Edwin Mellen Press.

Chapter 7

History

This book offers only a brief outline account of puppetry's history, and that with the accent on western developments, except where eastern techniques have impinged on those developments.[1] As the Russian researcher Boris Goldowski sensibly observes,

> The history of the puppet theatre is not a subject isolated from other phenomena. It is but one of the sections of the general history of theatre. It can neither be understood nor learnt without the knowledge of the history of the theatre arts. And vice versa, the general history of theatre is not complete and not objective without due reference to the course of history of the playing puppets. (Goldowski, 1994: 110)

The idea of the animated form can best be comprehended through the concept of animism, the sense of latent life in every thing, bringing with it the instinctive desire to instil breath and initiate motion in the inert form. Harold Segel considers that there is more to it than that:

> The fascination with puppets [...] reaches so far back into human history that it must be regarded as a response to a fundamental need or needs. It is, clearly, a projection of the obsession of human beings with their own image, with their own likeness, the obsession that underlies artistic portraiture, the building of statues, and the extraordinary and enduring popularity of photography. More profoundly, it reveals a yearning to play god, to master life. By constructing replicas of human beings whose movements they can exert complete power over, artists play at being gods instead of being merely playthings of the gods. (Segel, 1995: 4)

Research and archaeology have uncovered proof of the existence of articulated figures of animistic practices among aboriginal peoples and early developed civilizations all over the globe, including the Inuit, Indians and American Indians, Mexicans, the ancient Greeks, Persians, peoples of what is now Europe, Scandinavians, Africans, Asians and so on. The evidence underlines another of the primitive human's deepest compulsions – to bow

---

[1] Researchers will find many excellent works on the subject in the further reading list at the end of the chapter and in the bibliography. There are others which interweave the story with, say, treatises on religious practice and anthropology.

down to the spirit, *anima*, perceived in all of nature's manifested forms and humours. In ancient times the compulsion evolved into a wish to reproduce or symbolize these forms in depictions and crafted effigies.[2]

Where faith in the supernatural has not evaporated, in communities barely touched by secularism and consumerism, old beliefs in the power of the animated figure persist. In many cultures the puppet was and is thought to be a repository for a spirit, good or evil, seeking a home. Another belief which persists to this day is the association of the puppet with death. Instinctively, the first sight of a beloved's corpse brings with it the passionate desire to re-animate, to resurrect the lost person. In her book about the Awaji puppet theatre of Japan, Jane Marie Law says:

> Perhaps one of the most compelling reasons why puppet theater is so appealing is the human need to see and participate in the reversal of death. What is death but the transformation of the animate into the inanimate? In puppetry, this direction is reversed. (Law, 1997: 27)

A common *memento mori* is the display of an effigy of the deceased – a figurine, a photo – which may take part in funeral rites and may even be animated. There are places where the stiffening cadaver itself is used to prolong the physical and psychic proximity of the beloved:

> The need to propitiate the dead immediately after death has survived to the present and takes different forms. Even in Europe some rites involved the puppet, at least until the nineteenth century. On a small Catalonian port there were fishermen known to be passionate cardplayers. When one died the others replaced his body on the death bed with one of themselves and took the corpse to the inn for its final card party, animating it as though it were a puppet. (Jurkowski, 1996: 27)

PRE-THEATRE

On every continent much of puppetry is still associated with magic and the spiritual rather than the theatrical. The heads of the puppet figures of Japan and Indonesia are removed when the characters are at rest, to ensure that their 'life' is also removed and that no evil spirit may enter. Native American Indians like the Kwakiutl of the Pacific northwest and the Hopis of Arizona and New Mexico hold secret ceremonies, usually fertility rites, in which puppets feature strongly. The Hopi culture still survives, although the ceremonies are secret. The following, however, reads like an eye-witness account, provided by the American researcher Michael Malkin in *Traditional and Folk Puppets of the World*:

---

[2] See the Appendix to this chapter wherein I spin a tall tale of the imagined origins of puppetry in the first human societies.

Among the most spectacular of these was their ceremony of the Great Plumed Snake.

As the members of the Hopi tribe entered the ceremonial area, their eyes gradually adjusted to the dim and flickering light of a small fire. They could see a number of miniature cornstalks set in clay bases and placed about five or six feet in front of a brightly coloured cloth that was hung across one end of the ceremonial lodge or *kiva*. Suddenly, a masked dancer appeared in front of the cloth. Musicians hidden behind the backdrop accompanied his dance with drums, songs, and special wind instruments made from dried gourds. Just as the dancer retired behind the cloth, six large snake figures slithered into view, undulating through special holes in the backdrop. The puppet snakes moved in time to the chanting of the hidden singers and to the eerie howling and moaning of the gourds. Their hawk-feathered crests quivering they rose off the ground and stretched up and out toward the spectators. They hovered above the cornstalks, twisting and turning in a hypnotic aerial ballet, their sinewy five- or six-foot-long bodies weaving strange patterns in the air. Without warning the snakes swooped earthward and dashed the cornstalks to the ground. At this signal, the tempo of the music grew more rapid and the howling of the gourds grew louder. The *kiva* vibrated with the prayers and exultations of the worshippers as they shouted, prayed and threw offerings of cornmeal at the snakes. Slowly the frenzy subsided, and the ritually appeased snakes retreated until only their heads showed in front of the backcloth. Bulging eyes glowing in the firelight, the snakes were withdrawn as the next part of the ceremony began. (Malkin, 1943: 161–62)

Also by Malkin is this extended caption to the photograph of a pre-Columbian ceramic figure on a UNIMA[3] calendar of 1983:

The shamans and tribal elders of several Native American peoples were keenly aware of the ritual force and startlingly transformational power of puppetry. As law-makers and religious leaders they used puppets to impress, shock and mystify uninitiated participants in tribal ceremonies. Whether or not even the most devout spectators ever believed that the puppet animals, gods and demons were real, all were undoubtedly awed by their dazzling and splendid artificiality.

The earliest puppet-like figures in North America date from between 300 and 600 A.D. Some handmodelled and some clay statues with articulated limbs created by pre-Columbian Indian cultures in what is now Mexico have been preserved in a number of museum and private collections. The Teotihuacan culture of the central plateau region, the Central Veracruz culture of the Gulf coast and the Mayan culture of southern Mexico and Guatemala all produced articulated figures. Extant pieces, all of which are carefully designed and elaborately decorated, are of hollow clay and vary in height from approximately three inches to just over 24 inches. (Malkin, 1983)

---

[3] Union Internationale de la Marionnette, founded in 1927, is the oldest international theatre organization. Its headquarters are in France. See www.unima.org.

A snapshot of Asian pre-history, asserting the puppet's place in the earliest days of theatre, is given by the American historian Melvyn Helstien in the booklet of the Puppetry of India exhibition staged in Atlanta by the Center for Puppetry Arts in 1986:

> The history of Indian puppetry is obscured in antiquity. Scholars of classical Sanskrit have averred the puppet theatre of India to be at least four thousand years old based on ancient texts. Both Panini, the fourth century B.C. Sanskrit grammarian, and Patanjali, in the second century B.C. refer to puppets in their works. Material or oral manifestations are ephemeral, although first century A.D. poets in Bengal and Tamil Nadu states refer to puppets. ... Later scholarship has found fragments of data; references to puppeteers employed as spies; epigraphic references of lands gifted to performers; literary analogues; 'chayanataka' classical Sanskrit shadow plays such as *Dutangada*; stage directions for puppets and puppeteers in other theatre pieces (*Balaramayana* of the poet-playwright Rajacekhara): a Buddhist religious work, the *Therigatha*; to suggest they were known in India for at least two thousand years. (Helstien, 1986: 4)

In the 'classical' period of the Egyptian, Greek and Roman empires documentary allusions to the presence of giant hieratic moving figures and secular puppet shows testify to the presence of performative images in both high and low culture. These images include automata driven both by mechanisms and by human agency, and historians are almost certain that the same mixture of operating techniques was applied to many of the puppets (known in Greece as *neurospasta*, a word suggesting 'jumpy' figures, moved by threads or thongs). The references presume a familiar, if background, presence of puppetry, both as a popular itinerant entertainment and in a ritual context. The religious figures are rarely mentioned in the extant documentation, although, according to Jurkowski, the natural home of the puppets was in the hands of priests. The evolution of the puppet from moving idol to a character in a performance was one that lasted centuries.

> In the beginning the function of the puppet's ancestors had nothing in common with its future theatrical function. We may even be obliged to call these ancestors by other names more fitting to their social and religious applications: idol, fetish, talisman, magic doll, child's toy. ...
>
> At first these idols were clumsy and roughly shaped; we can see them still in anthropological museums, more often in stone than in wood. Later they became more elaborate as the skill of primitive artists grew until they became ritualistic statues [...] trapped in their immobile form. This imperfection does not simply reside in the view of a modern puppeteer but also in the view of contemporary practitioners of religion and magic. They believed that motion would increase the spectacular potential of these figures which would thus become more than a passive icon of divinity and assume a greater spiritual power in possession of a mysterious life.
>
> Throughout the following period the cult figure was transformed into the ritual puppet, that is to say a three-dimensional mobile icon representing a god, a

human, sometimes an animal, to be employed in rites, religious ceremonies and acts of magic ... all the stages of this idol's change from fetish to hieratic sculpture [...] opened the way to its animation and manipulation and thence to its metamorphosis into puppet. (Jurkowski, 1996: 20–21)

THE EARLY PUPPET 'SHOW'

To the great amphitheatre of Dionysus (Athens) came the first puppet showman to be named in the records: Potheinos. From the accounts of his performance (in the third century AD) the puppets were worked probably from above by a screened operator, while Potheinos, apparently a master showman, commented on the antics of the figures. The puppets played in some sort of booth on the spot where the altar or *thymele* of the great auditorium had been. This was in an era of decadence, but many were shocked that the theatre of Sophocles and Aeschylus was 'reduced' to this. Potheinos drew crowds and according to Athenaeus he was showered with gifts. The content of his shows was comic, perhaps satiric, but there would have been an element of low humour, in imitation of the farces known as the *Phlyakes*.

Even in the first years of the Christian era, and perhaps well before that, stock characters in the Phlyax comedies came with the Greeks into Byzantium and southern Italy via Sicily (known as Magna Graecia from the eighth to the seventh centuries BC). Judging from these characters who seem to merge naturally into those of the (Roman) Atellan farces it seems reasonable to suppose, as most scholars do, that the farces survived underground in the so-called Dark Ages, thanks partly to the play of glove puppets in the hands of the itinerant players, to emerge eventually as the resident stock characters of the commedia dell'arte, most of them little changed. Bil Baird takes the story forward:

> When great Rome toppled under the assaults of the barbarians, the humble art of puppetry dropped from sight. For some several hundred years there is no documentary evidence of any sort – official records, literary references, pictures – to give even the slightest hint of its fate.
>
> We know nothing of the invading Goths' and Vandals' tastes for puppetry, but its remaining Roman patrons were either too poor to afford the entertainment or too disorganized to write about it. To the emerging, once underground, Christian church any kind of show or idolatrous image was abhorrent. Too many of the faithful had been butchered as props and actors in the theatricality of the Roman circus.
>
> Under the circumstances the puppeteers probably lived by their wits. The individual artist does not stop the vibrating process of creation when the big show closes. We can be sure he was part of the restless movement of people traveling over the rude highways of Europe in that tumultuous age, finding an audience wherever he could in the streets and taverns along the way.
>
> It was not until the 7th and 9th centuries that we hear of puppetry again. By that time it had been put to the service of the steadily growing Christian religion.

It was not until the end of the 7th century that Jesus was represented as a man. Until then, he had been referred to and represented as the Lamb of God. Moving statuary was introduced into the churches – holy images rolled their eyes, nodded, and even bled, with the pull of a wire. Still later puppets appear to have performed in pantomimes while someone standing in front of the stage or booth recited a Bible story. The practice must have been effective and must have spread in the face of its detractors. But by the end of the 11th century an abbot of Cluny was denouncing puppets as smacking of idolatry, and by the 13th century even the Pope was inveighing against them – but apparently without success. By that time puppets had slipped into the educational pattern of the church.

While this kind of theatre was gaining a foothold in the church, we can be sure that the tribe of wandering showmen scattered over Europe was still busily engaged. Around the hearth in great halls and lowly taverns mountebanks, jugglers and mimes varied their turns with puppets.

These were undoubtedly hand puppets, since they are easy to carry and in no way as bulky as the heavy marionettes of Rome. (Baird, 1965: 64–66)

Victoria Nelson follows the same path 'after the end of the ancient West', regretting the absence of any historical documentation between the years 400 and 1200, but believing nevertheless that the popular comedic shows by travelling players in the 'low' tradition of puppets undoubtedly existed (Nelson, 2001: 48–49).

The wandering puppeteer burdened with his animals and often his family, cannot have had an easy time. The Christian Church of the western empire distrusted all popular entertainment concerned with the crafting of effigies whereas eastern Byzantium permitted the display of simulacra such as puppets, which were kept alive after the fall of the Roman Empire. In the west the 'barbarian' invaders and the iconoclastic regions of Christendom suppressed the entertainers, sometimes meting out cruel punishments.

Traditionally the itinerant players carried their booth, a glove puppet staging light enough to carry but strong enough to withstand the elements, made to be smartly packed up and transported away from snooping authority. Although gloves were the most convenient type of puppet for these showmen, the rod marionette (see Chapter 3 on Techniques), from the evidence of burial artefacts, was also known from antiquity through the middle ages. The shows were based on local folk traditions, naïve and distorted Bible stories, parodies of high life and the kind of crude libidinous humour that is threaded through the history of puppetry internationally (see 'Eroticism and Puppetry' in Jurkowski's *Aspects of Puppetry*, 1988).

THE MIDDLE AGES

Jointed dolls that could only have been operated from above by strings or rods certainly performed in classical times, and the prevalence of the fighting puppet leads one to believe that the combative qualities of the solidly-built, jointed wooden marionette would surely have been employed in Greek-influenced Byzantium. One such expertly carved and jointed marionette dates from the second century AD and can be found in the Antiquarium Comunale of Rome. Similar to this type were the tall, solid figures now known as *pupi*, like those still performing in Sicily and in Belgium. It is probable that even in ancient times they would have acted out topical stories of the glory of their emperor Charlemagne, and the triumphs of the wars and Crusades of Christians against Saracens.

Many writers believe that the *opera dei pupi* originated in Spain, others that they were imported from Italy and that they made their appearance in France and the Low Countries only in the early nineteenth century, as all the documentary evidence attests. However, given the extreme conservatism of the puppet show, the similarity of the marionettes of Belgium and those of Sicily, both acting out many of the same stories in praise of the monarch, it does not seem too far-fetched to imagine that these shows were played in the period of Charlemagne himself, whose court in Aachen was located on the borders of today's Germany, Holland and France, and whose conquests extended to Spain where he fought the Moorish invaders known as 'Saracens' in the time of the Crusades.

Under Charlemagne's rule as Holy Roman Emperor (from 800 AD), puppets were tolerated, mainly to illustrate sacred and morality plays in the churches. The status of the puppet showman must have moved up a step or two from his place at the bottom of the hierarchy of minstrels and players, as they were occasionally invited into courts and mansion halls and other respectable entertainment sites, without too much fear of the law, although there was always the question of obtaining permits and licences.

George V. Speaight's entertaining and elegant *History of the English Puppet Theatre* sheds a little more light on the European scene of the early medieval period:

> The traditions of the mimes with their mimicry and circus tricks, were gradually absorbed into that of the bard, with his staider recitations of epic poems, and by the beginning of the tenth century we begin to see the emergence of the great army of minstrels, gleemen, jongleurs, and trobadors [sic] who flocked to every court in Europe and followed in the retinue of every baron, with their old ballads and new love songs, their tricks and – sometimes – their puppets.
>
> Not all the minstrels followed the Court: there were some, we are told, who hung around taverns and village greens, strumming at some instrument, singing coarse songs, imitating birds' cries, and showing off the tricks of learned dogs. Such a one must have been the Perrinet Sanson, whose name a chance reference has preserved for us, who gathered his audience in a French village with a drum and trumpet to see the performance of his company – his wife and children, a bear, a horse, a nanny-goat and his puppets ['bastaxi']. This was comparatively late, in 1408, but for centuries before such little bands of human and animal entertainers must have wandered across Europe, carrying, sometimes, puppet shows with them.

Figure 7.1   A cabinet theatre, in this case a traditional Vertep from the Ukraine, still to be found playing in the 1990s.

© Penny Francis.

> Although the puppets seem for the most part to have been confined to the more lowly and popular minstrels, there were times when they too were seen in the houses of the great. (Speaight, 1990: 28–29)

The still familiar combative glove puppet in a booth, holding cudgel, stick or other weapon (a frying pan in the case of the Hungarian Vitéz László) is illustrated clearly in the fourteenth century illuminated text, *Li Romans d'Alixandre,* now in the Bodleian Library in Oxford. It contains two pictures of glove puppets in their respective booths whose playing space or playboard recalls the walls of a castle with a tower either side. The entertainment is watched in the first picture by an all-male group and in the other by a trio of elegantly clad women.[4] One puppet, a proto-Punch, holds some sort of club over his shoulder. These booths and puppets would not look out of place in a modern fairground.

From the thirteenth century many showmen carried a kind of box or cabinet booth with folding doors and tiered compartments. They were filled with scenes from religious, mythic, satirical and humorous tales, played by small carved figures that could be moved from behind by strings and levers operated by the narrator or showman. They are said to be adaptations of the high-relief folding altarpiece, the diptych and triptych, of the Christian churches whose carved hieratic figures, full of life and character, seemed to invite animation. Some of these were removed or copied and sent out into the countryside as a missionary exercise that often became a secular and even ribald entertainment.

> The tendency to visualise the episodes of the Christian stories in religious teaching led directly to the creation of a liturgical theatre which at first gave satisfaction to the church, since it served as an element to attract the faithful to the

---

[4] The original Flemish illuminated miniatures are by Jehan de Grise and are in the Bodleian Library, Oxford, England, dated 1344.

services. Later however the impulse to portray holy events brought enhancements in the form of theatrical effects, secular motifs and, inevitably, laughter. The shows became a cause for distress to the bishops who now hesitated between retaining the performances as an effective attraction, or condemning them as something blasphemous that should be forbidden. Finally they found a solution: they banned theatre from the church interior and permitted it to find its own way outside, first into the churchyard, then out to the marketplace, where it was transformed into the mystery play, placed in the care of the craft guilds and local authorities.

This new kind of theatre was so extremely popular and manifested itself so strongly that the Church, from the sixteenth century onwards (the time varying according to the local situation) eventually decided to forbid all religious performances, feeling that their theatricality went beyond the Church's control and thus did not serve its teaching.

[...] Puppets almost certainly assisted at the creation of mystery plays, although little documentation is now to be found. We know most about the exhibition of small crib figures in nativity worship, a custom started by St. Francis in 1223 which spread quickly all over Europe. It was a strong attraction for church visitors, and for some clerics the animation of the figures was a natural progression. (Jurkowski, 1996: 66–67)

The cabinet theatres were first reported in Spain (possibly brought there by showmen from Italian lands) whence they spread across Europe and have left their imprint in the eastern countries where the Belorus *batleyka*, the Ukrainian *vertep*, and the Polish *szopka* can still be found. I have enjoyed a *vertep* given in a decorated cabinet theatre from the Ukraine, playing a lively mixture of Biblical tales and parodies of everyday local life. Of the same provenance, the English 'raree' show, probably named after the church 'reredos', also employed animated figures in a box, and seems to have been the original of the 'peepshow'.

PUPPETS IN COMMEDIA DELL'ARTE

After the fall of Byzantium in 1453, the diaspora of Christian refugees to the west included artists and entertainers of all types. To give themselves status and proper remuneration and to distinguish themselves from the western itinerants (whose money was collected *ad hoc* depending on the generosity of their audience) many formed groups, calling themselves 'professional' players, the originators of the later *commedia dell'arte*. Their shows proved popular and by degrees Europe was peppered with these companies of highly skilled performers formed from the mimes, the jongleurs and the puppet players themselves. The repertory consisted mainly of secular stories which were gaining ground from the religious repertoire. The stories were variations on the farcical, romantic and/or physical antics of a number of stock characters, all stereotypes, of whom there is a long list, hardly varying from region to region except in name. Each character had a human and a puppet form.

An impressive body of evidence tells us that puppets were integral to the performances of *commedia*: many troupes are reported in words or contemporary illustrations to have carried sets of glove figures as an alternative and even a supplementary cast, to be presented when circumstances – the weather, the licensing laws, the content of the stories, the place of performance – made it difficult for the human actors. *Commedia* suited puppets well: the uncomplicated characterization, the minimal use of words, the comic business *(lazzi)* and the trickery of the *zanni* were and are ideal for puppet play. Jurkowski thinks that

> It is difficult to determine the true relationships between the actors and the puppets. What was the principle of their common presence? Were they inter-acting or was the puppet action only a decorative background for the more important performance by the actors? A reference from seventeenth century Poland offers another aspect of the possible relationship: some Italian comedians presented their show on the occasion of a session of the Polish Diet in Warsaw. A note, dated March 14, 1666 says: *Some Italians played a comedy in a particular room of the Castle. Here Pantalone intended to marry his daughter to the son of a rich Doctor, but the Doctor was mean.*

Figure 7.2   Punch draws crowds to Brighton Pier, 2008. The 'Professor' is Glyn Edwards.

© Mary Edwards.

The Son did not please Pantalone's Daughter and the Lawyer wanted to make him repugnant to her so when the Young Lady became ill, he offered Pantalone a medical man, who was his servant disguised ... The report continues on the next day, March 15th: *The Italians were expected to show marionettes in the chamber of his Majesty the King, but they quarrelled and never came to any agreement.* It was a pity the Italians did not play that day: we might now have a good description of their show; but at least we know that the same Italian company had the means to present both live and puppet performances. (Jurkowski 1996: 104–05)

The puppets traced much the same path as the live comedians, if more inclined to satire and parody, and with certain comic characters relied upon for action that was often vulgar and licentious. These were the zanni, and drawings of them reveal the exaggerated physical features we recognize in Punch and his cousins. At least three of them, Cucurucu, Captain Mala Gamba and Brighella, are depicted with humped back, protruding belly, hooked nose and/or exaggerated phallus, all of which were incorporated later into the puppet Punch, although middle class morality has hidden the phallus (though not everywhere) and replaced it, it is said, with the cudgel, the slapstick and all the other weapons of bastinado. Punch is descended from Pulcinella,[5] who appeared late in the lists of regular commedia zanni, having a curvaceous silhouette and a squawking voice like a chicken. Unlike Punch he was dressed in ruff, peaked cap, full belly and white tunic with a black mask over his upper face. The Dutch historian Hetty Paërl writes:

Pulcinella is one of the most intriguing masks of European culture. He enjoys a great reputation as a character of the Commedia dell'Arte, in which he plays the part of a comic servant.

[In] around 1600, Pulcinella appeared for the first time on the stage of a regular company of comedians, but even before that time he was already to be seen among the buffoons in the shows of the public squares [...] As a puppet Pulcinella [...] became the public's favourite, above all the other characters of the Commedia dell'Arte which had found a place in the puppet theatre. Like the comedians, Italian puppeteers travelled all over Europe, and even in foreign countries audiences highly valued Pulcinella. He was readily assimilated in many cultures and adopted a number of the traits of the local farcical figures already in residence.

Ultimately fourteen European countries have developed 'descendants' of Pulcinella. Amongst them are such well-known characters as the French Polichinelle, the Dutch Jan Klaassen, the English Punch and the Romanian Vasilache. The repertory of Pulcinella's descendants corresponds in broad outline with that of Pulcinella himself: the protagonist fights with the beast (a monstrous dog or crocodile), he has to combat Death, [and] he is confronted with the hangman and the gallows.

[...] But who is Pulcinella?

According to legend his original was a man who really existed.

---

[5] See the reading list at the end of the chapter, in particular Allardyce Nicoll and the specialist studies by G.V. Speaight, Robert Leach and Michael Byrom.

He was born in Acerra, a village of wine-farmers in the XVIth century. With his long nose and sunburned face he was grotesque in appearance, but also witty and astute. His comical talents were observed by the comedians, who took him to Naples and admitted him to their company.

Pulcinella became the mask of 'the Neapolitan', meaning a man who wishes to enjoy life, who wants to fill his ever-hungry stomach with pasta and wine, who wants to make music, to dance and make love.

But Pulcinella is more than that: he has a number of strange peculiarities, whose meaning is a matter of speculation. His mask has a nose in the shape of a beak and beady eyes like a bird. Performing in the booth his voice resembles the squawking of a cockerel, and for that purpose the puppeteer uses the *pivetta* or swazzle in his mouth.

The name Pulcinella means cockerel. There are pictures that represent the birth of Pulcinella out of an egg. When the Pulcinellini, his children, hatch they are identical to their father, with the black half-mask and the white vest, trousers and conical cap. Sometimes they even have his hunchback.

Pulcinella has human as well as gallinaceous characteristics. In addition he has a masculine and a feminine aspect. He often appears in multiples of himself. An [eighteenth]-century picture shows a room full of Pulcinelli. One of them – wearing trousers and with the bald head of an old man – brings forth children out of his boss [protuberant stomach]; in another picture Pulcinella bears children out of his posterior. It is clear that he is a hermaphrodite, sometimes uniting the hermaphrodite and the gallinaceous, as in the puppet-show known as 'The Egg'. This belongs only to the repertory of the Pulcinella booth and not to that of his descendants. In this piece Pulcinella makes love to a chicken, after which he kills her then grills her. He quits the stage to get knife and fork whereupon the devil appears. He enunciates a curse: if Pulcinella eats the chicken, something will happen to him that has never yet happened to any man on earth. Pulcinella returns and guzzles the chicken. His belly swells. He is seized with cramps. He calls a doctor, who diagnoses that Pulcinella is pregnant. A midwife helps him with the delivery. He delivers a large egg! He hatches it and there appear, one after the other, five Pulcinellini, all identical to the papa/mamma. The egg is the symbol of rebirth. The killing of the chicken leads to the pregnancy of Pulcinella and to the birth of the Pulcinellini, the idea being that out of death new life will be born. This idea is also to be found in many carnival rituals.

[…] So Pulcinella is a mask full of significance. He and his descendants are tricksters who tell us much about ourselves. (Paërl, 2007)

THE BEGINNING OF RECOGNITION

The first recorded sighting of a Pulcinella show in England is in the diary entry of Samuel Pepys of May, 1662. A showman from some region of Italy, probably Bologna since that was his stage name, was playing in Covent Garden, London, presenting the doings of the amoral Pulcinella (which in the English way with foreign names was found unpronounceable and finally shortened to Punch, having suffered a variety of names like Punchinello, Pollicinella, Policinelli, Puntionella). Pepys found the show 'very pretty', and, indeed, it was commanded to play at the Court of Charles II soon after, where the puppet showman, the said Signor Bologna, was awarded a gold medal and chain.

In the seventeenth and eighteenth centuries Punch became the star of the then successful English puppet stage, as a rod marionette and a glove figure. No play was complete unless he was there to provide the tricks, subvert the authority of his superiors and generally stir up trouble. The slapstick was and is his emblem (the stick being split down its length so that it inflicts minimum damage while making maximum noise); it is an evolution from the cudgel and the other weaponry that this kind of puppet has been pictured with since the thirteenth century at least. In Britain, time has endowed him, as it has most other popular puppet anti-heroes, with the characteristic features of every nation where he has put down roots. Punch's hunchback and belly have remained little changed, but through the years he has lost the white robe of Pulcinella in favour of the colourful motley of the English Jester, and Pulcinella's sly stupidity in favour of the cheerful insouciance of the amoral trickster.

George Speaight insists that in the fashionable marionette plays of London Town he was nothing like the glove puppet we are accustomed to now:

> The eighteenth-century Punch, in fact, was not at all the kind of person that he is usually imagined to have been [...] In fact he was a comedian, not a villain, a henpecked husband not a wife-beater, the receiver of slaps not the dealer of blows, the author of puerile vulgarities not a Don Juan, a naughty and mischievous wag not an insensate [...] assassin. (Speaight, 1990: 170)

By the middle of the eighteenth century the marionette Punch was the biggest draw both for the fairground booths and for the many metropolitan puppet theatres, as Polichinelle was flourishing in the Paris fairgrounds. Their universal attraction, as always, lay in the subversion and the comeuppance inevitably meted out to authority and his social superiors.

PUPPETS AND OPERA

The fashion in Italian artistic centres for ballet and opera (*dramma per musica*) gave puppetry its next significant step upward, in terms of its social status as a performing art with an aesthetic value and a distinct existence. Some fifty years after the beginnings of opera one or two composers turned to puppets – the first in 1668 – to act out and enliven the stories while the human singers and the orchestra remained by the side of, or behind, the stage. The use of puppets suited the baroque stylistic: artificial figures integral to an elaborated scenic space, lending spectacle and movement to an otherwise static concert played and sung by humans.

Opera with puppets became another Europe-wide success initiated by the Italians. This time the spectators were from a higher rung of the social echelon. Elaborate scenery inspired by the designs and perspectives of Sebastiano Serlio (1475–1554) and Nicola Sabbatini (1574–1654) and a variety of staging mechanics and costumed puppets were expensive, so this wave of the puppets' history became the prerogative of kings and bishops, the aristocracy and other rich patrons of the arts. In short, puppets took their place in fashionable society: to own a puppet theatre in one's palace symbolized good taste and wealth; to invite the best travelling professionals to set up their refined entertainment for the pleasure of your courtiers displayed your generous hospitality. The figures were rod marionettes, worked from above the stage by operators (who might be no more than servants of the great house), asked to do little more than move or jig any character(s) whose turn it was to sing. If sometimes the puppet was required to fly or dance or fight, there might be certain mechanisms to set in motion.

The composers and librettists included the likes of Scarlatti, Haydn, Mozart and Gluck. Anton Abbatini wrote the music for what is thought to have been the first puppet opera, *La Comica del Cielo*, (roughly translated: *The Heavenly Player*), with libretto written by a Cardinal, Giulio Rospigliosi (1600–1669) who became Pope Clemente IX. He invited guests to the papal palace in Rome for the opening. The scenery was graced by the illustrious sculptor Giovanni Bernini (1598–1680) who prepared the theatrical 'apparatus', which undoubtedly meant that some of the figures were moved by a system of counterweights. This high degree of patronage assured the success of the genre and the fashion for the puppet opera spread, though inevitably copied in humbler contexts as it became more and more popular.

All the puppet opera styles, *serio, comica* and *buffo*, drew their themes from classical and biblical legends and allegories, miracle plays, classical legends, romantic knightly exploits, and of course parodies of all these. Jurkowski affirms the initial recognition of the puppet opera as a 'refined and honoured genre':

> The new, highly respected operas with mythological themes had all the features of court entertainment, but it was unsurprising that this provoked some alternative versions by less pompous artists and musicians. The result was the creation of more popular forms of opera, opera buffa in Italy and opera comique in France. These presented hilarious topics and situations, not far removed from the folk tradition ... (Jurkowski, 1996: 118)

A fine example was the Portuguese poet Antonio Jose Da Silva, known as *Il Judeo* ('the Jew'). He wrote the libretti for (about) eight comic operas, each an entertaining mix of legend, spectacle, comedy and a strong story line, to be played by puppets for a less exalted audience than the court. His texts are now part of the national canon, but played mainly by actors. Da Silva found a musical collaborator in Antonio Teixeiras and the success of the partnership drew enthusiastic crowds to a well-equipped theatre outside the centre of Lisbon in the Bairro Alto. This, along with the puppets, was destroyed in the great earthquake of 1755. Much of the music has similarly disappeared, but may be in private hands. Although the Da Silva texts survive, only two have so far been translated into English, one of them not yet in print (see Perkins, 2004). Da Silva's work reflected the coming age of Enlightenment: humorous and humanist, it satirized the shibboleths of the age: for these and other reasons he fell foul of the Inquisition and was put to death at the age of 35.

The itinerant puppeteers continued to pitch their booths in the fairs and byways as they always had but by the eighteenth century most had dispensed with performing animals. Some were employed to perform with their puppets to halt the passers-by, aiding the charlatans as enticement into the enclosed booths of the fairs, where they might pay to see various entertainments and services such as freak shows, fortune-telling or even tooth-pulling.

The seventeenth and eighteenth centuries were ones of advancement for puppets in Europe, especially when the English and French authorities imposed a ban on performances by live actors other than those in the approved 'monopolist' houses, such as the two royal theatres of Paris, the Opéra and the Comédie-Française, and in London Drury Lane and Sadler's Wells. During the periods of the ban the puppet plays thrived – too lowly, it appears, to attract the wrath of the authorities, at least at first (Jurkowski, 1996: 134 et seq.). The ban in France lasted for nearly half a century, but the fairground puppets continued to draw audiences of every class. Some puppet proprietors even built large if temporary theatres capable of accommodating a couple of hundred paying spectators, alongside other traditional open-air pitches. In England the monopoly of the royal theatres was reinforced in 1737, when the puppet theatres entered a golden age of success with audiences which even included royalty.

At the end of the eighteenth century another Europe-wide attraction, the *fantoccini*, once more the invention of puppeteers from the Italian peninsular, was adopted and embedded in the repertory of the popular puppet show. The fantoccini were 'trick' marionettes, transformable figures both humorous and surprising. According to John McCormick, a specialist historian of puppetry, the term 'fantoccini' was used to describe 'puppets operated by rods and strings'.

It was initially applied to trick and variety figures but then extended to mean marionettes in general. The stringing of fantoccini was one of the secrets of their success, but this had to be taken in conjunction with the construction and articulation of the figure [...]

When John Holden [one of the most famous of the family marionette proprietors] visited Ghent, people remembered his 'fantoches' (fantoccini) and his 'metamorphoses' or transformation figures. One trick that is found in several repertoires is a box that opens out to become a dragon spewing fire, produced by sparklers placed behind its nostrils [...].Jim Tiller had a similar dragon and remembered a routine where the box began as a box of Yarmouth bloaters [herrings] loaded onto a donkey cart. With the arrival of the devil (and the release of a spring), the box became a dragon. (McCormick, 2004: 141)

The fantoccini had complicated controls that needed a high degree of manipulation skills to effect the changes that each one quite literally 'embodied'. One might be turned upside down to become quite another character, one would grow a whole family – smaller duplicates of herself – out of her hat or within her skirts. There were jugglers and Chinese bell-ringers and acrobats and slack-rope walkers and, most enduring of all, a 'dissecting skeleton' whose dancing limbs magically flew apart and then returned to the torso. Each 'turn' was brief and would be part of a programme of many other items, dramatic, musical and comic. They became the miniature theatre sensation of the age. The fantoccini rarely perform their transformations and tricks with the stiff rod to the head, which may have hastened the use of the fully strung marionette as the norm for most of the newer puppet companies in Europe, although many have perpetuated the rod version, particularly in the Czech Republic.

A GROWTH INDUSTRY

The inevitable social and philosophical reaction to the age of reason and classicism was manifested in the Romantic Movement. For the puppet producers, as for theatre in general, it was a liberation from the confines of the old biblical and hagiographic repertory. The puppet became a repository of subjectivism, invested by the poet-puppeteer with a soul. To an extent it regained its ancient supernatural existence. More mundanely, it became an instrument for the rediscovery of folk culture and a simpler, apparently more natural, way of life. The puppeteers thrived in the new cultural climate and as usual tracked and absorbed most of the changes in the actors' theatre repertory, bringing their own creative interpretations.

A herald of the Romantic attitude to the puppet, demonstrating the imagined attribution of human feeling to the apparently inanimate world of things natural and artificial (it may now be understood as the 'pathetic fallacy'), was an essay written in 1810 by the young but already distinguished German writer Heinrich von Kleist, *Über das Marionettentheater* (*On the Marionette Theatre*). Kleist was one of the first respected artists to apply serious consideration to the aesthetics of what was still thought of as a 'low art'. The essay which begins the chapter on aesthetics is not so much a study of puppetry as a philosophical reflection on the human's loss of innocence, exemplified by the puppet in performance, where its lack of self-consciousness and vanity is postulated as an enviable example of that innocence.

Other writers, including the historian Charles Magnin who produced the first serious history of puppetry, found the subject full of interest. A few socially distinguished producers and artists founded permanent theatres: in France, Lemercier de Neuville (1830–1918), and in Munich, Count Pocci (1807–1876) and 'Papa' Schmid (1822–1912) all gave puppet theatre an artistic and academic *cachet*. The amateur interest of the novelist Georges Sand (1804–1876) and her puppet-mad son Maurice (1823–1889) helped to bring it into the sphere of the educated classes. Maurice Sand researched the techniques and the history of his subject, particularly fascinated by the old *commedia dell'arte* themes and characters. He built a theatre for glove puppets at the family chateau in Nohant and enlisted the aid and contributions of some of the famous writers and musicians who surrounded his mother. She herself became closely involved in the making of the costumes for the figures. Maurice made and operated all the puppets, and produced a number of shows which may be read in published form (Sand, 1860). After the death of his mother he moved his puppets to a new home in Passy.

The role of the puppet continued to be strengthened in middle class and popular entertainment throughout the nineteenth century. Over the same period Harlequin rose to displace Punch in mainstream and puppet theatre, just as the French Arlequin rose to oust Polichinelle (who unlike Punch has never really returned to favour).

Perhaps most remarkable was the emergence of travelling marionette troupes run by generations of families. For a comprehensive account of their development see John McCormick's *Popular Puppet Theatre in Europe, 1800–1914*. His introduction gives a snapshot of the period:

In the early nineteenth century, travelling marionette theatres were an established feature of everyday life in much of Europe, and the main form of theatrical entertainment for many people. Street shows likewise were a key element of urban culture, most notably in Italy, and these provided a type of amusement that cost even less and came to wherever the audiences were. The growth of towns and industry led to a much greater concentration of puppet activity in certain areas, especially in the period between 1860 and the First World War. In Brussels in the 1890s a score of theatres mostly seating under a hundred people, were entertaining some 1500 to 2000 nightly, and by 1900 the town of Liège could count some fifty active puppet theatres. In Sicily the numerous active 'teatrini' of the back streets presented nightly episodes of chivalric adventure and were closely integrated with the popular life and culture of Palermo and other towns, whilst, in contrast, Milan and Turin possessed elegant 'bonbonnières' seating over a thousand spectators. Olf Bernstangel counted some 200 families travelling the roads of Saxony in 1900, whilst advertisements in the *Era* (a trade-paper for entertainers and precursor of *The Stage*) after 1860 reveal the existence of numerous companies with portable theatres active throughout Britain ... (McCormick, 1998: 1)

The elaborate fit-ups and a varied and spectacular repertoire attracted crowds from every social class and milieu, and the troupes were able to remain in a town or village for several days or even weeks at a time, wherever there was space to pitch the tents and the carts. Their shows included theatrical novelties, from waxwork to clockwork, mechanical marvels, dioramas, dramatic illustrations of popular science, magic lantern and shadow shows; while the puppets themselves performed folk tales and fantasy, melodrama and spectacle to give weight to the circus tricks and variety turns. By the mid-century, some proprietors found themselves for the first time running a commercially successful business, in demand at court as in the towns. Some troupes made extensive tours abroad, to North and South America, South Africa, Australia and New Zealand.

An addition to the puppetry of that era was the shadow theatre which in Europe became a widespread form of entertainment, though of uncertain origin: possibly the inspiration came from China, since it was known as the *Ombres Chinoises*; perhaps from the Middle East, since Egypt at least has a strong and ancient tradition of shadow play; possibly from the more local European fashion for silhouette portraiture, only a step away from moving shadows. Whatever its origins, the genre drew full houses to the best shows, for instance those by the French Feu Séraphin (Dominique-Séraphin François 1747–1800) who enjoyed royal patronage. In a handsomely illustrated book on shadow theatre David Currell writes:

> The shadow has been viewed at times as a disembodied spirit, a phantom or one's double and the shadow was how the ancient Egyptians envisaged the soul. Greek and Roman literature makes many references to the shadow as the soul after death and *the shades* was how they referred to hell, or Hades. In folklore only the dead, the dying or ghosts have no shadow and the Bible abounds with references to the shadow both as protection (for instance 'under the shadow of thy wings') and as the shadow of death. Even today in Indonesia, where the shadow puppets represent ancestral spirits, gods and demons, the *dalang* or puppeteer still performs a semi-priestly function. (Currell, 2007: 7)

Even in the Indonesian islands that have turned from Hinduism to Islam the stories from the Ramayana and the Mahabharata are told everywhere. In the near and Middle East shadow entertainments are tolerated by Islamic teaching where three-dimensional puppet or human theatre may not be. For this reason the Turkish Karagöz and the Greek Karaghiosis are the only popular puppet 'heroes' portrayed as a shadow figure.

In China and Japan many new dramaturgies for shadow theatre exist while the old traditions of delicately made and manipulated shadow puppetry, rooted in Buddhism and Shintoism, are maintained. The old Chinese shadows act out stories of battles, of their mischievous anti-hero the Monkey King, of Nature (the story of the Heron and the Tortoise is a classic favourite) and various national legends. According to the Sri Lankan historian Jayadeva Tilakasiri, writing in 1999,

China, India and Indonesia still possess established systems of this performing art backed by skilled support from design and production teams, preserving traditional methods. The shadow show has always carried a special appeal to the rural masses of many Asian countries, congregated in the south and south-east Asian region, particularly owing to the religious and cultural affinities they share and the common life-style the people follow.

[...] The secular elements which have been retained in the puppet show and the shadow show are intimately associated with the principal comic figure, the clown, whose counterpart in Sanskrit drama is the Vidūṣaka. The Indian traditional shadow show has been enriched and made to reflect the state of society and character types in the life-like portrayal of village clowns and their spouses.

[...] Of all Asian countries Indonesia has made the most [of shadow theatre] quite successfully, by enhancing the standard of the *wayang* as a performing art appealing to all grades of society and by transforming it into a vital force in the development of social and ethical values. [...] The organisation and spread of activities in the main cities and the impetus that the training in *wayang* is intended to impart to students in special schools and institutes are highly commendable [...] it has been able to cut across the barriers between the rural and the urban, the sophisticated and the illiterate and serve as a link between them [...] it has not remained static, varying types and styles created by artists and designers being added to the playing stock and the repertory, also enriched by the inclusion of varied romantic and adventurous stories reflecting ethnic and religious diversity but accommodating a multi-cultural literary structure. (Tilakasiri, 1999: 239–45)

The deep social changes of the nineteenth century saw a new kind of resident comic anti-hero, exclusively a puppet, this time a product of the urban industrial working classes.[6] The most notable example was born in Lyon in France, becoming so popular that his name is almost synonymous with 'glove puppet' both in France and Spain. This was 'Guignol', a worker in the Lyonnais cloth industry, the inspired invention of one Laurent Mourguet (1769–1844).

Guignol's fame spread throughout France, helped, perhaps, by Mourguet's 16 children, who fanned out across the country. The director of Lyon's Théâtre Le Guignol, Stéphanie Lefort, described the success of Guignol: 'He was the right puppet, in the right place, at the right time. I can't really explain it, it's a sort of miracle'. Guignol spoke for the man in the street, the working class, the poor, the downtrodden. He spoke for democracy at a time when the new French Republic and democracy were still precarious but rebellious energy surged through the country. While Guignol is unmistakably French, he is truly a son of Lyon. The Lyonnais are not only proud of being Lyonnais, they are proud of not being Parisian. Lyon has a history of rebellion – from the French Revolution to its place as the headquarters of the Resistance during World War II. This stubborn independence is also reflected in Guignol.[7] (see Bolitho, 2008)

---

[6] A useful article on Guignol by Andrea Bolitho for the magazine France Today can be found at http://www.francetoday.com/articles/2008/10/01/guignol.html, accessed 15 October 2009.

[7] Ibid. See first page.

Figure 7.3   Rod puppet of conjoined twin DJs on a submarine pirate radio station. Rod puppets designed by Marc Parrett and Chris Pirie for Green Ginger's *Rust* (2005). © Alex Scherpf.

Guignol took over from Polichinelle as the nation's favourite trickster, starring in myriad shows as the rogue workman or not-so-humble servant putting one over on his employer. He is less violent than Punch and Polichinelle, both characters out of favour by the beginning of the 1800s. Guignol's trickery was more subtle (invariably in the hope of obtaining money). Always a hand puppet, he had and still has a rough charm, relying on his friend Gnafron for badinage, instead of the showman out front; and not as unkind a husband to Madelon as Punch is to Judy. Although a product of his time, Guignol yet owes his origins to the *zanni* of commedia, to which Mourguet doffed his cap, adding a typical commedia after-piece to his Guignol performances, such as a Harlequinade.

While descendants of the zanni masks, including Punch, were by the end of the century familiar throughout Europe and the Middle East, the numbers of spectators for this kind of show gradually decreased, and the street players became poorer and therefore were considered less respectable than other puppeteers. The resident comic heroes had been forcibly separated from their original theatre context, and the shows looked isolated and run-down. Henry Mayhew, documenting the lives of the poor in nineteenth century London, gives a vivid description of a Punch street show that arouses compassion for the situation of these players.[8] (Mayhew, 1985 [1851]: 205–305). Things improved for them in time, but not until well into the twentieth century: Punch and his cousins are now part of a robust English tradition, perpetuators of another period in the history of entertainment, still with large numbers of practitioners and devotees, their own festivals and associations to uphold the presence of Punch.

Puppetry's cultural respectability persisted as recreation in 'home' theatres for the leisured, moneyed classes, growing through the century to be a dominant stratum of European society. Amateur family shows were given with silhouettes, marionettes or gloves, but the most novel and popular was the 'toy' or paper theatre sold as sheets of drawings. These were cut out and glued on cardboard to make an elaborate proscenium stage complete with changes of scenery and tiny actors moved laterally on wires. Each set of sheets, sold in England as 'Penny Plain, Tuppence [two pence] Coloured', was a miniature model of a production currently showing in the human theatres – chiefly those in London, Paris or Copenhagen. They included melodramas, sentimental plays with songs and dances, Harlequinades, myths and legends, pirate and robber tales and some of the more robust folk tales such as *Bluebeard* and *Ali Baba and the Forty Thieves*, since the miniature theatres were built and performed chiefly by the boys in the family.

During the same period there was an explosion of mechanical and semimechanical experiment with illusionistic scenic effects made possible by new engineering discoveries, all leading steadily to the invention of cinema.

But it was another new fashion that had the most profound, if negative, effect. The coming of Realism subverted the puppet's ontological essence of exaggeration and caricature. When marionette proprietors tried to follow the trend, the result was the belief that a puppet's highest achievement was to be the authentic reproduction of human appearance, movement and gesture. Gaston Baty wrote of the 'horrible perfection' of these puppets (Baty, 1944: 20), and Edward Gordon Craig was equally dismissive of their efforts to imitate human actors. (Craig, 1911: 82–83).

By the end of the century the English families of marionette players while still the most visible and widely diffused of all forms of professional puppetry, were in terminal decline. Where melodrama and spectacular magnificence, variety and circus tricks had suited the puppets well, realism and naturalism suited them not at all. Their determined attempts at human mimesis were leading them into an artistic cul-de-sac. Referring to the condition of these troupes at the approach of the twentieth century McCormick says:

---

[8] John Bell in the same book reports that the wife of Maurice Browne, Ellen Van Volkenburg, coined the word 'puppeteer' (Bell, 2008: 64).

... there was no renewal. The old repertoire had lost any potential for development and was completely out of touch with what might be happening in London.
The new showbiz ethos did not fit happily with the older tradition, and one result
of this was an increasing divide between those rural companies that perpetuated
the dramatic repertoire and the more urban ones that abandoned it in favour of
pantomimes and variety. The fantoccini acts had once been the novelty numbers
to complete the bill after the drama or to provide a short street or fairground
show. Once they displaced the dramatic material, a large part of what had been
fundamental to marionette theatre for three centuries began to fade [...]
     Audiences faced with far more choice, not to mention quantity, of entertain-
ment did not want to see the same acts again and again. Marionettes and popular culture in Britain were ceasing to belong together. (McCormick, 2004: 217)

Worst of all for the proprietors everywhere, the cinema had arrived to
seduce the public, so that for a time every form of live entertainment feared
for its future. The decline of the professional family touring groups and even
the single showmen continued over the next fifty years, and by the end of
the 1939–1945 world war the landscape was all but barren.

MODERNISM AND A NEW LANGUAGE

It was the emergence of Modernism at the end of the nineteenth century
which created a context in which puppetry was embraced and endowed
with an alternative language beyond Realism. It treated the poetic and the
metaphoric, the surreal and the spiritual, the grotesque, the sub- and the
super-human, all subjects wherein the puppets felt once more at home.
Harold Segel says that 'no period or movement in the history of the
European stage ever found as much creative relevance in the puppet figure
as modernism and the avant-garde'. (Segel, 1995: 75)
     The first tributary of the movement to gather up puppetry was
Symbolism, whose principal apologists included the poet Federico García
Lorca, as much a devotee of puppetry as Maurice Sand half a century before
him. Other writers such as the Irish W.B. Yeats and the Russian Aleksander
Blok were also committed adherents of the puppet. For all of them, (as
Edward Gordon Craig most forcefully expressed it) Symbolism was an open
door to a new theatre with great scenographic potential embracing its ideal
of the de-personalized performer, that is, the puppet which could symbolize
humanity and the human condition and could portray the new dramaturgies as actors could not. Maurice Bouchor (1825–1929), a French writer of the
Symbolist school, who wrote several neo-mystery plays for marionettes said
'the personality of the actor, too real and too familiar, destroys all impression
of the supernatural' (quoted in Segel, 1995: 83).
     For all their fascination with the idea of puppets as protagonists not many
of the Modernist producers actually employed them in performance, even
when the playwright stated that the work was conceived for them.

Maeterlinck and Lorca designated several works for puppets that ended as productions with human actors, even if the performers were directed to look and behave as much like puppets as possible, shedding any intrusive emotion and gesticulation. Alfred Jarry's *Ubu Roi*, the quintessential tyrant conceived as a student puppet satire, was first presented to a paying public in 1896 by human players and met with derision by the Paris audience. Ubu later returned to greater success in puppet form and has since become one of the perennial characters of the puppet theatre, alongside Faust and Don Juan.

Modernist writers, painters and sculptors often saw theatre as a work of visual art in motion, though almost none was experienced as a puppet performer or designer (with a few honourable exceptions such as Lorca, an enthusiastic performer, and Otto Morach, skilled artist/designer). Picasso, who made a few puppets himself, was closely involved with the Barcelona *Quatre Gats*, one of those cabarets which were newly fashionable in the culture of Europe. The intimacy of the small dark bars provided perfect conditions for performances of shadow and silhouette theatre. Harold Segel's comprehensive survey informs us that

The spectacular popularity of the shadow show at the turn of the century, above all among serious artists, cannot be explained merely by longstanding European interest in the form. Consideration has to be given, for example, to the stimulus represented by the new, more serious phase of Occidental interest in Oriental culture, especially painting and theater. Craig's enthusiasm for Japanese theater was anything but an isolated phenomenon […] The impact of this 'rediscovered' or newly discovered world of Oriental art on an emerging European modernism was formidable. Symbolist metaphysicality also responded well to the incorporeality, suggestiveness, and mystery of projected shadow figures. Spatially, the shadow play seemed to acquire the dimension of a strange, almost mystic or psychic area lying beyond the boundaries of conventional perspective. More important however than the stimulus given by symbolism to the cultivation of 'Chinese shadows' was the symbiosis of shadow play and mystery drama, which sank deep roots as we shall see in turn-of-the-century French theatre. But Modernist dramatists elsewhere – Valle-Inclán in Spain, Hjalmar Bergman in Sweden, and Massimo Bontempelli in Italy for example – explored the metaphoric potential of shadows in plays at a greater remove from the fashionable Symbolist neo-mystery.

Arguably the greatest single stimulus to the popularity of shadow shows in turn-of-the-century Europe was the extraordinary level of production achieved at the Chat Noir cabaret in Paris. Although virtually every form of cabaret entertainment was offered at the Chat Noir in its long history, chansons by popular singers and shadow shows soon became the greatest draw. The idea of introducing *ombres chinoises* at the cabaret originated with the artist Henri Rivière, to whom the founder and proprietor, Rodolphe Salis, had entrusted the production of the first puppet show. While working with puppets Rivière thought of adding shadow shows to the cabaret's program as well. One night, as the chansonnier Jules Jouy was singing one of his most popular songs, 'Sergots' ('Cops'), Rivière extinguished the lights in the auditorium and then, from behind a napkin suspended across the opening of the small stage used for the puppet shows, mimed Jouy's chanson with silhouettes cut out from cardboard.

It was from these modest beginnings that shadow shows went on to become one of the Chat Noir's leading attractions. (Segel, 1995: 65–66)

From the initial simple use of silhouettes made of cardboard to illustrate songs and stories, the shadows became ever more ingenious in their construction and capability of expression, and the repertory more ambitious. Its success – for an artistic élite usually – initiated a mushrooming of similar cabarets from Catalonia to Russia, and later across the Atlantic. In the 1920s the United States saw a surge of non-commercial ventures, 'art theatres' that included the cabarets, and a 'Little Theatre movement', deriving financial support from President Roosevelt's Federal Theatre Project. While certainly not abjuring text-based drama the movement provided an 'openness to the possibilities of alternative forms of performance in the name of artistic innovation [that] allowed America's little theatres to explore masks, puppets, dance and other aspects of non-realistic theatre traditions with relative ease' (Bell, 2008: 55–56). American theatre, as in Europe, was ripe for a reaction against stale commercialism and naturalism in theatre and eagerly absorbed the new Modernist ideas from various European emissaries. Among them were Lorca in New York and Argentina and Craig in New York. W.B. Yeats arrived from Dublin with revelatory productions by the Abbey Theatre, rapturously received. Maurice Browne, an Englishman living in America, was galvanized by the puppet productions of Paul Brann which he saw in Munich.[9] He returned to the States to found the Chicago Little Theatre in 1911, the first of its kind:

[The Little Theatres] pursued aesthetics antithetical to realism: the rediscovery, invention or appropriation of symbolic theatre languages that three centuries of mainstream European traditions had shunned as primitive. (Bell, 2008: 52)

Logically, other ideas began to be accepted by the Americans that came from the hitherto despised and marginalized practices of their own indigenous populations, for centuries concerned with performing figures, objects and masks. These at last received serious consideration as a valuable contribution to the culture of North America.

Among the twentieth century American artists who were not only puppeteers but wrote valuable books on the history of puppetry are Paul McPharlin (1903–1948) and Marjorie Batchelder (1903–1997), a couple whose works are still considered essential reading.[10] Bil Baird's *The Art of the Puppet*

---

[9] Japan Arts Council 2004 An Introduction to Bunraku http://www2.ntj.jac.go.jp/unesco/bunraku/en/contents/whats/history05.html, accessed February 2010. In addition there are many well-illustrated books on the Bunraku-za.

[10] Mayhew, Henry (1985[1851]) *London Labour and the London Poor*, London: Penguin Books, 205–305.

(Baird, 1965) remains a valuable resource, abundantly illustrated. Baird (1904–1987) ran his own New York theatre and entered cinema history with the marionette sequence in *The Sound of Music*. Remo Bufano (1894–1948) produced many shows, two of which manifested his admiration for Craig, interpreting Craig's concept of the Übermarionette with tall hieratic figures. Tony Sarg (1880–1942), the most commercially astute of the five, after early performances with marionettes, created mechanized puppet shows in department store windows and giant inflatable figures initiating the tradition of spectacular New York parades.

Returning to Europe, the first years of the twentieth century, as already noted, saw most of the puppeteers continuing to present a worn-out repertory, attracting ever smaller audiences and finding it increasingly difficult to make ends meet. In Britain the influence of the Arts and Crafts movement led to a decline in puppetry's dramatic value in favour of handcraftsmanship and the 'well-made marionette' as an end in itself. A formerly lively professional landscape gave ground to uninteresting performances by semi-amateur companies whose merit, at least in Britain, was judged by their puppets' ability to copy human appearance and movement, as they had since the middle of the previous century, but with this difference, that the productions of that era had also produced meaty plays alongside clever circus tricks, music hall songs and comic turns. By the 1950s few of the puppeteers had contact with or experience of the wider world of theatre, excepting a handful exemplified by the Hogarth Puppets whose directors Jan Bussell and Ann Hogarth were trained in acting and producing.

Major new developments happened in the 1960s when the first signs of a reinvention of the puppet theatre was brought about by a relatively small number of puppeteers whose artistry ensured a future for the art form in western countries. Another contributing factor was that international travel and exchanges were accelerating. International puppet festivals had been introduced by an organization founded in 1929 in Prague, the *Union Internationale de la Marionnette* (UNIMA) whose fragile beginnings were rapidly strengthened by the membership of many nations, each of which set up a national centre affiliated to the central organization. After an enforced break of twenty-four years, during the period of worldwide conflict, the festivals resumed in 1957, when the German UNIMA centre led by the great puppet designer Harro Siegel hosted an event in Braunschweig. Since then the UNIMA festivals with meetings of members from all over the world have been regularly held, and there are now UNIMA Centres on all six continents.

SOVIET RICHES

Towering over all other productions in these post-war festivals were the products of the countries of the Soviet bloc, hitherto hidden behind the 'Iron Curtain'. The rich resources awarded to puppet theatre by the Communist cultural authorities gave the productions a measure of excellence in their scenography and puppet operation that were unprecedented in Europe. These authorities were eager to exhibit their superiority in the festivals – in strictly controlled conditions. The groups and their performances were handpicked and supervised with all their movements monitored. But what performances they showed!

The fountainhead of the whole empire of Soviet puppet theatre was Sergei V. Obraztsov (1901–1992). A personality of the Moscow art cabarets during his early theatre career, he gave 'recitals' called *Romances with Songs*, illustrated with rudimentary but witty hand puppets. His performances were simple, satirical and ingenious, played in a small booth bare of scenery, narrated and sung by Obraztsov himself with his wife at the piano. He became personally and professionally popular, and it was not long before his name and reputation for entertainment value reached the Kremlin, where he was invited to perform on more than one occasion. In 1931 the authorities appointed Obraztsov as Artistic Director of the Central State Puppet Theatre, which was designated the hub and model for what became a conglomeration of puppet theatres established throughout the Soviet Union and its satellites. In 1933 Obraztsov and a company of performers, designers, craftspeople and administrators, moved into an enormous new Moscow building, purpose-built for the reception of thousands of children, created to radiate its influence, its repertory, its methods and messages to every other puppet theatre under the régime, even those in other Communist states, such as China, Cuba and West Bengal. Every major city had its puppet theatre, staffed by a large cohort of workers, supporting productions by a touring company as well as a resident company, producing a repertory of plays either provided or approved by Moscow.

> Large state children's theatres, a type of theatre that had never before existed, arose [...] Along with schools and Pioneer clubs, books [...] and thousands of clubs for [the] young [...], children's theatres were also drawn into the task of educating the country's future citizens. Puppet theatres joined the new forms of theatre. (Obraztsov, 1985: 145)

In all the countries of the Soviet empire, some of them with strong, age-old traditions of puppetry, the itinerant showmen and the independent groups faded away. In Russia itself a doomed attempt was made to harness Petrushka to the Communist cause, but Obraztsov soon gave him up, since, true to the puppet's character, he refused to cooperate with Authority:

> If the striving to make the traditional Petrushka the central character in Soviet puppet plays [had been] a correct one, good plays would have finally appeared. The problem was that time showed the very idea to be mistaken. Petrushka could not carry out the new tasks he had been given without losing his basic features, and it was these qualities that made him the choice of many theatres. (Obraztsov, 1985: 150)

Petrushka was tried out in social-realist plays where he was expected to give lengthy speeches to which he was entirely unsuited. His artificial voice, customarily spoken with a 'swazzle', made him all but incomprehensible, and had to be abandoned:

> The same thematic tasks which deprived him of his voice also affected his exter-nal appearance, taking away his costume and his most basic attribute – his stick.
>
> The hunchbacked, long-nosed, ridiculous figure in the peaked cap with a bell at the end who beat everyone at hand with his long stick, split down the middle to make a loud whacking sound … was too specific in time and space to be trans-ferred to another era and given inner features and functions that were alien to him.
>
> […] He could not be turned into a Red Army soldier or an outstanding worker because his primitive clumsy body and his special way of moving and gesticulat-ing contradicted the character he was now being made to play … The pre-revo-lutionary, traditional Petrushka beat those people whom it was forbidden not only to beat but even to criticise. He carried out the people's hidden wishes in Tsarist times. He established a justice that was lacking in life. Soviet government estab-lished this justice. The struggle against anti-social elements […] was carried out by Soviet legislation, which needed no help from anarchic rowdies. (Obraztsov, 1985: 152)

The establishment of many state puppet theatres created an urgent need for resources. The theatres had to ensure a continuous supply of performers, so a number of state schools were established to train actor-puppeteers and specialist directors via three- and four-year courses (five for the directors). Some designers and makers were needed too, and the cultural leaders decided they should be trained separately from the performers (a serious error, in the opinion of many), in existing art and design schools. An enor-mous number of administrators and stage hands were engaged, with the mandatory Party overseer.

A more pressing need was a new repertoire, for which the Central State Puppet Theatre at first could find no suitable models. Obraztsov's over-riding principle, in effect a powerful contribution to the aesthetics of pres-ent-day puppetry, was that no production should attempt to emulate a show for human actors. In the end the collection included fairy tales (after 1936, when the fairy tale was restored to State favour), animal tales, adaptations of classic stories and some original scenarios that earned the most success inter-nationally.

The world had never seen and may never again see so much energy, infra-structural resources and funds poured into the production of puppet theatre. Although the quantity of output could hardly guarantee its quality, the over-all result was a surge of artistic excellence which exerted a worldwide influ-ence, when the best and most suitable productions of the Soviet puppet theatre companies toured abroad. Their production values, the originality of the scenarios, their inventiveness, humour and colour, made Obraztsov, as virtual artistic director of the whole Soviet empire of puppetry, famous – one of the few names in puppet theatre ever to enter the consciousness of the general public. The shows most widely and most often toured were the product of the Moscow theatre directed by Obraztsov himself. They included *Don Juan,* a parody of the American musical; *The Unusual Concert,* a variety show on a large-scale, caricaturing a number of typical 'acts' held together by a solemn Master of Ceremonies, a tall nether-rod puppet whose movements, operated by internal stringing, were uncannily lifelike. One of the acts featured a massed choir (with perfectly synchronized mouths), conducted by a pigeon-chested conductor whose flailing arms and shock of hair recalled the Hollywood star conductor of the 1940s and '50s, Leopold Stokowski. More or less cutting satire targeting the capitalist, western way of life was a recurring theme of the Soviet productions. Obraztsov's *My Profession* is a revealing account of his life for any student of the Soviet era.[11]

Because generous subsidy was available, the best theatre designers and directors could be hired to lend puppetry their talents. One of the great scenographers of the puppet theatre was Adam Kilian, whose folk designs subtly reminded his Polish audiences under the Soviet yoke of their own national pride and origins. Like the Czechs, the Polish theatre resisted as much as possible the Soviet *diktats.* The director and professor Jan Dvořák wrote of the Czech experience:

> After the forceful arrival of the Communist régime in the 50s traditional puppeteering was eventually liquidated. Instead there was a new network of state puppet theatres. Arguments proving the decadence of the surviving tradition were imposed by the political *apparat,* which perceived the itinerant families of puppeteers as entrepreneurs surplus to requirements. Most of them therefore had to appear in shows organised by official cultural agencies, others were satisfied with work in fairground attractions, while only a few found their way into regional theatres. What a pity! (Dvořák, 1993)

The east European situation was in sharp contrast with that obtaining in the 'free' west where small groups struggled to survive. In the late 1950s and throughout the '60s French talent was exceptional because the art form was recognized and respected by the arts ministry which funded the puppeteers. Accordingly they led western Europe into an age of new and exciting techniques and dramaturgies. A number of French academic publications emerged, analysing the art form's mode of existence and its history.[12] The Netherlands was quick to follow.

In England the arts authorities refused recognition of puppetry as an art form, and statutory funding was almost non-existent up to the 1970s. A

---

[11] See the suggested list of further reading at the end of the chapter.
[12] The reading list at the end of the chapter has some publications on puppetry in France covering this period.

damning national survey of the professional groups commissioned by the Arts Council from an artist-puppeteer (Binyon, 1971) helped to confirm the belief that there was little artistic merit in the puppet productions on offer. When in the late '70s the advancing tide of new work could no longer be ignored the official bodies began to release small amounts of money (though the British Arts Council held out for longer than most). The making of puppet theatre is an expensive business, and Britain, Spain and other western countries were severely penalized by the national cultural policy.

A DISTINCT THEATRE ART

New hope arrived with the foundation in several European countries of a national centre entirely dedicated to the art form's recognition and development. These centres acted as dynamic and influential catalysts in bringing the attention of the arts world to the potential and needs of puppet theatre. The British centre in 1974 was the first on the scene and was awarded a number of grants, and the model of a staffed, accessible centre of this kind was adopted by other countries, resulting in a network which, added to the UNIMA network, underpinned puppetry, making it hard to overlook. The primary tactic was to promote the growing number of innovative artists in the field and their work. Other strategies included the publication of books and periodicals illustrating the work on offer, obtaining training and travel bursaries for artists in mid-career; running training sessions and workshops; and organizing festivals. The Centres provided a voice and a focus for the art form. Little by little results were evidenced in increased employment for the best groups, an accumulation of new performance venues and new audiences, regular subsidies and realistic fees, and a measurable elevation in the status of the puppeteers and their profession. The professionals acquired new confidence, a belief in puppetry as a valid performing art with its own language and skills. The British pioneers included Barry Smith who declared

> A puppet is a puppet – not an imitation actor. The actor can represent an idea – the puppet *is* that idea. It is the actor raised to an abstraction – the mask from which the actor has withdrawn. The less the puppet depends on naturalism, the greater is its power of illusion; but the more the puppet tries to imitate the surface of life for its own sake, the more it draws attention to its limitations.
>
> The puppet is lifeless unless it takes its movement from the mind and heart. It must create the illusion of reality – not reality itself.[13] (Smith, 1974)

Barry Smith's company was called Theatre of Puppets and was courageous in its intention to bring adults back to the puppet theatre, against all the odds, including those provided by BBC television where puppets were for a

---

[13] From a leaflet in the author's possession.

long time produced mainly for children of nursery age. Similarly struggling but determined, John Wright and Lyndie Parker founded the Little Angel Marionette Theatre in a London temperance hall in 1961 where it flourishes still, having always been a leader in the field, catering as much for discerning adults as for children. Violet Philpott and her company 'Cap and Bells' gave new life to children's work with her own original stories, witty designs and performance skills. Christopher Leith was singled out by the newly founded National Theatre which sponsored and presented his version of *Beowulf* in 1979.

Everywhere in the west new audiences were being discovered, older children and adults attracted to animation *per se*, but still wary of a form of theatre supposedly made only for the very young. A major advance was in the burgeoning of a specialist dramaturgy, scenarios adapted or written for the new puppetry environment by a few companies and writers which offered a genuinely original kind of theatre.

In 1971 Josef Krofta became the artistic director of an already highly regarded Czech company called DRAK, one of the most influential in the history of the art form. Krofta introduced fresh ways of thinking about the potential of performance with puppets, and a new methodology for producing the work (see pp. 112–14, Chapter 5). The company was a pioneer of the devising, collaborative, multi-disciplinary way of working with a theatre group. Guiding principles in the adaptation of any text were that the verbal element was minimized, and the music and the 'stage picture' always remained paramount. Although the first years of Krofta's incumbency were in the time of the Soviet occupation, DRAK avoided the aesthetics and the texts of the Moscow formulae.

Meanwhile in France the Philippe Genty group was the first in the west since World War II to attract international plaudits. The company used illusion and magic, lighting effects and trompe-l'oeil to create a series of large-scale productions that attracted audiences to prestigious venues, Genty himself is another in the line of fine puppeteers who came from the cabarets. He has been a major contributor to the launch of a 'theatre of objects', consisting of all kinds of animated forms, materials and things.

This narrative omits the work of scores of solo artists and small groups which in this period rose to play in every country save those of the Soviet states. When the Iron Curtain dissolved in 1989 and the Obraztsov influence faded (as it did almost immediately), western puppetry was ready to replace it and the work of the liberated east Europeans was quick to follow. Many of their puppet-and-actor theatres and schools have survived (Poland, for instance, still has over a score of subsidized theatres and two university-level schools), but the Soviet style of the large rod puppet playing a mandatory repertory has vanished.

In the late 1980s and for a period in the 1990s a new phase of development that many commentators found disturbing was observed in the productions of the proliferating puppet festivals. Broadly, the puppet was being treated as a prop, a dead figure hardly articulated held in the hand of the actor-puppeteer apparently as an icon – a visual ideal – of the stage character being enacted. Little or no attempt was made to 'animate' the thing, and every attempt was made by the actor-puppeteers to perform the role themselves. The new puppet ontology was difficult to accept, and in 1990 George Speaight remarked on the trend:

> [The] age-old distinction between human and puppet theatre is breaking down. In innumerable productions, human actors and puppets are to be seen performing side by side and sometimes the puppet seems no more than a stage prop for the human actor. Whether this tendency demonstrates a loss of faith in the puppet as a pure theatrical medium will be for the future to determine. What is certain is that puppet theatre no longer exists as a separate artistic and theatrical form, but that it can take its place alongside mime, mask, dance, music and speech in the totality of theatre art. (Speaight, 1990)

The practice has now declined, though not disappeared, but Speaight was accurately observing a strong post-modern development: a new genre of theatre with manipulated objects, but without animation.

THE CONTEMPORARY REVIVAL

Seven years after Speaight's observation, the history of theatre with puppets, not limited to Britain and the United States, received further impetus in two productions: *Lion King*, a musical mixing dance, masks and puppetry, which opened on Broadway in 1997 followed in the same year by. *Shockheaded Peter* which opened in London. The latter was a production played by actors and animated figures with the live accompaniment of a quartet of musicians. The work of two designer-directors, Julian Crouch and Phelim McDermott, its aesthetic was that of a macabre parody of Victorian melodrama that was nonetheless enjoyed by children and adults. Subtitled a 'Junk Opera', the piece was chiefly remarkable for the integration of the music with the poems, the puppets, the music and the puppetesque set which recalled a colourful toy (paper) theatre, one which contracted and expanded. A counter-tenor sang the cautionary verses of the well-known German book *Struwwelpeter*, although in this version each tale ended with the demise of a number of transgressive children, played by grotesque, floppy puppets manipulated by two actor-puppeteers in early nineteenth century dress. The production was the first fringe production to attract large audiences of all ages and it toured internationally for many years, often returning to a city by public demand. It enjoyed four seasons in London, all in mainstream theatres. Its run-away box office success hastened changes in modern theatre, such as the increasing employment of animated figures and objects by directors and designers who despite a lack of any specialist training are nevertheless discovering new dramaturgical uses for puppetry.

As for the dedicated puppet theatre practitioners, the itinerant by-way puppeteers have more or less disappeared, and in their place have come the respected, often high-art, solo artist and the two- or three-person touring groups working for all ages in all kinds of spaces. Innumerable groups all over the world, which are more or less self-sufficient, will be found playing for an unfailing public of young people, in theatres, arts centres and schools; and there are others interpreting exclusively adult themes which may be dark and intellectually challenging.

Jurkowski points to some of the ingredients prevalent in the puppetry of the twenty-first millennium, including

> ... the visibility of the acting subject (the puppet manipulator) demonstrating the artificial character of puppet theatre; the return to ritual forms of theatre; the play-ing with elements of drama, especially with time, space and characters which have undergone the process of atomisation; and the extended meaning of the word 'puppetry' which now covers all kinds of impersonal presentation using, for example, objects or raw material. (Jurkowski, 1998: 453)

Ten years later we can add to this list the increasing involvement of puppeteers with modern image-generating machines, projections, computer graphics and filmed sequences.

A global pattern is emerging. In Asian countries the traditional is comple-mented by the modern, whereas in others such as France, the modern has almost completely replaced the traditional, although Guignol and a few other local heroes survive. There are religious communities defending themselves against an age of secularism and the machine which still practise ritual and ceremonial puppetry; many ancient forms are respected, excavated and regen-erated. Ever more sophisticated societies try to obliterate puppetry's spiritual associations, concentrating instead on secular matters, psychology, pedagogy, science fiction, sex and violence, and – still – mimesis or substitution. Clearly puppetry is a dynamic presence in the history of the performing arts.

FURTHER READING

Adachi, Barbara C. (1979) *The Voices and Hands of Bunraku*, New York: John Weatherhill.

Adachi, Barbara C. (1985) *Backstage at Bunraku*, New York: John Weatherhill.

Baty, Gaston (1942) *Trois P'tits Tours et puis s'en vont. Les théâtres forains de marionnettes à fils et leur repertoire 1800–1890*, Paris: Odette Lieutier.

Bell, J. (ed.) (2000) *Strings, Hands, Shadows: A Modern Puppet History*, Detroit, MI: Diagram Series, Detroit Institute of Arts.

Besnier, Patrick (2007) *Alfred Jarry*, Paris: Cultures France, 44.

Binyon, Helen (1971) *A Survey of Professional Puppetry in England*, London: Arts Council of Great Britain.

Byrom, Michael (1983) *Punch in the Italian Puppet Theatre, Its Origin and Evolution*, London: Centaur Press.

Byrom, Michael (1996) *The Puppet Theatre in Antiquity*, Bicester: DaSilva Puppet Books.

Dagan, E. (1990) *Emotions in Motion; Theatrical Puppets and Masks of Black Africa*, Westmount: Galerie Amrad African Arts Publications.

Darkowska-Nidzgorska, Olenka (1980) *Théâtre Populaire de Marionnettes en Afrique Sud-Saharienne*, Bandudu: Centre d'Études Ethnologiques.

Efimova, Nina (1935) *The Adventures of a Russian Puppet Theatre*, trans. E. Mitcoff, Birmingham: Puppetry Imprints.

Gibson, Ian (1989) *Federico García Lorca*, London: Faber and Faber, 117 et seq.

Impe, Jean-Luc (1994) *Opera Baroque et Marionnette*, Charleville-Mézières, Editions Institut International de la Marionnette.

Keene, Donald (1990) *Major Plays of Chikamatsu*, New York: University of Columbia Press.

Leach, Robert (1985) *The Punch and Judy Show: History, Tradition and Meaning*, London: Batsford.

Magnin, Charles ([1862] 1981) *Histoire des Marionnettes en Europe*, Paris: Editions Slatkine.

Mayhew, Henry ([1851] 1985) *London Labour and the London Poor*, London: Penguin Books.

McCormick, John (2010) with Cipolla, A. and Napoli, A., *The Italian Puppet Theater, A History*, Jefferson, NC: Mcfarland.

Paërl, Hetty (2007) *Acerra and Pulcinella* www.pulcinellamuseo.it/museo/eng/acerra_and_pulcinella.php.

Perkins, Juliet (2004) *A Critical Study of Antonio Jose da Silva's Cretan Labyrinth*. Lewiston, NY: Edwin Mellen Press.

Speaight, George V. (ed.) (1981) *The Life and Travels of Richard Barnard, Marionette Proprietor*, London: Society for Theatre Research.

Stalberg, Roberta, (1984) *China's Puppets*, San Francisco, CA: China Books.

Conclusion

Some may view puppets as manifestations of human spirituality, symbols of man's union with the divine. Others view them as little more than children's toys, or wooden heads made for the simplest birthday party show. Some puppets are obviously conceived as works of art, to be performed in an artistic, esoteric context. Still others are made to please crowds with their transformations and tricks. Each view is one in a panorama, each valid to a degree.

Whatever one's conceptions and prejudices, it is true that contemporary mainstream theatre has grasped the metaphoric and symbolic significance of puppets and is making use of their theatrical power and their value as performers, in the myriad situations where the human actor is impracticable or intrusive.

Puppets, animated objects in performance mirror, emphasize and interpret. They speak to and are understood by the entire world, having little need of a spoken language. Pragmatically they respond to the demands humans make of them. More abstractly they respond first to the spirit of the puppeteer who makes and controls them, then to the spirit of the individual spectator. They are a blend of sculpture and actor, of scenographic entity and cynosure.

In presenting a brief overview of the contemporary world of puppetry, I have tried to mirror this duality of perception, the spiritual and the mundane. Victoria Nelson says,

> Truth does lie in recognizing both. [...] the two world views are actually complementary; neither perspective qualifies as rigid dogma or superstition so long as it is applied to its own turf. We get into trouble only when we mix territories, expecting the transcendental to do the work of the empirical and vice versa. (Nelson, 2001: 189)

Puppetry, this dead-and-alive phenomenon, belongs on both territories, enriching the soul-seeker and the pleasure-seeker – and life.

London, 2010

Bibliography

Adachi, Barbara C. (1979) *The Voices and Hands of Bunraku*, New York: John Weatherhill.

Adachi, Barbara C. (1985) *Backstage at Bunraku*, New York: John Weatherhill.

Amaral, A.-M. (1994) *Le Théâtre de Marionnettes au Brésil*, São Paulo: Secretaria de Estado da Cultura de São.

Arnott, P. (1964) *Plays Without People: Puppetry in Serious Drama*, Bloomington, IN: Indiana University Press.

Artaud, Antonin ([1933] 1970) *The Theatre and its Double*, trans. Victor Corti. London: Calder and Boyars.

Badiou, M. (1992) 'La Valeur de l'Objet Animé dans le Processus de Dramatisation', in M. Waszkiel (ed.), *Present Trends in the Research of World Puppetry*, Warsaw: Institute of Art of the Polish Academy of Sciences, 57.

Baird, B. (1965) *The Art of the Puppet*, New York: Ridge Press.

Baker, Rene (2009) 'The Puppet as Teacher of Acting', in E. Margolies (ed.), *Theatre Materials*, London: Centre of Excellence in Training for Theatre, Central School of Speech and Drama, 50–54.

Baldwin, P. (1992) *Toy Theatres of the World*, London: Zwemmer.

Banham, Martin (ed.) (1992) *Cambridge Guide to Theatre*, Cambridge: Cambridge University Press.

Barker, Howard (1993) *All He Fears*, London: John Calder.

Barker, Howard (2001) *The Swing at Night*, London: John Calder.

Barthes, Richard (1971) 'On Bunraku', trans. Sandy Macdonald, *TDR: The Drama Review*, 15, 3, 76–79.

Bass, Eric (2007) 'The Puppet's Nature' in Nancy L. Staub (ed.) *Breaking Boundaries*, New York: Center for Puppetry Arts, 10.

Batchelder, M. (1948) *The Puppet Theatre Handbook*, London: H. Jenkins.

Batchelder, M. and Comer, V.L. (1959) *Puppets and Plays*, London: Faber and Faber.

Baty, Gaston (1942) *Trois P'tits Tours et puis s'en vont. Les théâtres forains de marionnettes à fils et leur repertoire 1800–1890*, Paris: Odette Lieutier.

Bell, John (ed.) (2000) *Puppets, Masks and Performing Objects*, Cambridge, MA: MIT Press.

Bell, John (ed.) (2000) *Strings, Hands, Shadows: A Modern Puppet History*, Detroit, MI: Diagram Series, Detroit Institute of Arts.

Bell, John (2008) *American Puppet Modernism*, New York and London: Palgrave Macmillan, USA.

Benavente, Jacinto ([1908] 2004) *The Bonds of Interest/Los Intereses Creados*, trans. S. Appelbaum, Mineola, NY: Dover Publications.

Bensky, Roger-Daniel (1969) *Structures Textuelles de la Marionnette de Langue Française*, Paris: Editions A-G Nizet.

Besnier, Patrick (2007) *Alfred Jarry*, Paris: Cultures France.

Bicât, Tina (2007) *Puppets and Performing Objects*, Marlborough: Crowood Press.

Binyon, Helen (1971) *A Survey of Professional Puppetry in England*, London: Arts Council of Great Britain.

Blackburn, S. (1996) *Inside the Drama House*, Los Angeles, CA: University of California Press.

Blackham, Olive (1948) *Puppets into Actors*, London: W. Taylor.

Blackham, Olive (1960) *Shadow Puppets*, New York: Harper and Bros.

Blumenthal, Eileen (2005) *Puppetry and Puppets*, London: Thames and Hudson.

Boehn, Max von (1972) *Puppets and Automata*, New York: Dover Publications.

Böhmer, Gunther (1971) *Puppets,* trans. G. Morice, London: Macdonald.

Bolitho, Andrea (2008) 'Guignol', *France Today* Jan, 2008. See http://www.francetoday.com/articles/2008/10/01/guignol.html.

Boyle, Kirsty (2008) 'Karakuri Info', http://www.karakuri.info/history, accessed 19 January, 2010.

Bradbury, Malcolm (1977) 'Romanticism', in Alan Bullock and Oliver Stallybrass (eds), *The Fontana Dictionary of Modern Thought*, London: Fontana/Collins, 548–550.

Brecht, Stefan (1988) *Peter Schumann's Bread and Puppet Theatre*, New York: Routledge, Chapman and Hall.

Buckmaster, Sue (2000) 'Object Relations', in A. Dean (ed.), *Puppetry into Performance: A User's Guide*, London: Central School of Speech and Drama, 14–16.

Burkett, Ronnie (2002) *Tinka's New Dress, Street of Blood, Happy,* Canada: River Books.

Burkett, Ronnie (2005) *Provenance*, Toronto: Playwrights Canada Press.

Burkett, Ronnie (2006) *10 Days on Earth*, Toronto: Playwrights Canada Press.

Burkett, Ronnie (2009) *Billy Twinkle*, Toronto: Playwrights Canada Press.

Butler, R. (2003) *The Art of Darkness. Staging the Philip Pullman Trilogy*, London: Oberon Books.

Byrom, Michael (1983) *Punch in the Italian Puppet Theatre, Its Origin and Evolution,* London: Centaur Press.

Byrom, Michael (1996) *The Puppet Theatre in Antiquity*, Bicester: DaSilva Puppet Books.

Calliès, Gregoire (2000) 'La marionnette ne peut pas être bavarde' ('The puppet cannot be talkative'), *Alternatives Théâtrales*, 65–66, 86–88.

Camerlain, Lorraine and Vaïs, Michel (eds) (1989) 'Ecrire pour la Marionette', *Cahiers de Théâtre Jeu*, 51.

Carroll, Tim (2007) 'Puppet Love: Why the Best Actors are Wooden', http://blogs.guardian.co.uk/arts/author/tim_carroll, accessed 26 January 2010.

Chase, Michael (2007) 'Who Am I Anyway?' *Total Theatre*, 19, 2, 13–14.

Cixous, Hélène (2000) 'Theatre Surprised By Puppets', in Marek Waszkiel et al. (eds), *The Worldwide Art of Puppetry*, Charleville-Mézières: UNIMA and I.I.M, 16–21.

Connor, Steven (2000) *Dumbstruck, A Cultural History of Ventriloquism*, Oxford: Oxford University Press.

Coult, T. and Kershaw, B. (eds), (1999) *Engineers of the Imagination: the Welfare State Handbook*, London: Methuen.

Craig, Edward Gordon (1911) *On the Art of the Theatre*, New York: Theater Arts Books.

Craig, Edward Gordon (1912) 'Gentlemen, the Marionette!' in J.M. Walton, *Craig on Theatre* (1983) London: Methuen, 24.

Craig, Edward Gordon (1918) 'The Marionnette Drama. Some Notes for an Introduction to "The Drama for Fools" by Tom Fool', *The Marionnette*, 1(1)–(2), 4 et seq.

Craig, Edward Gordon (1921) *Puppets and Poets, The Chapbook – a monthly miscellany*, no.20, London: The Poetry Bookshop.

Crouch, Julian and McDermott, Phelim (2000) 'The Gap', in Anthony Dean (ed.), *Puppetry into Performance: A User's Guide*, London: Central School of Speech and Drama, 21–23.

Curci, Rafael (2002) *De los objetos y otras manipulaciones titiriteras*, Buenos Aires: Instituto Nacional de Teatro and Universidad de Buenos Aires.

Currell, David (1974) *The Complete Book of Puppetry*, London: Pitman Publishing.

Currell, David (1986) *The Complete Book of Puppet Theatre*, London: A & C Black.

Currell, David (1999) *Puppets and Puppet Theatre*, Marlborough: Crowood Press.

Currell, David (2007) *Shadows and Shadow Puppets*, Marlborough: Crowood Press.

Dagan, E. (1990) *Emotions in Motion; Theatrical Puppets and Masks of Black Africa*, Westmount: Galerie Amrad African Arts Publications.

Darkowska-Nidzgorska, Olenka (1980) *Théâtre Populaire de Marionnettes en Afrique Sud-Saharienne*, Bandudu: Centre d'Études Ethnologiques.

Dean, Anthony (ed.) (2000) *Puppetry into Performance, A User's Guide. Colloquium Papers and Interviews*, London: Central School of Speech and Drama.

Down, Mark (2009) 'Voices', *Total Theatre*, 21, 2, Summer, 2009.

Duncan, Ronald (1961) *Chambers Encyclopaedia*, vol.9, London: George Newnes, 140.

Dvořák, Jan (ed.) (1993) *Josef Krofta: Babylonska vez – La Tour de Babel –The Tower of Babel*, Prague: Pražská Scéna.

Dvořák, Jan (ed.) (2001) *DRAK. A Plague O' Both Your Houses!!!* Prague: Pražská Scéna.

Efimova, Nina (1935) *The Adventures of a Russian Puppet Theatre*, trans. E. Mitcoff, Birmingham: Puppetry Imprints.

Enckell, Johanna, (1999) 'Sitting Astride Live Theatre and Animation', in *Theatre of Animation: Contemporary Adult Puppet Plays in Context 1, Contemporary Theatre Review* 9(4), 57–58.

Eruli, B. (ed.) (1995) 'Ecritures et Dramaturgies' in *PUCK: La marionnette et les autres arts*, no.8, Charleville-Mézières: Editions Institut International de la Marionnette.

Fenton, Rose de Wend and Neal, Lucy (2005) *The Turning World*, London: Calouste Gulbenkian Foundation.

Fettig, Hansjürgen (1973) *Glove and Rod Puppets*, trans. S. Forster and J. Wright, London: George G. Harrap.

Fettig, Hansjürgen (1997) *Rod Puppets and Table-top Puppets: A Handbook of Design and Technique*, English version by Rene Baker, Bicester: DaSilva Puppet Books.

Fisler, Ben (2002) 'Exposing Intercultural Gestation: A Study of the Engineering of non-Western Puppet, Mask, and Costume Traditions in The Lion King', in James Fisher (ed.), *The Puppetry Yearbook Vol. 5*, Lewiston, NY: Edwin Mellen Press, 33–61.

Foulc, Thieri and Jurkowski, H. (eds) (2009) *Encyclopédie Mondiale des Arts de la Marionnette*, France: UNIMA and Editions l'Entretemps.

Fournel, Paul (ed.) (1982) *Les Marionnettes*, Paris: Bordas.

Francis, Penny (1999) 'Interview with Howard Barker', in *Theatre of Animation: Contemporary Adult Puppet Plays in Context 1, Contemporary Theatre Review*, 9(4), 37.

Francis, Penny (2007) 'Ancient into Modern', *Móin-Móin – Teatro de Formas Animadas Contemporâneo*, 3, 4, 148–71.

Fraser, Peter (1980) *Puppets and Puppetry*, London: Batsford.

Furse, Anna (2008) 'Committed to the Other: the Ethics of Puppetry', *Puppet Notebook* 13, 20–21.

Ghulam-Sarwa, Y. (1994), *Dictionary of South-East Asian Theatre*, New York: Oxford University Press.

Gibson, Ian (1989) *Federico García Lorca*, London: Faber and Faber.

Gilles, A. (1981) *Le Jeu de la Marionnette: l'objet intermediaire et son métathéâtre*, Nancy: Université de Nancy.

Gioco Vita, Teatro (1995) Company brochure, no named author. *Un mondo di Figure d'ombra*, Piacenza: Gioco Vita.

Goldowski, Boris (1994) *The Chronicles of the Puppet Theatre in Russia in the 15th – 18th Centuries*, Moscow and Warsaw: Nina Gallery.

Green, T.A. and Pepicello, W.J. (1983) 'Semiotic Interrelationships in the Puppet Play' *Semiotica* 47, 1/4, 147–61.

Hadamowsky, Franz (1956) *Richard Teschner und Sein Figurenspiegel*, Vienna: Eduard Wancura Verlag.

Helstien, Melvyn (1986) *Puppetry of India, An Exhibition by the Center for Puppetry Arts*, Atlanta: Center for Puppetry Arts.

Henny, Sue et al. (1985) *Karakuri Ningyō: An Exhibition of Ancient Festival Robots from Japan*, London: Barbican Art Gallery.

Hutton, Darryl (1974) *Ventriloquism*, New York: Sterling Publishing.

Huxley, M. and Witts, N. (eds) (2002) *The Twentieth Century Performance Reader*, Abingdon and New York: Routledge.

Impe, Jean-Luc (1994) *Opera Baroque et Marionnette*, Charleville-Mézières: Editions Institut International de la Marionnette.

Johnstone, Keith ([1981] 1989) *Impro*, London: Methuen Drama.

Jones, Basil (2009) 'Puppetry and Authorship', in Jane Taylor (ed.), *Handspring Puppet Company*, Johannesburg: David Krut Publishing, 253–268.

Joseph, Helen Haiman (1922) *A Book of Marionettes*, London: George Allen and Unwin.

Jurkowski, Henryk (1988) *Aspects of Puppet Theatre*, London: The Puppet Centre Trust.

Jurkowski, Henryk (1991) *Ecrivains et Marionnettes*, Charleville-Mézières: Editions Institut International de la Marionnette.

Jurkowski, Henryk (1994) *The Human Among Objects*, British Centre of UNIMA.

Jurkowski, Henryk (1996) *A History of European Puppetry*, vol.1, Lewiston, NY: Edwin Mellen Press.

Jurkowski, Henryk (1998) *A History of European Puppetry*, vol.2, Lewiston, NY: Edwin Mellen Press.

Jurkowski, Henryk (2000) *Metamorphoses, La Marionnette au XXe Siecle*, France: Editions Institut International de la Marionnette/L'Entretemps.

Jurkowski, Henryk (2002) 'Aesthetics of Puppetry at the Beginning of the 21st Century' in James Fisher (ed.), *Puppetry Yearbook Vol. 5*, Lewiston, NY: Edwin Mellen Press.

Kantor, Tadeusz (1993) *A Journey Through Other Spaces: Essays and Manifestos 1944–1990* (ed. and trans. Michal Kobialka) Berkeley, CA: University of California Press.

Keene, Donald (1973) *Bunraku, The Art of the Japanese Puppet Theatre*, Japan and USA: Kodansha International.

Keene, Donald (1990) *Major Plays of Chikamatsu*, New York: University of Columbia Press.

Kentridge, William (1999) 'Director's Note Faustus in Africa', in *Theatre of Animation: Contemporary Adult Puppet Plays in Context 1*, *Contemporary Theatre Review*, 9(4), 45–46.

Kleist, Heinrich von ([1810] 1983) 'On the Marionette Theatre' (trans. C. Halsall) *Animations*, 6, 6.

Klima, M., Makonj, K. and Balogh, G. et al. (eds) (2003) *Josef Krofta*, Prague: Pražská Scéna.

Knight, Malcolm (ed.) (1992) 'Proceedings of the Soviet/British Puppetry Conference, Glasgow, November 1989', *Contemporary Theatre Review*, 1, 1.

Kohler, Adrian (2001) Episodes: Catalogue of an Installation of Puppets from Seven Productions over Sixteen Years, Grahamstown: The Albany Museum.

Kominz, L. and Levenson, M. (eds) (1990) *The Language of the Puppet*, USA: Tears of Joy Theatre.

Kott, Jan (1984) *The Theatre of Essence*, Evanston, IL: Northwestern University Press.

Kurokawa, K. (2001) 'The Philosophy of the Karakuri', in *The Philosophy of Symbiosis from the Ages of the Machine to the Age of Life* http://www.kisho.co.jp/page.php/308, accessed February 2010.

Law, Jane Marie (1997) *Puppets of Nostalgia*, Princeton, NJ: Princeton University Press.

Law, R. and Chester, L. (1992) *A Nasty Piece of Work: The Art and Graft of Spitting Image*, London: Booth-Clibborn Editions.

Leach, Robert (1985) *The Punch and Judy Show: History, Tradition and Meaning*. London: Batsford.

Lecoq, Jacques (2000) *The Moving Body*, trans. D. Bradby, London: Methuen.

Lee, Miles (1958) *Puppet Theatre Production and Manipulation*, London: Faber and Faber.

Mądzik, Leszek (2000) 'Temoignage/Testimony', in Marek Waszkiel et al. (eds), *The Worldwide Art of Puppetry*, UNIMA, 26.

Magnin, Charles ([1862] 1981) *Histoire des Marionnettes en Europe*, Paris: Editions Slatkine.

Malkin, Michael (1943) *Traditional and Folk Puppets of the World*, A.S. Barnes: South Brunswick, NJ: and London.

Malkin, Michael (1983) *UNIMA Calendar 1983*, Dresden: Henschel Verlag.

Margolies, E. (ed.) (2009) *Theatre Materials*, London: Centre for Excellence in Training for Theatre, Central School of Speech and Drama.

Mayhew, Henry ([1851] 1985) *London Labour and the London Poor*, London: Penguin Books.

McCormick, John (2004) *The Victorian Marionette Theatre*, Iowa City: University of Iowa Press.

McCormick, John and Pratasik, Benny (1998) *Popular Puppet Theatre in Europe 1800–1914*, Cambridge: Cambridge University Press.

McCormick, John (2010) with Cipolla, A. and Napoli, A., *The Italian Puppet Theater – A History*, London and Jefferson, NC: McFarland Inc.

McKechnie, Samuel (1931) *Popular Entertainments Through the Ages*, London: Sampson Low, Marston & Co.

Meschke, Michael (1992) *In Search of Aesthetics for the Puppet Theatre*, New Dehli, India: Indira Gandhi National Centre for the Arts.

Michener, James (1968) *Iberia*, New York: Fawcett Crest.

Millar, Mervyn (2007) *The Horse's Mouth, Staging Morpurgo's 'War Horse'*, London: Oberon.

Morley, H. ([1866] 1899) *Journal of a London Playgoer*, London: Routledge (1891 edition).

Myrsiades, Linda (1988) *The Karagiozis Performance in Greek Shadow Theatre* (trans. K. Myrsiades) Hanover and London: University Press of New England.

Nelson, V. (2001) *The Secret Life of Puppets*, Cambridge, MA: Harvard University Press.

Nicoll, Allardyce (1931) *Masks, Mimes and Miracles,* London: Harrap.

Obraztsov, Sergei (1981) *My Profession* (trans. D. Bradbury) revised edition, Moscow: Raduga Publishers.

Paërl, Hetty (2007) 'Acerra and Pulcinella' www.pulcinellamuseo.it/museo/eng/acerra_and_pulcinella.php, accessed November 2009.

Paska, Roman (1990) 'Notes on Puppet Primitives', in L. Kominz, and M. Levenson, (eds), *The Language of the Puppet,* USA: Tears of Joy Theatre.

Paska, Roman (1992) 'Statements', in Nancy L. Staub (ed.), *Breaking Boundaries,* Atlanta, GA: Center for Puppetry Arts, 20.

Paska, Roman (1995), in (no ed. given) *Teatro Gioco Vita, Un Mondo di Figure d'Ombra,* Piacenza, Italy.

Paska, Roman (ed.) (2000) 'Jeux de Miroirs', *Alternatives Théâtrales* 65–66, 36.

Pasqualino, Antonio (1978) *L'Opera dei Pupi,* Palermo: Sellerio.

Pavis, Patrice (1998) *Dictionary of the Theatre, Terms, Concepts, and Analysis,* Toronto: University of Toronto Press.

Perkins, Juliet (2004) *A Critical Study and Translation of Antonio José da Silva's Cretan Labyrinth,* Lewiston, NY: Edwin Mellen Press.

Philpott, A.R. (1969) *Dictionary of Puppetry,* London: Macdonald.

Plowright, Poh Sim (2002) *Mediums, Puppets and the Human Actor in the Theatres of the East,* Lewiston, NY: Edwin Mellen Press.

Podehl, Enno (2002) 'Parlament den Dingen – Gedanken zur Entwicklung einer Theaterform', *Das Andere Theater,* 41, 4–5, trans. Zeller.

Proschan, F. (1983) 'The Semiotic Study of Puppets, Masks and Performing Objects' *Semiotica* 47, 1/4, 3–44.

Reusch, R. (1997 and 2003) *Die Wiedergeburt der Schatten, The Rebirth of the Shadows,* trans. F. and M. Zirkel, Schwäbisch Gmund: German Centre of UNIMA, Shadow Play Study Group and the International Shadow Play Centre.

Sand, Maurice ([1860] 1915) *The History of the Harlequinade,* London: Martin Secker.

Schechner, Richard, (1991) 'The Canon', *TDR: The Drama Review,* 35, 4.

Schechter, Joel (ed.) (2003) *Popular Theatre: A Sourcebook,* London and New York: Routledge.

Schumann, Peter (2003) 'The Radicality of the Puppet Theatre', in Joel Schechter (ed.), *Popular Theatre: A Sourcebook,* London and New York: Routledge, 41.

Segel, Harold B. (1995) *Pinocchio's Progeny,* Baltimore and London: Johns Hopkins University Press.

Shaw, P. and Allen, K. (eds) (1992) *On the Brink of Belonging: A National Enquiry,* London: Calouste Gulbenkian Foundation.

Sheehy, Colleen (ed.) (1999) *Theatre of Wonder: Twenty-five Years. In the Heart of the Beast,* Minneapolis, MN: University of Minnesota Press.

Sherzer, D. and Sherzer, J. (1987) *Humor and Comedy in Puppetry: Celebration in Popular Culture,* Bowling Green, OH: Bowling Green State University Popular Press.

Silk, Dennis (1996) *William the Wonder Kid: Plays, Puppet Plays and Theatre Writings,* Riverdale-on-Hudson, NY: Sheepmeadow Press.

Silk, Dennis (1999) 'The Marionette Theatre', in *Theatre of Animation: Contemporary Adult Puppet Plays in Context 1, Contemporary Theatre Review,* 9(4), 73-83.

Smith, Beccy (2007) 'Burkett in Britain!' in *Animations Online,* http://www.puppet centre.org.uk/animationsonline/aonineteen/burkett.html, accessed 20 November 2009.

Smith, Derek (2003) 'A Brief History of Automata', http://www.smithsrisca.co.uk/automata-history.html, accessed 30 September 2010.

Speaight, George V. (1969) *The History of the English Toy Theatre,* London: Studio Vista.

Speaight, George V. (1970) *Punch and Judy: A History,* revised 2nd edn, London: Studio Vista.

Speaight, George V. (ed.) (1981) *The Life and Travels of Richard Barnard, Marionette Proprietor,* London: Society for Theatre Research.

Speaight, George V. ([1971] 1990) *A History of the English Puppet Theatre,* London: Robert Hale.

Spieler, Sandy (1999) 'From the Mud', in C.J. Sheehy (ed.), *In the Heart of the Beast,* Minneapolis, MN: University of Minnesota.

Stalberg, Roberta, (1984) *China's Puppets,* San Francisco, CA: China Books.

Staub, Nancy L. (ed.) (1992) *Breaking Boundaries,* New York: Center for Puppetry Arts.

Steadman, Ian (1992) 'Variety', in Martin Banham (ed.), *The Cambridge Guide to Theatre,* Cambridge: Cambridge University Press.

Taylor, Paul, (1994) 'Hamlet?' *The Independent,* 22 April.

Thanegi, Ma (1995) *The Illusion of Life – Burmese Marionettes,* Bangkok: Orchid Press.

Tilakasiri, J. (1999) *The Asian Shadow Play,* Sri Lanka: Vishva Lekha.

Tillis, Steve (1992) *Towards an Aesthetics of the Puppet,* New York: Greenwood Press.

Tillis, Steve (1996) 'The Actor Occluded: Puppet Theatre and Acting Theory', *Theatre Topics,* 6, 2, 109–119.

Tillis, Steve (2001) 'The Art of Puppetry in the Age of Media Production', in John Bell (ed.), *Puppets, Masks and Performing Objects,* Cambridge, MA: MIT Press, 172–185.

Tribble, Keith (ed.) (2002) *Marionette Theater of the Symbolist Era,* Lewiston, NY: Edwin Mellen Press.

Vella, M. and Rickards, H. (1989) *Theatre of the Impossible: Puppet Theatre in Australia,* Roseville, NSW: Craftsman's House.

Venu, G. (1990) *Tolpava Koothu, Shadow Puppets of Kerala,* New Delhi: Sangeet Natak Akademi.

Vitez, Antoine (1976) 'A propos de Mister Punch', *UNIMA France, 53.*

Voisard, Claire (1989) 'Écrire pour la Marionnette', *Cahiers de Théâtre Jeu,* 51, 108.

Vox, Valentine (1981) *I Can See Your Lips Moving,* Tadworth: Kaye and Ward.

Walton, J.M. (ed.) (1983) *Craig on Theatre,* London: Methuen.

Waschinsky, Peter (1980) 'Théâtre de Marionnettes: entre illusionisme et distanciation', *Theatre/Public,* 3me trimester, 56.

Waszkiel, Marek et al. (eds), *The Worldwide Art of Puppetry,* UNIMA.

Whinnery, Steven (2007) 'Hidden Art', *Total Theatre* 19, 2, 14–15

Williams, D. (ed.) (1999) *Collaborative Theatre; The Théâtre du Soleil Sourcebook,* trans. E. Prenowitz and D. Williams, London: Routledge.

Williams, Margaret (2007) 'Including the Audience: The Idea of "the Puppet" and the Real Spectator', *Puppetry and Visual Theatre in Australia and New Zealand: Australasian Drama Studies,* October, 51, 119–132.

Wilshire, Toby (2006) *The Mask Handbook, A Practical Guide,* London and New York: Routledge.

Wilson, P.J. and Milne, G. (2004) *The Space Between,* Sydney: Currency Press.

Wood, G. (2002) *Living Dolls: A Magical History of the Quest for Mechanical Life*, London: Faber and Faber.

Wright, John (1951) *Your Puppetry*, London: Sylvan Press.

Wright, John (1986) *Rod, Shadow and Glove*, London: Robert Hale.

Yarrow, Ralph and Chamberlain, Franc (eds) (2002) *Jacques Lecoq and the British Theatre*, London: Routledge.

Zaloom, Paul (2007) Statement in Nancy. L. Staub (ed.), *Breaking Boundaries*, Atlanta, GA: Center for Puppetry Arts, 30.

Index